I0082686

REVIEWS

"Martin Kari is obviously a deep thinker and an observer who has developed some deep philosophies on life, death, and the hereafter. Martin encourages us all to open our minds and thoughts, not just isolate them to any chosen pattern. He is a self-admitted 'everyday' thinker and potential problem solver. If you, like me, are fed up with hearing the experts bully and chivvy us all into coming around to their beliefs, Martin's book might be just the one that can help you unlock your innermost thoughts. John Morrow's 'Pick of the Week'

"Kari's ponderings on education, health, justice, and religion are presented with in-depth historical research. This is an extremely interesting book with much background detail and contemporary analysis. At no time does Kari exert his opinions; he merely invites readers to ponder the points and to 'join in the thinking process' with him."

—Robin Fleming, *Acres Australia*

"This is a thought-provoking book on the many facets of today's society. It is based on the author's own observations and a lifelong inside experience of the nature of human societies on four continents and in many countries. The book was a refreshing reading experience for me. Working myself in the field of science, I appreciate the author's method of approach: He first sets the scene by taking an 'objective look' from a vantage point far outside the topic under study, e.g. when observing the life of the anthill society in the first chapter of the book. But, as it goes further into the essence of the topic, the author brings in his own 'insider's view', often based on his own immediate experiences or independent personal thinking.

"One central message of the book, contained already in its title, is that the things in society are seldom only 'black or white' (two faces of a coin), but there is always a whole spectrum of different nuances and colours between them. This state of affairs is systematically demonstrated in the balanced and well thought-through discussions in the twelve chapters of this book. The author is not out for 'selling' his own world view or interpretation of things, but he rather sets the scene for the reader's own thinking process to start and continue after he has laid down the book.

"Unlike with many books on philosophy or social affairs, the author of this book is not trying to enforce another '-ism' on the reader. The central message is rather to avoid any '-isms' that have, in general, brought much misfortune and act on the basis of common sense as exercised by a responsible, awake individual. 'Look at things from different viewing angles, solve problems through conversation.' This recipe might be especially worth considering in the case of one of the most burning issues of today: terrorism. The author discusses this in the chapter 'Terror: A Disease'. His central message is that this disease cannot be cured solely by hard sentences passed by a judge but rather by the 'medicine of conversations' prescribed by a doctor.

"One final point on the chapter on education may be allowed since the undersigned has himself been working as an academic teacher. I fully subscribe to the principle of 'on the job training' or 'learning by doing' as opposed to 'formal education' through mass lectures and reading textbooks. Even with more theoretical topics, like pure science, real learning is possible only via a student's own 'hands-on' activity."

—Professor Dr. Kalevi Mattila, Sipoo, Finland

ACKNOWLEDGEMENTS
"All's well that ends well…"

THE
THIRD FACE
— OF —
COINS

MARTIN KARI

Copyright © 2025 Martin Kari.

All rights reserved. No part of this book may be reproduced, stored, or transmitted by any means—whether auditory, graphic, mechanical, or electronic—without written permission of both publisher and author, except in the case of brief excerpts used in critical articles and reviews. Unauthorized reproduction of any part of this work is illegal and is punishable by law.

ISBN: 978-1-63950-343-8 (sc)
ISBN: 978-1-63950-344-5 (hc)
ISBN: 978-1-63950-345-2 (e)

Because of the dynamic nature of the Internet, any web addresses or links contained in this book may have changed since publication and may no longer be valid. The views expressed in this work are solely those of the author and do not necessarily reflect the views of the publisher, and the publisher hereby disclaims any responsibility for them.

Writers Apex

Gateway Towards Success

8063 MADISON AVE #1252
Indianapolis, IN 46227
+13176596889
www.writersapex.com

Dedicated to the Memory of Arja Kari

Every page of this book carries with it the quiet strength
and wisdom of my beloved wife, **Arja Kari**.

Her life was a reminder that love is not measured in
years but in the depth of its presence. Though she is no
longer here to walk beside me, her spirit endures—guiding
my reflections, softening my judgments, and reminding me
always to see beyond the surface of life's many "faces."

The Third Face of Coins is more than an exploration of society;
it is, at its heart, a continuation of the dialogue Arja and I shared.
Her memory is the compass by which these words find their
way, and her love remains the third face of every coin I turn.

CONTENTS

ABOUT THE AUTHOR

Born 1941 in Romania/Transylvania during World War II, Martin Kari's life followed many pathways.

Technical and then formal higher education prepared the author for life with a sense of exploration, adventure, intellect and humanity.

Having worked and lived on four continents as a global citizen, he settled in Australia with his Finnish wife and six children in 1981. It was only in retirement that he found the time to take up the pen again, proving that it is never too late to take on something new in life. Martin has published worldwide a number of books so far ranging from: politics, novels, travel-stories, biography, practical philosophy, children's book, lyric poetry (in the English and the German language). (https://martinkaribooks.com.au)

INTRODUCTION

How many faces does a coin have? One face shows a number and another a picture, which makes two faces. What then is the third face of a coin? Take for instance the 'gambling factor' of the two coin sides. Tossing a coin gives one option out of two—heads or tails. The third option is an imaginary third face being the 'common sense' version, which refers to both other faces, regardless of the chance tossing result.

In the same 'common sense' way, writing should serve a purpose of a wider dialogue with people, which we couldn't otherwise reach. There are so many issues surrounding us today that it has become a near impossible task to comprehend everything concerning our modern existence. One way out of such a bottleneck is to break down this complexity into single issues in order to initiate a better understanding.

My twelve chosen topics—from 'The Ant Society' to 'Religion'—highlight general aspects of a society and their reflections on the individual and vice versa, where the individual finds himself in a constantly changing society. In a search for answers to the big questions of life we will never reach an end, but we should update in our lifespan our inherited understanding. We will always fall behind in upgrading the present and our movement away from any given position that expresses our current beliefs seems only to occur as a last resort.

The 'experts' look from too close at a task, losing in this way the general view in relation to other tasks surrounding them. Many sit their lives out in a 'glasshouse' watching the world from their 'educated' perspective. But there is also a need to recognize the world as it is, in order to understand and act more responsibly in it. Such efforts should be recognized as a creative positive contribution. We all have knowledge, some of it written down, but much of it incoherent 'bits and pieces' floating in our minds.

By writing, thoughts are collected and eventually a better-organized perspective is gained, which can then be passed on in a dialogue with a reader. I consider also that it is essential to follow a path, which starts in the past, showing where we came from. This then opens up an understanding of our present situation: updating, opening up clichés for changes, and elements of constructive criticism are all essential to energize a future responsibly.

After all these supporting elements have been considered and a dialogue has developed with a reader, we are asked to contribute in measured practical steps when the occasion arises. Knowledge that does not go out into its practical field for the real test is like an appendix—of very little use. I don't want to see my writing as an appendix but as a useful contribution.

You, the reader, are not asked to agree with everything outlined here but to join in a thinking process, because from there we get the motivation for better judgements. Even by disagreeing with something, as long as we have thought about it, there is the chance for real progress. Historical, social, psychological, philosophical, biological, and futuristic considerations are brought together in a way that everybody can gain an understanding and follow my objectives.

Everybody has his/her way of thinking; a difference between individual thinking and writing is that we can think only in the moment, whereas writing allows us to collect thoughts over a period of time. When put on paper, they can become organized into a more complex overview, enabling a reader to follow it through and compare it with his/her knowledge. A writer's preparation opens up a reader's own moods and views. So much is said; therefore, I think that it is worthwhile to collect a personal understanding, organize it and then go out to the reader's world to experience how it is received.

CHAPTER ONE

THE ANT SOCIETY

PROLOGUE

All societies are subject to changes throughout history, deriving from internal and external developments. Societies have experienced rises and declines, always leaving a mark of these changes either willingly or forcibly. What nature have these changes taken? Did they point in a certain direction, which, while consistent, was not obvious as long as the society was punished by the rise or decline. It is only from a distance that a view of historical matters can be developed. Where are these cycles of societies—democratic, socialist or whatever label we have chosen—today in 2008 and beyond it?

Let me develop for you, the reader, a concept, in which we are bound to follow a destiny inherited by all living forms. By observing a life form such as the ant, it can be established that they are advanced in the evolutionary process. Looking at the ant 'society' an absolute 'mega-society', we can learn where our path could lead in a quest for a human mega-society. Hopefully, the thoughts gathered here will enable every reader to connect in one way or another to this understanding.

AN ANTHILL OBSERVATION

One Sunday, on a warm summer's day, I walked to the edge of a forest. My pace had slowed down. It could have been anywhere in the world that forests are left. A pile of wood, cut clean to even lengths, invited me to have a rest on the side of the track before entering the dense forest. I climbed the small pile in a single jump and sat down to enjoy the tranquility of the late afternoon sun. Not long after, I had to move because ants had reached my legs dangling down from the side of the timber pile. Where had these creatures come from?

Just around the pile, on its front side, sat a heap of fir tree needles piled evenly nice and round up to its top. An anthill was next to me and a number of ants were quick to bring their message across: you are in our territory and are not welcome! As a matter of fact, the bite of the first ants reaching my legs caused me to move instantly. They remained on my legs while a few more had moved onto my shoes on their way upwards. There was only one way to shake the ants off and that was to stamp my foot down hard onto the ground.

The sun still reached the anthill, keeping up its warmth on it. With nothing special on my mind during this outdoor walk, I took my time first to find out how best to observe this hectic ant life. Partially blocking the sun out with my body instantly changed the movements of the ants. As I moved out of the sun the ants settled back to the activities they had been following before the sudden change. All moved again in both directions up and downhill, whereas the ants had stopped going in both directions during the interruption of my shade. With all the rushing ants, the whole hill seemed to move and, at first glance, everything looked like chaos. In order not to disrupt these activities, I had to find a position acceptable for the ants to be observed—out of the sun and away from the pile of wood. The track in front of the woodpile had to be left open for ant visits to the forest so that only one corner allowed me to remain at a distance of half a meter from the center of the ants' activities.

A few minutes later, they no longer seemed to become disrupted any more through my presence. This was the beginning of a closer observation to find out what understanding I could develop out of this seeming chaos. The more I looked at the scene, the more I realised that all of the movements were in fact carefully coordinated. There was a dense traffic line from the forest across the dusty, stony track heading in both directions towards the anthill and the forest. The 'traffic' from the forest carried all sizes of waste material, exceeding in most cases the size of the ants. Not every ant coming from the forest carried something. Some followed the 'workers' for a distance, while others turned around, joining the opposite 'traffic' to the forest. Occasionally support came for a worker carrying a burdensome load. When a load caused a 'worker' to be stuck on an obstacle in the way, the ones carrying nothing were instantly at the scene in constantly increasing numbers helping to free the load, until the 'worker' became unstuck again.

Ants from the opposite direction had mainly joined to keep the 'highway' free. The moment they joined and came face to face with a homecoming ant, their head feelers and front legs came into action, testing each other. Some confirmation must have taken place as to whether or not the ant belonged to the family. Was the outgoing colony checking on the homecoming 'worker's' response with the right 'key word'? Only then, other 'family members' pulled their weight on the operation.

While the 'traffic' kept moving in both directions, I could not miss the sudden presence of an insect in the ant line. It must have been a friendly visitor known and accepted by the mainstream population, sharing life with the ants in a highly cautious way. The ants are very alert and make sure no parasite sneaks in under camouflage. A small beetle landed out of the air obviously too close to the ant highway, causing immediate interruption to the steady routine. Even 'workers' carrying a load abandoned it straight away and rushed with all the others towards the beetle. Not much of a choice remained for the unwanted guest but to take off again and leave the defenders on the ground. It had to prove its superiority to the ever increasing number of the much smaller ants. The beetle decided to get out in time. Other ants rushing to the scene took over the abandoned load; only a few of them secured a continued transport of their goods, taking it further away from the battleground. The battle over, everybody moved back into normal gear.

Raging war is apparently a steadfast element in an ant society when a provocation is started. I had not long to wait to watch a sudden upheaval on the ant highway. What I first observed was what looked like the ants getting stuck into each other. Looking closer however revealed that there were a number of ants at which this onslaught was directed. The ants must have been from another society in the area, having mixed initially on this busy ant road until somebody unveiled this 'cover up'. Everything I saw before was only a minor disruption compared to what was to follow. From as far away as the anthill, all ants changed their direction immediately towards the 'enemy'. War bells were ringing and relentless defense became the order of the day. The invaders were pushed and in turn pushed back while the pile of ants grew. It was not possible to see from outside just who was invader or who was defender. Steady reserves moved in from the hill becoming finally so overwhelming that the picture became clear: the smaller number of invaders was pushed off the highway and bitten by a dominant majority of defenders and dumped in bits and pieces as a reminder for other 'would-be-intruders'.

The battle worked this time in favour of the local ant regiment because they were alerted by their own defense in time. They could call up the numbers for an effective victory. It would only be quick and effective outside their own hill, because they could lose the 'principal' of their existence in a battle raging close to their 'queen' and 'nursery'. Other people have also observed smart foreign ants sneaking into another ant society under the cover of a well-wishing 'guest', stealing the 'queen' and large numbers of the nursed eggs. Due to a lack of vigilance and alertness this deprived the ant society of their purpose for living. Wars rage also in ant societies. Are they regulating life in order to stimulate renewed survival efforts?

Once a routine returned to the ant society, I could better continue with my observations. Other ants arriving at the bottom of the hill joined immediately in the local march, always ready to assist. The opposite traffic checked for the right 'key word' on their way up the hill. Entrances around the hillside appeared as holes in irregular patterns. In front of an entrance a 'procession' came to a halt. Some obviously larger ants emerged from inside, moving constantly around the arrivals while a few others remained at the entrance 'interviewing' first a 'worker' or an 'assistant' with their head feelers and front legs before moving on to the delivered 'goods'.

There must be a 'scent' related to the 'queen', which is a 'passport' for entry. An ant matching this 'scent' is welcome; if not the case, 'police' and 'soldiers' would raise an alarm at the entrance, announcing a war. Many insects produce signaled messages like ants do. In the case of the ants they rub their tails against their ridged under body surface. There must be a whole language behind this communication method: intensity, frequency, tone, duration, timing, identification, mimicry, positions; all this is hidden from us. What cannot be comprehended is that its existence is usually written off so quickly.

Besides the 'police' and 'soldiers' of the ant society, other ants must have appeared at the entrance from inside, all making sure that everything was all right. Among the crowd more 'workers' mixed, assisting from inside to bring in the 'goods'. Eventually a 'nurse', an 'administrator' or probably a young offspring caught a first glimpse of the outer world, a 'good guest' and a 'cleaner' never far away. An especially good delivery sparked curiosity among the young females, who then joined the scene to have a quick look at how their 'hero' of the day looked. Mating messages can go many ways.

New workers from inside went straight back on to the road into the forest. Despite the large number of ants moving in all directions, every single one knew exactly what to do when a situation asked for it. In other words, there were 'actors' and assistants constantly mixing so that the assistants could prove that they moved on purpose in the ant society, acting only with the assistance of many other ants in order to sustain their society. Everybody's involvement meant that no one had to carry too much of a burden and was therefore always ready to assist because of its reduced task.

Watching an anthill begs for patience. It must have been the time of the year when young hatched female ants appeared with their large pair of wings. Compared with the size of the ants, the wings were huge but they later fall off in an early stage of development. The wings of the young female ants enable them to propagate the colony for a better chance of survival. If there are enough of them, they can start a new colony. Nature holds options also for the ants to survive, simply by the fact that any hatched ant can be a male or a female, depending on an incidental fertilization or not. Every egg can bring out an ant; a fertilized one will be a reproductive female, whereas a non-fertilized egg will be a reproductive male.

Strong male ants are around to fertilize young female ants. The male then becomes obsolete in the ant society, existing predominantly on female ants. A new colony would need also a queen and in most cases she is forcibly kidnapped from another colony, which triggers a major ant war. Young, winged female ants visiting another colony divert the strong male ants through their presence, which gives followers of the winged females the chance to enter the other colony. Under the cover of distraction, a foreign 'queen' is then kidnapped and brought as a new addition to a colony in exchange for new female ants. Interbreeding within one colony is also hampered this way. It is also said that a clear moonlit night is used for an escape with a foreign 'queen', outsmarting the rest of an ant society while it is in a low state of alertness. Even craftiness has its place in an ant society as long as it serves a survival strategy.

To make better use of my observation time, I decided to try a couple of tests on the ant colony. Outside interference instantly alarms the ants and they change their routine as I experienced with my first test. In order not to alert the ants too early on their busy road, I slowly picked up a small piece of bark from the ground. As soon as I dropped the bark piece near the anthill, lightning seemed to strike the ants around the immediate area. This made them stop their routine and all turn towards that piece of bark.

The quicker ants stumbled over the slower ones, all head over heels towards the 'intruder', to establish first-hand, the message of this foreign object with their eyes and head feelers. The first ant arriving at the scene pushed, with the support of a rear guard, the 'foreigner' up from the ground and off the ant road, leaving the remaining task to only a few ants who had to remove it further to a safe distance from the hill. The message spread visibly around the area right into the anthill. No matter which direction an ant took, every ant was subjected face to face approach with front legs and head feelers of each other to confirm the right 'key word', either the specific colony scent or both. While every ant was doing so, a message spread instantly. The message reached the whole of the watchful ant society, losing its urgency through the insignificance revealed by the bark piece. Routine quickly returned.

I thought to test the ants also with something more useful for them, a crumb of bread, which I found in one of my pockets The breadcrumb went on the ground near the anthill. The ants' reaction was again instantaneous, this time however it was more aggressive. They must have somehow realized the difference between a useful and a non-useful object. The few first ants on the scene couldn't handle the breadcrumb on their own. Some of them became entangled underneath in the heat of the moment while help from more ants arrived to finally turn the 'intruder' over in a common effort. Unlike the bark piece, the breadcrumb was instantly directed towards the anthill. On its way, smaller pieces came off which alerted other ants to assist in the shifting of an increased number of breadcrumbs towards the anthill.

The breadcrumbs were obviously recognized as a staple food source and consequently directed in unified efforts into storage facilities within the anthill. Even by looking closer and trying not to disturb the ants in their task, I could not recognize that some of these breadcrumbs was eaten on the way. Ready to check the new 'arrival' in front of an entrance, the 'police' allowed other inhabitants from inside to take over the job and drag the cut-up breadcrumbs out of sight. I was not able to see any more what happened inside the anthill. With the further changes around however I could relate to the in-house life of the ants. On the side of the woodpile opposite to where I stood, ants appeared, each carrying a small white object downhill towards the woodpile. Watching this from a close range, I recognized a group of ants not seen before on the outside, moving one tiny egg each away from the hill. Why were they doing this? Had I caused an exodus through my persistent presence? This was hard to comprehend because I had kept to myself, was as quiet as possible, and therefore could not see any cause for hasty changes in the ants' routine.

From other sources and observations, I also knew that ants sense severe weather conditions twenty-four hours earlier than they happen. Outside in the late afternoon it was still very hot, indicating already a possible storm in the near future. The ants probably sensed the onset of a low pressure system in the atmosphere and therefore knew that their house would receive more water out of the sky than it could normally accommodate by runoff. Consequently they started to move the most vulnerable part of their society early. The unhatched eggs were moved to a place higher above the ground.

I have also seen ants going up posts and trees with their eggs, before severe flooding in the area took place. The ants here had chosen the woodpile for their escape, because it was closer than the forest. Now I knew why I was prevented from sitting on top of the wooden logs on my arrival. The woodpile was a refuge for the ants' next generation. Ants' routine focuses on communication aimed at in-house food storage, internal as well as external security, home construction and maintenance, cleaning, health care, grooming, reproduction, raising offspring and administration of the colony.

Most of these activities take place inside their declared home, which is difficult to judge from an outside position. But basic behaviour patterns could still be established from persistent observation and patience. Inside anthills a very stable temperature is maintained between 25°C and 27°C. This is created by the ants within their hill galleries. The height of the hill is directly related to the outside average temperature: a lower average temperature asks for a lower hill, whereas a higher average temperature for a higher hill, because of air-regulating differences. The ants however live in the ground underneath the hill. The hill serves as a protection against temperature differences from outside.

Technology set foot in ant colonies long before we knew about technology at all. Air-conditioned housing is an 'ant invention'. Galleries in the hill compress slightly the internal rising warmer airflow allowing, through decompression of it near the outer surface, to return cooler air. This keeps a very stable temperature underneath the hill in the ground during such constant exchange of warm and cooler air. Excess heat is transformed and returned into cooler air, insulating and regulating the underground temperature. The housing temperature corresponds with the ant body temperature delivering an environment for a minimum energy requirement at home.

Composting of organic materials is a vital aspect of an anthill, where, under a stable temperature, biosynthesis is nurtured by bacteria colonies. Only they can break down the cellulose into sugar, on which lice feed and the ants again cultivate the lice to gain their honey. The nursery is also located underground, where the eggs are kept in an even temperature environment. Ant nurses have the task of shifting the eggs constantly, 'signaling' eventually from outside to the inner eggs 'messages' for a more prosperous development of the young ants. They must receive from an early stage, life messages from outside; this special care is crucial for their development in the ant society.

Once hatched, the care continues. Young ants are taught from an early stage by 'nurse' ants in cooperation with a 'teacher' to become workers, soldiers, cleaners, guards, administrators, nurses, teachers, ant husbands or ant wives to take care of the upcoming generations. Education from the first moment into one direction ensures in the ant society the unconditional follower into one preset direction. How ants find and determine the suitability of a young ant for a community job is a well-kept ant secret. The survival of the ant community relies on that early 'career choice' in a young ant's life. Failure in such an undertaking would mean, the end of the ant society's function. Young ants are taught what to know and do from the beginning of their lives. It is all they can do and nothing else interferes. Humans also do what they know or in a limitation, a master emerges.

As the sun had set near the horizon with quickly diminishing daylight, the ants on their 'forest highway' had almost returned to the hill. Only a few could be seen still heading home, but none was taking the direction towards the forest. The remaining 'outside hill citizens' had also considerably slowed down their movements and sought protection through the numerous hill entrances from the approaching night. Only single, watchful guards remained almost immobilized near the entrances. They must have been the night guards.

As the anthill came to a complete rest, I wanted to find out while some daylight was still left what will happen while disturbing with a twig a small outside area of the hill's surface. The few ants took notice of it retreating slowly into the nearest entrance holes but nothing else happened after that. The majority of the ant population had moved into the ground under the hill and could feel safe. Even normal rain would run off the hill directing water away from the underground living galleries. An approaching deep weather low with a heavy storm to follow makes ants sense in time that a situation is coming, when their community and especially their nursery would be at risk from excess water. Then is the time that the ants move with their nursery to higher ground.

When tree fellers pursue their activities, as I have seen happen in certain forests, an anthill can be destroyed. The ants can then be observed taking off in all directions, searching first for places to hide. When later calm in their judgement had returned, the ants went back to the place of the destroyed hill in small numbers. Somehow they must have been able to judge whether it was feasible to rebuild at the same place after an observation period or abandon it and find a suitable new territory. I am sure that not necessarily the whole community moved into a new place as they might have developed different decisions about a new direction.

Nobody can really say when looking at the ants, to which social group they belonged. Except for the very young hatched ants, they all look very much the same. For a long time studied behaviour patterns only could eventually tell to which group of an ant society an individual ant belonged.

The anthill that I visited for over four hours during the remainder of an afternoon caught my attention again the next day. A big storm started to build up exactly twenty-four hours after I watched on the previous day the ants shifting their eggs up into the woodpile next to the hill. When I returned to the scene well before the sky opened its sluices, I found the hill abandoned. Not even one ant moved on its surface. More frequent lightning followed by steadily approaching thunder brought heavy rain for a number of hours to the area. There was no proper shelter for me to hide and nothing could be seen on the anthill.

I returned again on the next day after the storm. What could I see then? The ants had returned to the hill. Water from the storm had eased especially around the hill sitting further away in puddles of depressions on the road. A day routine in an ant society had come into a full swing again.

How do ants deal with death in their community? An aged ant not fulfilling the task any more of a 'soldier' or a 'worker' is pushed to go out and away from the anthill and when the time comes to lose its appointment with life, it remains aside not being a burden to the community. Survival is a priority in an ant society. Only in special circumstances is a dead ant removed with a joint effort from an anthill. For such reasons a dead ant's removal from the community can hardly be watched. Even in that phase of life, ants have strict regulations.

What conclusion can be drawn from these fragmented observations of an ant society in order to reflect on our human society? The hypothesis of this topic – 'Our destiny, the ant society'—is best established by analyzing both 'camps' and finding similarities which point towards the hypothesis. Let me sum up my first observations.

THE MAKE-UP OF THE ANT SOCIETY

Ants are one of the most prolific living forms on earth. They live in colonies inside a community residence. Community tasks subordinate each individual ant to a class within the wider ant family. These classes are workers, soldiers, guards, administrators, nurses, teachers, cleaners, guests, reproductive females and males and at least one queen.

All have a limited task to do to allow the overall number of their colony to survive. No task for the individual would involve staying outside the community and not surviving. As long as everybody contributes to one and the same task, the ants will be much stronger than any individual could produce with its single effort. Their emphasis is on action. Everything done outside the anthill keeps the colony inside happy so that it can be organized for what is best for all. Their parole would be: 'We take on everything that has to be done. Don't mess around but just do it.'

Close observation of the various classes of the ant society reveal the following attributes.

Workers are all small non-reproductive females that make up the majority of an ant family. Workers bring the sacrifices within a society and make it function. This is a natural law and any deviation leads to a degeneration of the society's function.

Soldiers are the ant giants. Because of their physiques, the task is given to them to defend the colony when necessary. Their numbers are not large, operating in small 'guerrilla groups'. First they try to frighten a suspect off. If not successful, they defend themselves with everything they have inherited—legs, bites and also a sting from the tail. When one ant struggles with a defense the others join in straight away to assist. Every organization excels in its efficiency and so do ant soldiers. Their presence and field of activity is mostly outside the anthill. Soldiers head a colony; dominant features like size and strength support their position as long as they gain the respect of the other classes in the colony, which is vital in a mutual aspiration for continued survival of the colony. Respect is gained through consistent approaches towards the other classes. Inconsistency would mean loss of respect, which leads to a loss of unity, the key to the survival.

Guards are recruits from the ant giants, staged at the entrances of an anthill in a regular shift change. The guards check with a 'key word', a 'scent confirmation' or behaviour pattern, the membership of a new arrival. An alarm in the case of suspicious circumstances calls the soldiers into action.

Administrators live near the 'queen', overlooking and supervising the colony's organization. Dominant features support their selection. The focus is on the 'Queen' and the colony's eggs, to overlook the nurses, receive and analyze outside messages for internal distribution. The well-being of the colony depends largely on the command chain starting from administrators and its follow-up. First consequence of a disruption causes a split in the colony leading to its reduced function and eventually to disintegration of one colony into another. Renewed efforts can only then ensure the continuation of a new colony, which could be called a generation change.

Nurses take care of the offspring of the colony. They determine largely the destination of an egg as they constantly care in many different ways about the developments of the new generation by changing positions of the eggs, exchanging in time messages from outside with them, controlling the temperature in the nursery, accidental pre-natal conditions. All this determines from an early stage of the development of an ant its membership within an ant class. When hatched, this membership is recognized by nurses and teachers. The emphasis is then on recognition to direct the hatched young ones to the appropriate classes of the colony to learn to practice what they were endowed with.

Teachers are all those who are a good example to others. The many teaching inputs from within the colony give the individual ant the best option whether or not to follow a direction. This becomes a natural selection in which an ant positions itself in a class. A teacher on the other hand receives recognition in a free teaching exercise across the colony through the numbers of students joining the teacher's practical ant lessons. Good teaching integrates the individual into a class, whereas less successful teachers cause a student to struggle in front of the other ants, which then asks for correction by another teacher. The better teacher in such open 'game' qualifies for a leader position in the colony, which is justified through a constant superior teaching input and recognised as such in a well functioning society.

Cleaners belong to the workers and are stationed inside and around the anthill to keep the house tidy for everybody. Looking after this side of ant business, nobody else in the colony has to worry about cleaning and can exclusively look after its own job. Everybody respects a cleaner, because it is them making the home look nice. With so many inhabitants, the whole colony is always kept busy with something. Every so often when the place is clean again, they spend the time cleaning themselves to encourage all the others to do the same.

Guests are allowed to come and see the ant members because of the open society. They can eventually share life, but under conditions set by the house rules. The guards and soldiers constantly check the guest's behaviour. If it remains acceptable for an ant majority and does not interfere with the colony's routine, the guest is allowed to stay. Bad or even dangerous guests are expelled forcibly without delay. The whole colony then rises up to that task. Allowing guests to join the colony keeps the ants alert, becoming less likely for an enemy to creep in unnoticed.

War is also present in ant societies when all measures have failed to prevent an escalation in hostilities. More than one queen in a colony will eventually cause disharmony in the ant population, which receives its orientation strongly from the scent of a queen. A multiple scent orientation within a colony often becomes a trigger for hostilities, which commands protection against overpopulation. Conditions from outside can also contribute to a situation, when survival is provoked changing from a routine into a defense. War is always costly; usually the best are sacrificed so that after a war bigger efforts have to be made again to bring back a renewed survival situation. War takes place also between neighbouring ant societies so that eggs and a queen are kidnapped. When territory claims, superior aggressions of another colony meet a routine of a colony's well-being, it triggers a contest involving all the ants. The stronger will prevail and continue with its routine, even with a reduced colony. In Brazil I watched how young birds in a nest in banana trees were eaten alive by myriads of ants, because the nest happened to be in the 'wrong place'. The ants were also very determined so that it was no use to try and save the young brood as they could have even defeated me. These large black ants cut anything that came into their way and also defended themselves with a lasting painful sting. Another species of special ants made its presence noticeable when working the soil with a spade. Almost invisible tiny 'lava-pes' (wash-the-feet) of Brazil give your legs the instant feeling of having stepped into fire. Running away from the spot and shaking off the tiny pest becomes the most sensible answer. A lasting, burning pain will prevent everybody from returning too early to the ant spot.

Male ants owe their existence to non-fertilized eggs. Only some become reproductive as a male. Strong, big males fertilize young females and then become obsolete. Males are clearly in a minority in an ant society because they are of little use in a colony's daily routine.

Female ants form the vast majority in the ant society, owing their existence to fertilized eggs thereby becoming reproductive females. Female superiority belongs to a very early evolutionary stage of living forms, which indicates that ant societies still operate on ancient evolutionary patterns. Their affiliation to the insects becomes evident by newly hatched female ants. They initially have a pair of wings, which enables them to move away from their home nursery in a quest for diversified reproduction.

Queen ants are young female ants who have disposed of their wings and become fertilized by big reproductive male ants. A colony can have more than one queen, which makes it stronger in a quest for survival and at the same time vulnerable to aggressions within the family, when the nursery becomes too crowded. A queen is the centre of an ant family, constantly attended to, fed, looked after and she contributes with her rich scent the sense for the unity within a family. Everything works around her. Her gift is to deal with everybody in an exchange of services qualifying her for a longer lifespan than the rest of the colony can expect. Ants feed from mouth to mouth supplying this way certain hormone ingredients from across the entire family to the queen, who in return spreads the centralised scent in the colony.

FURTHER THOUGHTS

Where do the indicators point in these observations of a hypothesis: does our destiny parallel that of an ant society? Our destination is not different from that of other living forms; each living form has its own way to reach it, which it has developed through evolution. We are all 'animals' and differ from each other only by the degree of ignorance between us.

Before highlighting our human society in order to find out where the associations are, I'd like to point out a fact that was only recently established—that all living forms have in common one and the same DNA double helix, responsible for life's evolution. This leads to the conclusion that all living forms are basically built from the same material—DNA (Deoxyribonucleic Acid)—making them equal in a universal perspective. The mixed diet customs of both species, ants and humans, have a strong biological bond with a bearing on our common developments.

We are the ones overestimating our level of existence and therefore failing in our coexistence with other living forms! New knowledge should support a new understanding; we 'excel' at failing to follow such an adage, as change is never easy for us. We would be better advised to play a much more humble role in our existence and not to lose our bond to other life forms which together represent the vast majority of life itself.

I'd like to refer here to this understanding so that my statements are also seen in relation to it. There is another point of interest, which should be taken into consideration. We claim our intellectual superiority is above what we call the 'instinct' of other animals. Aren't we also animals? Where are our 'instincts'?

Besides reproductive instincts, we are also locked into narrow margins of what we really can do. A maximum of ten percent of our brain capacity is available to us for the creative learning process. The remaining ninety percent is reserved for our physical functions. The more we create and learn, the more we shift away from a sound function of our body. Neuroses are common results of this, which feed back to unbalanced behaviour. With our progress and understanding we constantly shift a certain amount of effort in relation to our ten percent capacity. To gain more, we have to leave something behind, allowing a constantly growing deficit on other sides, but nature redirects us to our origins.

Many today use a mobile phone, a car, a television, a video camera, a watch and so on—but how much do we really understand about all these things? To know how to use something has very little to do with our inherent know how! Consumerism leads us into a self-confidence that can lock us into ignorance. As long as we don't recognize it, we think we do not have any reason to worry about what we don't know. All dependencies have in common consumption, in that they feed on our existing rules that are placed above a common understanding.

A mass of individuals becomes through its activities over time a coordinated society in order to survive, which is a natural 'mechanism' to which we are also bound. As a result, an individual is more and more restricted in his actions, allowing more individuals to participate through a reduced function in a quest for survival. Other living forms are locked into behaviour patterns relative to their survival needs.

Are we really better off diverging from such directions? Every intellect in us is equipped with a capacity, which is constant and not variable; it drives our physique and our mind. Would an ant-like society become our final destiny? Also, we live with limitations. We recognize the limitations of animals with their instincts only on a very superficial level, because we have very little knowledge in real terms about other living forms, especially when it comes to communication.

What we call instinct allows other living forms to learn about their destination in a roundabout way, which ultimately is the same for all living forms—"*Vivat, crescat, floriat*" ("Live, grow, flourish")—for a purpose we can only guess. Our drive for progress accelerates our evolutionary race. Failure to recognize this in time will affect the environment around us and feed back to us in strong messages. Goethe said, "*Die Kraefte, die ich rief, die werd ich nun nicht los.*" ("The powers we unleashed will take over and control us.")

I encourage everyone to take their 'blinkers' off: everybody wants to see the world through his own eyes; the technician sees the world as a technical field; many others see opportunities to make money, a chemist sees it through a test tube, a bricklayer wants to see the world 'bricked' up, a teacher sees an uneducated world, and a clergyman sees it through a devoted vision.

Where is the all-connecting 'looking-glass', which could keep us on a more sustainable common track instead of diverting our blinkered path towards our personal 'hobby-horse' directions? Philosophy is meant to bridge those gaps in a new understanding, but it is lacking dramatically behind a quickly advancing reality. All these preliminary thoughts serve as an introduction into a continued analysis of the human society versus the ant society. I'd like to foreshadow a result a bit in advance to indicate where the direction leads: We are on track with the ant society and not all that far away from it.

HUMAN SOCIETY VERSUS ANT SOCIETY

Are there parallels between human society and the ant society? Where are the commonalities today? What are the determining facts to show this parallel direction between an ant society and a human society?

Our skyscraper residences (right down to the cellars) are not much different from an anthill, when built close together in our towns and cities. Only in small numbers we can act more individually, whereas in masses, we respond more to needs, which drive our existence. Looking at our own 'anthill', it also swarms with moving residents. Passages control the movements inside and outside both domiciles. Rushing around—often for no apparent reason—is quite common. Our movements by other means than nature has given us, only add to a busy scene that asks for increased attention. We conform, often almost unconsciously, to restrictions; they are the result of our own activities. Controlled activities are again the reality associating us with the ant society.

What do our activities look like and reflect in terms of the classes of our society? We are not as clever and independent as we pretend to be; we are all more or less followers like the ants. We all indulge in something, whether it is meeting a goal or making money. In recent times consumerism has taken over so that even money becomes subordinated. Consumption has become the indicator of our activities, which is questionable, because of its distance to our efforts and actions in today's exchange economies. In our streets we mainly look busy.

Workers pursue their employment, which in return supplies them with the commodity money. Money is said to drive our world. In other words, money largely determines our actions. We have subordinated ourselves also to a 'mechanism' that drives us just like the ants are driven but not necessarily exactly the same.

Soldiers in our society are not only the military. There are also police and to a certain degree banks, which all 'defend' through control. They become the '*status quo*' in a society. In some countries I have seen even banks fortified inside with life-ammunition to secure their 'title'. This is the same thing that the soldiers of an ant society do. Their defence is, in comparison, rather sophisticated with 'keywords', 'scent-confirmation' and character analysis.

War also seems to be a necessary 'commodity' in our lives. So far we could not prove the opposite. War returns everything to basics from where we try so hard to escape efforts to advance us. Every advance is also accompanied by its 'club-foot', which makes sure that we don't run out of control. The more we push for 'progress', the more another side demands balance. Everything in the universe exists in polarities and so also are our actions.

War is among us in many forms in everything we do—as an individual, a family, a society, and the world. Original war-signs are not always visible, but they follow the signs of confidence versus depression—conviction versus disbelief—victory versus defeat—success versus misfortune—intellect versus ignorance—effort versus failure—health versus sickness—construction versus destruction—help versus indifference—honesty versus lies—birth versus death. They all co-exist in a so-called neighbourhood, waiting only to change over as soon as the balance is lost. The extent of a re-balance determines the scale of the war. Do we know about balance needs? Obviously we don't know much, because our actions cannot be translated into a balance even when we claim to know it. Acting and knowing seem to be another polarity, therefore we are bound to keep them together in a constant struggle.

Guards are the soldiers for specific classes within a society. In many ways we guard our advantages against others, whether it is through 'status', education, competition or even war. By often being our own guards, we tend to distance ourselves from others, which is one significant difference from the ant society, where all individuals of a mass society are subordinated to one main task, survival. With our mass society on the increase, we are also increasingly bound to one main task, namely to survive. Nature returns us to our origins even in the case of humans, through roundabouts ways.

Administrators in our society are identified as the ones notvisibly doing much, but claiming instead responsibilities in our societies. They successfully interpret with 'delays'; at the most, they prompt a constant potential between wishful thinking and reality. Their position relies on acceptance by a majority, which they secure eventually with 'vote rigging' and other things that help their case temporarily. Long term, our administrators fall back on 'mechanisms' driven by majority demands. How does this compare with the ant society? The 'masses' need guidance in a direction they know how to accept. The reason for changes lies within that process bringing claims and acceptance closer together. Adaptation is evident in both camps, ant and human, for a broader acceptance, whereas dispute over principles leads to disunity.

Nurses operate in a human society mostly in line with doctors. In many developed countries hospitals take centre-stage today in society through their impressive complexes, which constantly grow in size. Can we afford or sustain such a direction? Will there be enough healthy people left to support the less healthy ones? More and more people are sick today requiring the services of doctors and nurses to eventually stabilise them. Hospitals are like the nurseries in an ant society; they are central to the community, but with the difference that the ants obviously have to deal less with sickness than we do and this is not just by accident.

Lack of the necessary insight drives large portions of our ever-growing society towards the health industry, which again is, to a certain degree, working hand in hand with an industry favouring conditions of ill health. Education hasn't come far in that field yet. Asking questions about a healthy life, there would be as many answers as there are individuals, indicating confusion on the matter. A healthy life is not only knowing about it, but also following it in order to understand it. We are in many ways good at substituting new ideas by economizing them, until we register a loss, when it is by then too late.

When conditions aren't 'right', most other living forms refrain from reproduction; what about us? In socially imbedded societies much less of such a consideration exists. Recently some societies have started to throw money towards a younger generation—money they haven't got in real terms—and pay to have off-spring all in the name of keeping a future consumer economy afloat, regardless of the individual's living conditions.

Questions about life-quality to be passed on are not raised; a reproductive cycle is downgraded to short-term gains to score political points. Doesn't this take the shine off our 'superior existence' for the purpose of adjusting us towards an ant society, where an individual responsibility is not asked any more, even if at a price of lowering our 'sacred' living standard?

The question arises again: what makes us so superior to the ant society? Don't we create our own problems and consequently struggle in then finding ways to overcome them? We are again on the 'circus of the roundabout', which the ants and all other living forms are equipped to avoid in the first place. Also they have to deal with diseases, but on a different scale, as they do not promote and maintain an industry out of it. We are regularly caught in our own activities as we have the choice of 'good' and 'bad', which delivers us the varied options in our lives.

I consider it a phenomenon of our human understanding: We can talk relentlessly about health issues while most of us would only agree about it, but finally very few can practice it. Are we largely incompetent in dealing with our actions, when words proceed? Wasn't the action first and the word always followed afterwards? If we really think about it, this statement would not only relate to health, but also to other vital issues concerning societies. We talk conveniently; many pretend to know and at the end, most of the time nothing is done about it? Are we by nature 'drivers' and 'dampers' at the same time?

Teachers are needed by societies to support its people in a task just as ants do. We however tend to isolate teaching from actions, creating an adaptation problem for the individual pupils later on. This is how the 'convention' has always slanted it. Teaching is brought into the world of action only in fragments; teaching and reality have traditionally been separate. Is it human nature seeking expressions of power through systems? A teacher finds him or herself in a class cemented within our society, where constant adaptation is not a priority. To a large degree this spares the teacher a life in the real world. We have run the world for a while like this and it will stay in place for quite another length of time. Others are always asked to make the changes as long as the others are still available.

Couldn't we learn from ant society, where teaching is a constant partner with life's actions and not isolated like we have it? It is better to remember: the action was always first and only from there can we learn further. Learning first and acting accordingly is in fact a system, but a very inflexible one, because it requires an individual translation into the reality. The teacher, who comes out of the world of action, would understand much better how to assist in teaching requirements as they emerge. He/she would then be part of the process. The economy and efficiency out of such team efforts could support a broader field in our societies.

What we teach, we claim to know. What ants teach or pass on, can only be guessed at. As a matter of fact, all the ants know what to do to fit into their society. Is this accidental or a result of the broader effort? One can only watch and try to analyse what is going on when ants meet, moving their head-feelers into specific directions like antennas towards each other. What do eye contact, subdued sounds from their mouth, leg movements partly towards each other and the rubbing of their legs at the lower part of their ribbed body mean? Specific movements of a single ant and in a company with a few others or in their numbers, express moods and thoughts not able to be interpreted by us. All these are likely levels of a complex communication, which we haven't inherited to that degree of sophistication. We should be more cautious in declaring ants or any other living form inferior to us, especially as long as we know so little about them.

Cleaners pursue an activity, which each individual should perform for himself in the first place. As our society explodes, controlled or uncontrolled, into constantly larger numbers, these masses bring in new rules. Whether present at an event or watching it on television, the huge crowds leaves each time in their aftermath a perfect mess. People have unthinkingly disposed of their rubbish. It is not any more a matter how to prevent this occurrence; it is always accepted that cleaners move in after an event and restore a cleaner environment.

We all hate to look at a messed-up environment from our wanton disposal of rubbish and yet it happens without fail each time people gather in huge numbers. Masses of people are driven by different rules from those of individuals. We reluctantly accept this and employ our cleaners to correct what we have abandoned, individual discipline. Ant masses operate the same way; cleaners do the work in order to keep the home with its immediate environment tidy for everybody.

Guests can also bring into human society a welcome change to daily routines, but not always. If not going out all the time to see other people, guests can make up for this and with properly developed contacts they come in return to us. It is up to us to cultivate knowledge of human nature, which tells us who to trust and who to allow entrance to our private territory. Wrong judgement can lead to negative experiences. Guests are like an open window to the outer-world for us: a lifeline with others reaches also our private lives under the condition that both parties find common ground.

Developing such better judgement, keeps us alert towards our fellow citizens just as with the ants. Only then we can gain a better judgement by learning whether a guest is a wanted or unwanted one. Cutting guests out of our lives sends us into isolation. A constant open approach to guests teaches us however the all-important knowledge of human nature, which qualifies us to make better judgements that are so crucial to our coexistence with others, whether in private, at work or in public. The ants could show us even here a way to learn more eventually, if we understood their way of life better. Their survival depends on their judgement as well. It is only more likely, they can look back much further in evolution than we do and have therefore as a consequence more proven experiences. Are the ants surviving for that and many other reasons?

Males and **Females** are another 'polarity', ensuring the continuation of our society with offspring resulting from their relationships. For some reason our human society is reasonably balanced in numbers of males and females; whereas ants dating in evolution much longer, their females are dominant. Is this also a way we are heading? Our quick answer would be: the ants are more 'primitive' than we are. Females still have by nature the task to bear the offspring. Survival is the dominant reason for our existence and therefore females are endowed with more dominant features in order to fulfil the survival purpose.

Where men have failed in recent times, women step in more and more to balance the often one-sided claims of their male counterparts' power. As in our society the sexes are almost balanced, it relates also to our mainly traditionally established monogamy keeping families more controlled and smaller in order to manage our existence better. Mathematically, multiple differences in the sexes of societies lead to an average distribution—the bigger the number, the closer the mean distribution.

Ant evolution must have gone further by reducing their male numbers only to one task, namely fertilizing young females. One male can fertilize a huge number of eggs, which become females in the ant society; non-fertilized eggs end up as males. What does this establish? Increasing masses select one sex preferably to control a society, which will naturally be the one more related to a survival demand. Even numbers in a selection process lead to unclear solutions jeopardizing a long-term survival in a mass society. Here is a future 'switch-signal' also for the human society. Nature demands survival techniques and therefore only a small number out of the larger mass can survive in a universal quest.

A new definition emerges out of the latest science. To secure survival of living forms during a new 'big-bang', masses collide after an expansion of the universe and then move again into a contraction in order to regenerate new energies for a new start. A pool left invariably from all living forms is the one and the same DNA, connecting them to the same origin, the 'new start'. Such a DNA pool from all living forms has to be the largest possible one to secure again a 'minimum', generating selectively life. In view of all this, we are also bound to follow a request that other living forms like the ants already do. All individuals are subordinated to majority rules and we are not exempted; divergences from it are only temporary in a larger timeless picture.

Whether it is a **Queen** *or* **King** in our societies, they represent a focus on a majority within a population, which is mostly underpinned by traditional elements. This is not a question about right or wrong. As a matter of fact, our society also needs to look at a 'personalized figure' in whom they can put their hopes and wishes that they otherwise wouldn't see becoming materialized. Religion has also prepared us for such a vision. As changes have taken over the world, much is today in a 'transit situation'; we are better at throwing 'things' out than replacing them wisely. The Queen and King personality cult might have changed, but a focus on a personality cult still remains in place. Who can best tell people what they want to hear?

Back in history, a leader emerged from a superior background, becoming institutionalized for coming generations without a new justification towards its superiority. The queen cult in the ant society serves a centralized function for survival. Indirectly, a personality cult does the same in our society, whether it is a king, queen, president, party, teacher, parents or even a friend; they all serve in a direction vital for a society's function from the smallest of its cells up to a leader role. How right or wrong a direction had been was always left to history to answer. We rarely direct ourselves without compromising our actions at the same time; a polarity-law is behind it, allowing action only with built-in controversy. Only time shifts it out of our immediate perception.

Personality cult speaks also for authority, which claims a leading role in any form of society; our experiments show well into the present time its divergences have always led back to the basic rules. Ant societies have been around longer and established more successfully their numbers than we have and reached through their masses a more stable situation in which everybody restricts himself, allowing also others to live. We are on the identical track; a queen and a king might have been only an interim stage, but 'we can rarely see past the end of our own noses'.

More recent developments have favoured the creation of a new form of society: multiculturalism. New countries especially supply better starting conditions for such a new formation; a classical example of how a society heads towards an ant society: everybody who joins such a new society has to step back from their 'high horse' and practice the language, culture, work, knowledge required for integration. The 'bigger picture' demands restrictions from everybody; no one can emerge any more as the stronger one, only when such a contribution is asked for within a majority ruling. Such a process is fairly new and takes therefore time to work in an environment where many cultures, languages and races sit at one and the same table. This step-back process in a multicultural society points in the direction of the ant society; it will be the only answer for our human society to survive longer. An amalgamated human society is still far away from becoming a reality, as long as cultures, languages and borders support the barriers already in place.

Way back in history, when fewer individuals had to answer a surviving quest, language, culture and borders worked as survival mechanisms. Masses of individuals today cannot achieve their survival claims through individually structured defences out of the past. An individual has to step back from his/her claims to allow others to coexist. Failing to do so sends a society back into individually structured aspects of language, culture and borders as long as spaces are available. If space were not any more an option, broad conflict would become inevitable where multiple interests collide. The transition from an individually focused human society into a mass society becomes a reality through a multicultural society towards an ant society. Multicultural societies of today are in real terms experimental models on which we have still to do a lot of work to make it viable.

Other living forms also use sign language for communication considerably more often than we do. Their communication is on different levels compared with our straightforward recognizable one. It is interesting to look at one—a meeting with a dog. We mainly understand the aggressive signs of a dog, but very little of its peaceful communication; whereas the dog can show us many times that he understands us quite well by the position of its ears, head, body and legs, tail action, and eye contact. The dog's enhanced smell instinct identifies adrenalin from a human body's perspiration telling it, 'there is some contradiction with a personality'; a dog receives information and responds with his understanding. I'd strongly suggest, there is more behind a sign language than we conveniently recognize. It's certainly not only a communication in bits and pieces like words; it is more like whole stories.

Another observation regarding communication techniques of animals has been evident on our rural property. Over twenty-two years, we have had first two and now one donkey. For some reasons, we generally perceive donkeys as stubborn and stupid, which is definitely not the case. A donkey knows for instance what to eat or not eat, making it already superior to a horse. It realizes from a distance the character of a person, whether a person can connect to it or simply 'likes animals'. Somebody with a negative attitude towards animals will receive no attention from a donkey at all; the donkey will stay away from that person, even when a carrot is offered. Our donkey can tell us a whole story about another person outside our family, whether the person is positive, calm, has a straight mind and no hidden agendas, 'likes' us and therefore also animals. A donkey connects to a person predominantly with its hearing and eye contact; whole messages and pictures are likely received and returned.

It is also worth mentioning briefly that birds also have a high communication intellect. They have a beloved preference in a communication with music, on which they reflect with exceptionally positive attitudes; music seems to be a higher communication level especially for birds. We keep around our house on a rural property a variety of Australian birds and therefore we can easily make such observations. For instance, when harmonic music reaches them from inside the house, they sit peacefully in one place moving their heads in the direction from where the sound comes. They mimic unmistakably with their own 'music' and move also excitedly in between. Disharmonic music-noise causes however a very different response. Movements are then their main response, no 'music' of their own is added, and no calm and peaceful settlement becomes visible. I don't think we have yet made enough efforts to understand the correlation between humans and all the other living-forms.

Looking at the environment in which the ants and our society on the other side live, it can be established that ants live without irreparable changes to their environment; they are the 'biological cleaning-machine' by turning waste into material strictly for their own use and assist with a healthier regeneration of their direct environment. When it comes to waste, we have created a problem out of our unlimited consumerism. Everything nowadays has to serve our consumption probably until nothing will be left to consume.

Also, we are locked into behaviour patterns, which control us just as it does with the ants. The one outstanding aspect would be our behaviour towards a consumer item; consumerism drives individuals away from the knowledge highway. It is becoming impossible for the individual to retrace and comprehend how knowledge has driven progress; a deficit of comprehensive knowledge is building in us. Reluctantly, we all press buttons today, whether on a mobile phone, a computer, air-conditioning, or a camera; hardly anybody has a clue about the know-how behind the buttons. Such superficial comprehension of a deeper knowledge leads to a self-knowledge, which increasingly lacks basic intelligence. An 'information highway' removes individual uncertainties and keeps circulating assurances that you are in 'control' of your 'possessions', even if you are ignorant about it. Trusting the consumer message gives you a false sense of self-confidence. We are not cultivating coexistence with other living forms in order to gain something from them as the ants do with their lice and bacteria cultivations. We exterminate many living forms and eventually raise them afterwards and use them for our own benefits. We leave therefore a trail of destruction in nature's diversity-chain, which will return in due time, jeopardizing our coexistence with nature. We subdue ourselves inadvertently to the powers we have unleashed and get caught in our own 'games'. Ants on the contrary live with more restrictions—what we should be aiming for as well. How good would that be, us becoming closer to an ant society? There is no such thing in nature as what we consider 'good' or 'bad'. Only through our isolation in nature we produce other outcomes in our lives, outcomes that are different from those nature holds in store.

What are the messages out of these reflections in a comparison between an ant society and a human society? By looking closer at these two living forms we can reveal an understanding common with other living forms that reflects more than we are prepared to admit. We are probably the most disadvantaged ones among all living-forms. By disconnecting ourselves from nature's mainstream—which all the others adhere to—we have become lonely creatures in the midst of an originally diverse, rich environment. Only by reducing our claims, can we reconnect to mother nature again. Doesn't a master prove himself in the restriction?

Instead of accumulating our so-called achievements, let us step back and master the first achievement at the time. We will find out that there is still plenty left behind of what we could have done better. The 'races' in our lives constantly leave too many behind; a restriction however allows more people to participate in efforts for a better society. Stepping back would be a real challenge for all of us. As we push ahead with our intense need for progress, we should also be able to turn the table, step back and work with 'zero-growth'. Instead of shivering with inflation, let's take decisive action and also reduce gradually cost and income to counter inflation. Economists will probably cry foul, but they have never made efforts to think and act responsibly this way. Our ideas of liberty and liberalism stand in our own way. Liberty in real terms is a subordination of one's own accord with necessary rules and not a license to do whatever one likes. Adhering to the examples of other living forms could teach us a more steady order, in which animals and plants around us live without harming their existence. In contrast, we are on a constant 'school bench' trying to learn not to harm ourselves. We will probably only wake up after 'the child has already fallen into the well'.

I am not going to suggest here that we could change immediately towards restrictions as outlined, but that we should gain an insight, which could facilitate our existence into a better coexistence with other living forms. Even if this is done in very small steps we would be following what is a well known recipe: everything that will succeed starts off small. This is a bit of a mind-blowing exercise, something different from the every day's vision, when we mostly have our blinkers on. A universal law tells us: the efforts we bring forward in advancing, is the same, as to make a halt and redefine our position by turning the clock gradually back in order to catch up with ourselves. If we don't do so, our own misery catches up with us instead through conflict and war. It is not only us but also our actions, which cause controversy within nature's polarities, where we are caught through our self-declared 'superiority'. One thing is sure however; we all stay on the same path in evolution, only we have chosen a short cut to get us there.

EPILOGUE

We think the humble ant is no match to our existence; we think we can exterminate it just by stepping on it with our foot. I wanted to correct this in an observation and a 'play-of-thoughts'. We wouldn't lower our standards if we were to recognize the 'small elements' surrounding our existence more often. Ants are just an example of this. The 'right' or 'wrong' has to be left for the future to discover. Doesn't everything that lives have the same aspirations and values? From that point of view, all living forms are on one and the same evolutionary track, differing mainly in their expressions relative to the species and its timely position on the 'evolutionary ladder'. It is therefore reasonable to suggest, our society's function is nearing the ant society in many ways as we also grow into a mega-society.

CHAPTER TWO

DEMOCRACY VS. 'DEMO-CRAZY'

PROLOGUE

How much actual knowledge is available to answer the question, "What is known about democracy?" Many take democracy for granted and therefore it would be no surprise as to how little actual knowledge might surface. While pursuing this question, it is important to include a common-sense approach when delivering questions and answers in order to involve the reader in a necessary dialogue—a dialogue that is vital for the individual to distinguish whether he/she lives in a democracy or in a 'demo-crazy'.

What has been said in principle throughout history is reiterated here but with a more up-to-date understanding. By nature we are good at forgetting the past, but we should maintain the effort to understand it, so that we can judge better where we stand in the present. A collection of thoughts related to 'demo-crazy' will be presented to the reader. Is there something 'crazy' in democracy that makes us talk a lot about it today, but always in bits and pieces—never as a complete picture. We can hardly form a more cohesive opinion than that of a 'demo-crazy'. Additionally, we are constantly blocked by 'classified information', which makes forming an independent knowledge of democracy rather difficult. This is the environment in which many live today without question.

The reader is also invited to ponder the big questions and agree or disagree with the views expressed. Naturally, sometimes the reader will experience his/her own viewpoint surfacing during this dialogue. Having collected some of these thoughts, it was somewhat of a surprise to realize just what can be grouped together in this one topic—'demo-crazy' or democracy. Hopefully a broad base of readers will connect to it and activate more knowledge, which starts with democracy and eventually answers the questions surrounding 'demo-crazy'.

HISTORY OF DEMOCRACY

Democracy (*demos* (people) and *kratein* (rule/ruler)) has come a long way since ancient Greece, when Socrates first introduced his revolutionary ideas by teaching in public that a growing city like Athens should be run by its people. Socrates went out to the people spreading his messages to them in a direct way. The more people live together, the more representation by them is required in order to find ruling directions, which reach everybody in the community and can therefore be followed by everybody.

Only with the perception of being part of the ruling process of daily life can individuals contribute positively and not stand off to one side indifferent to what is happening around them. By eliminating the all so important involvement in the control of decision-making, an insurgence of corruption can occur. Socrates, and later his student Plato, made citizens aware of how to develop a positive outlook with high moral standards in their lives. They demonstrated that this is only achieved by taking part in deciding issues of public matter.

Socrates, during his public awareness lessons, didn't write anything down, out of fear of being prosecuted by those few who ruled at the 'head' of the community.

Nonetheless, imprisonment with an imposed death sentence brought his activities to an abrupt halt. Already the early beginnings of democracy were marred with difficulties. Instead of the more disgraceful execution, Socrates chose instead to drink the poison, hemlock, to end his life. His ideas however lived on, especially through Plato, who tried unsuccessfully to implement the democratic principles Socrates had expressed. In Southern Italy the *polis* (city) of Syracuse was not ready for these changes.

Despite a bumpy start, democratic principles survived not only history, but also in more recent times the 'demo-crazy' societies, absorbing on its way other principles and emerging more and more as a composite government. Monarchy (rule by a single person) and oligarchy (rule by a few) continued to exist alongside democracy. Probably the element of compromise helped all three forms to continue to coexist.

The new 'people's power' rule received significant impact going back to the thirteenth century in Urkantone of Switzerland. Then in the seventeenth century in transit from England to North America, it was the basis of the *Declaration of Independence* and a *Bill of Rights* (Human Rights) in 1776. Puritan religious thinking mixed with colonial daily life became in those early days the trigger for the 'Wild West' civilization of North America. Many controversies in the rising democracy had to be carried through over centuries by societies and this process seems to continue as we are constantly torn apart by our never-ending power claims. History has shown the movement from a modified democracy to today's 'demo-crazy' in many societies but why have we specifically chosen this move? It is up to us as individuals in these societies to answer this!

The initial democratic movement in America came at a high human cost. Nothing concerning the democratic movement has ever been achieved easily. The formation of a majority carrying the ruling authority has struck obstacles throughout history. There have always been parties coming face to face, where one opted for change, whereas others have tried to stop that process, which could have had implications on their behalf in a power struggle. Where humans are involved, there is always a struggle for superiority.

Europe on the other hand experienced fundamental changes in its power base through the French Revolution (1789-1799). Lack of adaptation within a growing society to social changes caused an upraise from the people's power base, violently pushing the *ancien regime* (the Old Guard/Regime) out of the political scene. The use of power to protect the interest of a small select number of citizens within a society was renounced in the French Revolution opening decisively the way to a 'civilian' republic.

Despite the 'royal' and 'clerical' part of society trying hard to keep their foot in the 'power-sharing' door of a new Government, it was established for the first time by a third party, the people's representation, a referendum which counted the heads of all represented in the 'National Assembly'. This was the first time in history that people's representation had by law the majority voice in a shared political arena of 'royals', 'clerics', and 'the people'.

Social ideas were born during that time, starting in its most radical form the ideology of communism. The whole of Europe was taken by storm through the changes in France. Nothing could stop this new way of thinking. The growth of societies exposed the sorry state of their affairs growing proportionally and building a powerful response in due time with its first silent majority.

War against France started in Austria and Prussia and spreading to England and Spain, mostly because the ruling powers became insecure. Napoleon Bonaparte restored the predominance of France for the time being in his military campaign and introduced with it changes across Europe. The 'spark' of the French Revolution flashed over to other parts of the world, in a slow but sustainable way. Simon Bolivar tried to unite Latin America, starting with Venezuela, against foreign colonial interference.

Democracy caused many waves on its voyage throughout history. A shake-up in more recent history happened again in Europe after World War I. The war had brought down more than one society in its aftermath, favouring conditions in which democracy was temporarily abandoned by the rise of the 'Third Reich' under Adolf Hitler. The cost of such moves in a society became clear—renewed war. A consequence of World War I was that it neither solved the then current problems nor allowed Europe to recover sufficiently.

CHALLENGES IN A DEMOCRACY

The most stable society emerging in recent history is the one participating in a wider social responsibility, because only from there can everything else receive its proper direction in a society. Social responsibility is the anchor of democracy; social irresponsibility tends more to cause 'demo-crazy', which is still widespread even in today's democratic societies, often living side by side with democracy.

Democracy always had difficulties finding a calm 'anchorage', as the focus of societies has constantly changed by influences, either from inside or outside. Every time 'upsets' occur in societies, whether economic, social, or strategic, societies have to stand up as in the past and redefine the changed circumstances of a 'demo-crazy' in order to regain firm political ground in a democracy at least for a period of time.

Everything that lives constantly remains on the move, as does democracy. In our quest for progress, we sometimes lose contact with the past—from where we came—and therefore confuse ourselves with the underlying principles that ground our current beliefs. It seems to be too much for us to keep on track of everything, especially with the past. A past however gives us the understanding from where we have come and also, why something is happening the way it is now. Only by recognizing and understanding this past are we able to make decisions that are not disconnected from previous ones. If we ignore the past we could easily become 'derailed', jeopardizing what progress has already been achieved. Continuation with new input is the key direction for progress.

Where do we stand with democracy today in 2008? Are there trends towards 'demo-crazy' as well? Do we administer democracy's legacy appropriately as we have inherited it? Naturally we all talk about democracy. How do individuals of today's society understand democracy? Doesn't our understanding connect to the past mainly by expressing our immediate wishes? This wishful thinking has become a powerful political instrument, of which the ruling parties take advantage, especially today. As we have no need to fight for basic rights any more, but still want to be heard, we continue to raise our demands to representations of governing levels which are simply asked to respond.

Voters historically embody one camp; it is not necessarily the individual any more who influences opinions and outcomes. Voters providing the mandate to a ruling party are also organized in interest groups, as is the case with ruling parties in order to give more weight to their brief. The greater influence the parties gain on either side, the more an individual opinion retreats from a political discussion, where systems take over individual responsibilities. The reason could be that individuals cannot answer the complexity of a society ruling any more. On behalf of individuals, interest groups form opinions and go to their constituency, meeting also their opponents. Power sharing has become one answer to put the brakes on controversy. We cannot deny that expressions in a political process are one thing, whereas the actions with their outcomes can differ substantially from the original task.

Isn't today's society more like this—the ones claiming the responsibility sit inside a 'glasshouse' making sure that they don't get hit by the 'stones' from outside, where the majority of society finds itself. Many views are formed inside the 'glasshouse', which aim in their translation to the people outside that no stones should be thrown. The emphasis inside the 'glasshouse' is to a great extent on self-protection. Inside the 'glasshouse' is a 'sandbox' in case of a 'childish outburst' so that its inhabitants can throw sand into each other's face regardless of class or party membership. As a consequence, the vision of the 'glasshouse inmates' becomes at times understandably blurred.

Is not an understanding of someone's situation a good way to better our 'glasshouse-inmates'? When it comes to a 'stone-throwing situation', the 'glasshouse' has then to stand up and be accountable for what it has delivered to the outside. In power lines, power is travelling in amplitudes of sin-alternating current, changing constantly from positive to negative and back to positive. The power of our efforts is travelling a similar path. It would be impossible to maintain constant positive efforts in a society; the negative field needs that visit to allow efforts to be renewed. Isn't everything, including us, a form of power expression? A direct current is the desirable option, but also it has its downsides; a change that makes life interesting by bringing new challenges.

Communism has adopted 'direct current', not realizing how to recharge, as there is no constant power available from a 'direct current'. Everything that lives, that exists with its polarities, is a given universal condition. Polarities in a democracy are expressed through different party opinions aiming for a majority and the right to govern. A mandate to govern and express the will of the people is predominantly given in elections. One major polarity in a democracy would be the wishes expressed by voters, which are consequently taken on board as 'good' as circumstances allow by want-to-be-rulers. On the other hand are the necessities for changes to the present set up of a democracy so that it doesn't deteriorate into a 'demo-crazy'.

Human nature plays a vital role here. Say something the other side doesn't like to hear and you are marked unpopular. Saying something however and doing something different later, suits the power base more and seems to work in many cases for a short time at least. Where does this leave the democratic system? An 'idle' motion seems to be a price we all have to pay from time to time to keep the regeneration process alive. A running engine needs a service from time to time to allow it to continue running. There is no such thing as a constantly smooth running 'engine' as communism has claimed on occasions throughout history. Even if we preferred our conditions cemented only in 'good' terms, the good cannot exist without the challenge of the less good or bad. The only 'good system' handled by humans will be run down under the pretext of good government becoming poisoned in a power grab by the so-said 'bad sides'. Enough 'poison' on one side calls for 'immunization', an injection of new efforts, eventually through new 'actors'.

The initial role of the individual has been transformed by the growth of societies. As each field of a society has grown, representation of a field has overtaken an individual's mandate, because the complexities of issues have developed beyond the average individual's comprehension. Interpretation can help to bridge the gap of understanding, which however diverts from a direct individual expression to a 'body' or party. Where does an individual stand today in such a democracy? Since using a mandate to participate in an election from early beginnings, democracy has changed its image considerably when expressions of power came on the agenda.

Initial basic demands have turned into an ocean of demands relative to the growth of societies; the original, relatively small basis of demands has changed into a complex process within a democracy.

In a democratic election citizens are asked to cast their votes to express their will. The quality of a vote has not become an issue yet as everybody's vote is valued equally. Looking however at each individual voter reveals that from a standpoint of social background, dependency and independency are by no means equal. How would such a fact translate into a vote? How much impact does a vote still represent today? Here is a start for a future thinking, how we could 'move' the system and return more responsibilities to citizens, thereby reducing the 'overheads' through excessive representation. This is what makes governing so costly that sooner rather than later we cannot afford any more to be governed, if we don't keep reverting to simpler forms of democracy.

All service industries in today's societies, including government, have dangerously unbalanced the other industries providing the justification for service industries to exist. If efforts don't match the expectations of a society any more, the balance diminishes, which causes a deficit, destabilizing a society. The call for government can reduce citizen responsibility by stressing the adage, "Let them do it; they get paid enough for it." A lessening effect of responsibility awareness is also given in prosperity, where a society has the closest 'threshold' before an 'abyss'. All efforts call sooner or later for a renewal; the higher we aim, the further we can fall. 'What goes up has to come down again.' Nothing has and will remain permanently on either side unless we really engage our brains and stay on a constantly renewable path.

With democracy in as many forms as we like, freedom is truly understood. Is this all democracy is really about? Unlimited freedom doesn't exist; it is the path to 'demo-crazy', towards which we are increasingly heading today. By crossing a road, we have to respect traffic, a simple limitation in our freedom out of innumerable others. Freedom can only truly be available by accepting the accompanying limitations, which we are asked to recognize and accept. It is not an understanding of an unlimited right to use freedom as one would like. Freedom is the insight of accepting restrictions! Restrictions can only raise awareness towards the real needs in a community, because they are the necessary 'attachments' to keep a balance between needs and wants.

The key question remains with the individual citizen, how his vote relates to his contribution in a society. Groups representing different interests compete with each other for the votes of individuals.

A 'thinking process' is diverted away from the individual, which leaves the way open for other interpretations. The further a mandate departs from a voter's intention, the more likely a political 'backlash' is to follow, which needs rectification. Each time, the bill has to be met by the voters, not by the governing body. Why do elections take place and vote rigging is sometimes claimed later? Observers try to monitor the ballot while the whole process of voting remains open to irregularities committed by party representations.

What are the problems of today, when after more than two thousand years since the birth of democracy, we are still 'fiddling' to get the system right? Multiple 'inputs' from voters multiply the options on a table, but prevent simple, straightforward solutions. Outcomes other than simple ones are more likely to become 'watered-down' and 'mediocre'. The simple input on the other side lacks diversity, which functions as a control mechanism.

Societies have grown since democracy started, with the result that the changes in a democratic system always lacked behind the advances of societies. Instead changes took place most of the time from outside a system, bearing however its influence on the system. The 'human factor' from the numerous voters out of different camps (parties) twists a direct vote into an indirect one, changing therefore the nature of a voter's mandate.

In addition to this, the 'international capital' has become very dominant by downgrading individual efforts for the benefit of a multinational power base. Money still drives the world and has entered all areas of a society assigned to affect everything the way the 'wire-pullers have threaded it'. Such a dominance of capital can make voters dependent on interest groups, who can take possession of mandates and manipulate them to their own benefit. Capital has taken over efforts in today's societies, controlling many more aspects than simple freedom of expression should allow in a democratic system.

The only answer for an individual to gain more control lies in critical views supported by a broad education. Well-informed citizens are less likely to become manipulated and therefore can deliver a more independent vote. Whether there are many manipulated or independent votes, one result is however emerging; the more often voters cast their vote, the closer an absolute winning margin ensues. For that reason, all outcomes are marred with a possible vote rigging—many often cast votes to help equalize the nature of different outcomes. We use then a second ballot to get us out of a 'deadlock', which changes the original voter's mandate.

Are limitations attached to democracy? It really appears so. In our technological era we should have implemented more useful technology for voters and governing bodies into a democratic system in order to reduce 'duplicated representations'. Instead, voters seem to favour more and more bureaucrats into a system, which is still conveniently called democracy. When will the time come that we cannot afford to be governed any more under the currently stressed democratic system of a 'demo-crazy'? When the accountability of ruling parties cannot satisfy voters' majority regarding the promises made and when original democratic principles about personal freedom cannot be delivered any more, then the time has come to return to the 'drawing board' and restore the concept of democracy in its simplest form.

All ballots will then be forced into a much-reduced governing body. These cycles are relevant to our constant drive for progress. Adversity has always been the mother of renewed progress, shrinking from lack of sacrifices across whole societies. A call for freedom has already been well known throughout history. When a system is run-down, it makes us pay dearly to regain what we have lost. Looking at television and its daily reports of the ups and downs of societies around the world, democratic or not, reveals that there is a competition between established systems and power-elements of a society. Liberalism is pushed more quickly for the benefit of the society, which could not move as freely or as quickly. There are also 'holes' in systems used by the 'smart ones' for their benefit, while the establishment is most of the time on the back-foot correcting those backlashes.

Here we are again with the polarities with which we are bound to live. Nothing will ever go in only one direction, because we are fiddling with everything in all possible directions and trying to gain the little advantage that puts us temporarily ahead of the others. It is a race for wants and needs. Everybody's individual life depends on a vision in which a quality of life can be seen that will bring contentment. As a matter of fact, as long as we live, we will err (*errare humanum est*) and therefore remain on a move to 'patch-up' what is considered useful. In life, complete freedom cannot be reached, because there will always be opposition at our borders.

What does all this mean for a democracy? Democracy can only re-emerge out of 'demo-crazy' if we remain on a constant lookout for the competing opponents and stay in a balance. Neither of the opponents must move too fast thereby leaving too many behind. Not only has the number of citizens increased in societies, impacting profound changes on democratic systems, but also the changes from within societies have affected a democratic system. Progress has diversified intellect in a sense that traditional social levels do not necessarily hold the 'intellect'. Broader education and new technological as well as scientific directions demand a new intellect to help advance our progress aspirations. A traditional intellect claiming superiority of government in the past today finds many more intelligent levels competing side by side.

Traditionally lawyers, doctors, influential and wealthy people were considered to be at the pinnacle of a society. In recent time in society, intellect has created many more levels, which can take part in power sharing within a democracy. The power base has widened. More interests enter political agendas asking for changes in the power distribution, and with it, a 'tug-of-war' naturally takes on new dimensions. Many more interest groups shift the focus from an individual citizen into new power expressions, which in return translate their agendas to the voters. Voters face prepared agendas by interest groups and it is up to the voters to find out how ruling parties handle their mandate. The discrepancy between wants and needs keeps the political arena mobile, being sometimes more desirable than other times. Groups representing their interest in parties play an ever-increasing role in today's mega-societies.

SOME 'DEMO-CRAZIES' OF TODAY

Where has the democratic movement gone today in 2008? Here are six cases of societies highlighting how democracy has developed from a humble start into today's societies: Georgia, Russia, Kenya, England, United States, and India.

Georgia is a relatively new independent state formerly ruled by Russia and has just left the ballot box trying to confirm a government in its aspirations to become more like the West. On the short list were two candidates: one a pro-Western candidate, the other pro-Moscow. These options were presented to the voters. Behind the scene two power blocks were pushing their interest into the internal affairs of Georgia. The West—Europe and America—pushed their case under the democratic cover of liberation from Russian dominance, whereas Russia used its power to keep up its influence in its former satellite state. Two interest groups from outside determined the voting campaign in Georgia. The end result revealed that the party officially left behind by the ballot box used the seal of its disapproval.

Despite all the assurances, nobody could really prove if the election had been marred by vote rigging or corruption. The actions behind the scene were so dominant that the public could not differentiate between official and unofficial election campaigning.

In elections everybody initially claims to be the winner until a result becomes available. The loser has to demonstrate his/her disappointment and start the blame-game; otherwise he/she would discredit himself from being a winner. New democracies seem to have more of these disputed outcomes in an election. The expectations are raised higher in traditional democracies by new electorates than where the outcomes have already 'worn out' some controversies.

Democracy receives the 'nimbus' of a 'doctor', who can raise the hopes of a cure for the many 'diseases' of which a society is poised to rid itself. Interest groups represented in parties play a vital role in societies' endeavour for changes, because they produce strong expectations with the usual trust attached to it. 'Honest' as well as 'smart' election campaigns reveal only after an election the capability and real intention to the public. In a new democracy an election is a virgin process—full of expectations. Only the ensuing experiences bring caution to the electorate and changes also to the party representations. Nobody is spared from taking part in these experiences.

Polarities in a democracy move with time towards an integration of opponents into a governing process. Through a constant democratic election process opponents lose gradually the 'sting' of controversy. Time erodes everything, and as a result, opponents draw nearer in the election results. When no clear mandate can be reached any more through an election process, the time has arrived to renew and re-energize the system, before corruption can change a concept like a democracy into a 'demo-crazy'. Changes have never been easy; they ask for sacrifices. Bad times are usually the best times for changes, because the fewer options become less disputed as everybody is reduced to more equal conditions.

Traditional democratic societies are also not spared painful changes. Let a society come to the brink of prosperity and everything becomes different from then on. Claims, opinions, actions—only renewed efforts can restart a new 'spiral' towards a future prosperity. Changes have always been around and if we don't deal with them constantly, something else will change us. Stability and prosperity can also receive changes from outside as happens when people from other parts of the world push a new migration move into more stable and prosperous societies, forcing them into changes. Our social progress can become our own 'stumbling block'. Everything asks for balance and we are not exempt.

Returning to the subject of Georgia, it is worth mentioning that even its mighty neighbour *Russia* is currently going through its own democratic changes under the rule of President Putin. The initial euphoria towards democracy under Gorbachev received its damper through Western influence into Russia's own internal affairs.

Putin turned this unlimited freedom for everybody down to an interest, which he was determined to serve as Russia's interest. As a matter of fact, the democratic start of Russia under Gorbachev and Yeltsin brought most of the Russian people to the brink of their existence

Liberalism allowed only a few to prosper regardless of the all-over failure to address a wider Russian population. A population, which has been for generations under the 'knout' of totalitarian systems, was lost with a sudden democratic change. Only a few managed to use the new democratic system for their benefit with support coming often from outside of Russia at the expense of the wider population. In order to safeguard Russian interests, a correction was waiting to happen. It might have been smarter to pay Russia to dismantle its military arsenal, but the 'Russian bear' woke up out of hibernation and it is no surprise that the 'bear' doesn't fail to respond today.

Changes towards a democratic rule in Russia were the result of inflexible government in the past. Throwing the past out and replacing it with something 'better' had to come at a price; again it had to get worse before getting better. The initial entrance of democracy into Russia licensed a minority in its society to apply the advantage formula; first to come, first to win. Most Russians became simply disconnected from what they had before and as a consequence the call for change to a democracy lost its initial enthusiasm asking increasingly for an adjustment to Russian condition. The 'human factor' changes everything in societies, satisfying the interest and power aspirations.

Today in 2008 Putin and his nominated successor are making the adjustments, which the traditional establishments of other nations argue is its democratic state. The new Putin initiatives obviously seem to work better for Russia and the people therefore honour such a move at the time. Has democracy failed in Russia, as other democracies want to see it? Aren't we all moving into compromised positions between democracy and socialism? No system can live without the necessary changes. This is also the reason why democracy has changed since its birth in Greece and is still doing so. We have to watch that democracy doesn't turn into 'demo-crazy' (*demos*: people—crazy people). Russia is on a long 'voyage' to find the democracy that best suits its country and people, a process only Russia can go through. Nobody else can do this for Russia because of its unique circumstances.

Kenya, in the opposite hemisphere, also went through the democratic process of electing a government in January 2008. The dominance of interest groups was especially evident here. Two main rival tribes found themselves at the ballot box. Old rivalry going back in history surfaced and turned the election process into tribal rivalry. Past rivalries were staged with tribal war and this happened again after the election, when one tribal party would not accept that the other side had won. One blamed the other for vote rigging and corruption. During this process close to a thousand people were killed and many more displaced, creating their own humanitarian catastrophe. What a price for a 'democratic election'! In view of this, it appears grotesque that a government pursues its governing right in comfort, while it stays in a strong contrast to the situation in which the people are left.

One could ask; what is the price for a democratic rule? In Kenya, the price appears too high. Why did such a situation suddenly arise, in which all previous understanding diminished? Differences between the ruling party of the society and its population had gradually increased. The ruling party of Kenya took too much advantage of its position, neglecting people's broader constituency in the course of the events. With the disappearing justification for government, the call for a balance erupted into a traditional tribal dispute based in the past.

A calm, self-confident government representing itself in luxury in front of an impoverished population amounts to an irresponsible contrast! Also, deep mistrust towards past colonial rule prevents many countries even today finding a new identity through a process of reconciliation, whether related directly to the population or its leading institutions. Kenya's antagonistic parties dug-in for a continued fight as they used to do in the past to sort out their differences instead of seeking dialogue without engaging its people in their controversies. Finally, it is the people who have always to carry the burden of the failures in political systems.

Democracy in Kenya has deteriorated into a 'demo-crazy', raising queries about democratic justification. Painful sacrifices are again asked of people to restore what a governing body has allowed to disintegrate. A situation deteriorates usually quicker than it can be restored. Unfortunately government failure comes also in a democracy at the expense of the population and on top of this, a 'golden handshake' releases government officials very often from their duties.

Government ideas of 'work' and 'responsibility' are more easily expressed in words than to address their constituency with action. All governments like to present themselves in style in order to underline their importance. Is that really what people want—a stylish, costly representation? Would a government otherwise manage to present itself as important? The formality commonly used around governing bodies can divert from an original task, most of all from a working environment, which could more efficiently keep the focus on issues other than work. The political arena appears like elegant visitors to a theatre, in which the actor's role is exchanged with spectators.

Some politicians are not helping their own image by declaring publicly, as happened recently here in Australia in a wage address in Parliament, "It is impossible to live on an income under $100,000 a year." What did the public think about such a comment when the average qualified income at that time amounted to $40,000 a year? 'The bastards should come into the real world and learn what life is all about,' was one common response of the public. It is no wonder that many politicians are held in such low public esteem. Such unnecessary disrespect for players in the democratic game doesn't help its case much. Politicians should live outside the 'glasshouse' and in the real world more.

England, belonging to a more traditional 'hub' of democracy, has maintained to date a mixed form of a democratic system. As long as the supporting 'columns' of the system remain in place, a governing power can operate with both forms—traditional as well as a more modern representation of Parliament. With the consent of the population, this representative system of quite different views has so far survived in transferring the 'battlefield' from within the nation into its Parliament, even though efficiency always remains questionable.

Traditional institutions in a democratic government have so far proven to be a successful 'braking' system for changes that are occurring too quickly. Tradition can maintain a balance with progress, which is a desirable outcome. Despite tradition stabilizing the society of England in the past, there is a definite move away from it today. People adopt different views in exchange with other societies, which happens today more than in the past because technology facilitates people's communication and movement across societies. A broader exchange then takes place, exposing people to new views, which in turn affect the political system.

As long as the present government can deliver, within reason, what the mandate of the people have entrusted them with, tradition has been respected if not completely accepted by a generation change. England cannot be excused from sitting with its government in a 'glasshouse', but has company with another branch of society—tradition. Tradition working for a society depends on the readiness of an upcoming generation to identify itself at least as a good 'neighbour', because 'neighbours' are there to be respected.

What could eventually replace tradition in a society is demonstrated across the Atlantic in the *United States of America.* A branch of Calvinist ideology, in which individuals were encouraged to live a restless, active life in order to overcome a passive existential attitude, was widely established in Europe. In the early American civilization, when the Pilgrim Fathers moved from England to the 'New World', this ideology came with them. Early changes from such a guided religious life toward a more practical life led to 'Puritanism', introducing strict rules for a society under 'moral principles'. This became the starting point for the democratic movement and its Declaration of Human Rights in America.

First consequences out of such firm ruling became the developments we call today the 'Wild West' life. Marks from this time remain in the political reality of today's America, still claiming to be the leader of democratic nations in 2008. Looking from outside at the election processes of the country, one could also ask, since when has democracy become a 'circus'? The power concentration with the President at the pinnacle is a contradiction of a democratically shared representation of the people's power.

Politically miscalculated maneuvers have in recent times undermined America's title of leader of the democratic world. Opposition through terror unfortunately became one of the dominant responses. Whether legitimate or not, people's power responds to power misuse as it is warranted by democratic rights. It is up to America to correct the loss of image and restore some international trust in itself as a democratic leader. 'Demo-crazy' is the most extreme form of a democratic ruling, meaning it has also mostly withdrawn from the original democratic principle.

The 'circus' around the election of a presidential candidate could be called at best a 'show', where the number of words and the amount of money divert from the real issues. Since when has money determined beforehand the capacity of an 'actor'? If an 'actor' turns out to be good, money represents a confirmation. People are simply misled in an exchange of roles; "does money also speak in advance for performance?" What are the chances after such an election 'circus' of confirmation for what money has produced in advance? Once elected, such concerns can easily be 'pushed under a carpet' by the winner. Testing freedom of power then becomes much more tempting.

Issues are turned here into a person cult, a form of representation that democracy wanted to have abolished. The presidential candidate in America is scrutinized at great length for truth finding facts and character references. The syndicate of interests backing him/her for a race in superlatives of money and promises has only to make sure that their candidate can physically also stage their show to an end, when the electorate becomes confused with the issues and the personality. There is so much going into an election beforehand that it should be alarming for a rational electorate. What will be left for the real issues after the election?

Stressed parties will resort to a compensation-recovery attitude once the 'show' is over. Those efforts in an election process beforehand come at the expense of a democratic process that is to follow. An understanding has been established in the name of democracy that no expense should be spared in its process. The winner of such a pre-election 'circus' must virtually be on his/her knees by the end of the pre-selection process. Instead, they should be fit and ready when it comes to taking on political responsibilities. The alternatives for a newly elected leader are: if he/she is weak, people will pay anyway for the fallout; if a leader is strong, he/she faces the dilemma of a mountainous task, which will minimize outcomes in time even with the best intentions. One fact often remains; the 'actors' moving out of the political arena receive their 'golden handshake' as an incentive attached to their job. Under these conditions, lasting, clean political solutions are harder to achieve. Watered down solutions are more common.

The democratic system has developed into interest representations moving away from its original task relating only to the people's demands. Today interest-group brokers translate their version to the electorate and it usually remains to be seen just what emerges. The individual voter's responsibility is taken for a ride and a voter is left behind to form an independent opinion in whatever capacity he/she can manage.

When such a process of guardianship stays long enough in place, it leads to a back-seat mentality, where the voter is not the judge any more, leaving the hard work to the 'brokers'. The election process is often on a back-foot, waiting to be repeated in the event that promises couldn't become a reality or take a direction far enough. The 'circus' remains open; 'shows' become more frequent.

Also democracy/demo-crazy has become expensive today, eventually to a degree that we cannot afford to be governed any more in the way it has developed. What then?

A democratic process has then to be returned to a more sustainable level of representation. As humans, we have always pushed for progress and in the past eventually had to retreat from it through war. War has become our 'creator' for everything. Today it is starting to change, as power is more widely distributed, thereby preventing controversies flaring up easily into the open. Problems seem to stay nowadays more with the originators; as a consequence they have difficulties shifting their own problems somewhere else and making others pay the bill.

An interesting 'mechanism' has entered the ever-growing societies that political activities—when departing from their goals—generate. More activities keep the carousel in the circus going and the politicians therefore remain always in business.

It depends on them how they translate their cases to the electorate. No problems would mean fewer politicians are required. Problems or no problems, what remains is our impact on the environment, which will respond in due time. Such a response could strip us of all our options regardless of how significant are the actions with which we associate.

A democratic race staged in America or anywhere else then cannot respond any more to people's power as it has become irrelevant. New efforts on much reduced expectations will be the only way out of such an impasse. We would be well advised to take this into consideration and develop our democratic ideas with more foresight. Our efforts always aim at big steps towards progress in as little time as possible, which ends up regularly in steps sending us also backwards, a bit like 'one step forward, two steps back'.

Returning to America's case as it stands in 2008, it is easy to see exactly what is outlined here: a state of internal and external 'mess' due to a wrong understanding of freedom in a democratic society. Freedom is not necessarily what we like or want, but must accommodate the restriction towards priorities in a society, which we have to learn to accept. Setting the right priorities and monitoring them is a real political responsibility within a democracy. Then, and only then, could they be presented openly to an electorate to cast its vote.

In 2008, America finds itself not alone in a 'mess'. There are the 'followers' finding themselves in the same boat and all this in the name of democracy in a free world. Would taking more people into a boat help to keep it afloat better with the efforts of others? Keeping that boat afloat will amount to a mammoth task. Our expectations have been plagued by severe shortfalls in nearly all aspects of society. Who is to blame for that? The bill will once more remain with the public. Cycles to realise higher and lower expectations are natural elements in a democratic system. However, all efforts can only be renewed once the bottom has been reached. A high is always not far from a decline and vice versa with the difference that it goes down more quickly, taking much more time to raise again what has previously dropped so low.

In relation to America and its claim for superiority, financial market concentration has developed arrangements, which affect economies right across the globe. This **globalization**, the official version of which multinational companies endeavour to use as their market strategy, amounts to an interest concentration, which they consider to also serve other countries. At the same time however, multinational companies exercise such powers that they can interfere in a democratically balanced power distribution of individual countries. Companies can become more powerful than governments, overriding finances, employment and the democratic control by a majority with their power.

Such a process could lead to another **French Revolution**, where a majority turns against a minority rule. Let's hope our insight towards continued changes will prevent democracy stalling in the face of growing non-appointed power concentrations. A measure of hope won't be enough. We will have to stand up and respond continuously to such provocation to avoid a deadlock with an emerging power.

One of the main supportive 'columns' of a democracy is public vigilance, to embark on dialogue and implement changes by democratic means. Sitting back and doing little eventually strengthens the other side, offsetting the balance to which a democratic system is committed. A prosperous life is one common trigger for losing vigilance. When retreating from efforts towards our expectations, we have arrived at a point so that other efforts will override ours. History has always worked this way and will not cease to do so.

Time can eventually be given a helping hand, where we are able to extend our chances for a stable life before changes force us to lose our 'nest eggs'. Governments appointed by us introduce changes often. One government usually works its way up a 'ladder' while the next one goes down, drawing us with them. This said, if one government manages to save something in the 'money box', the next one will certainly spend it, and the cycle restarts.

Are there political systems other than democratic ones, and if so, how do they operate in comparison? In a search for better living conditions that can be sustained, it is reasonable to look over our own 'fences' with which we have isolated ourselves over time. Looking in an unbiased manner at each other's political realities could only help to open all eyes for a just vision and to find out where we stand in comparison.

One of the last strongholds of communism can be found today in **Cuba.** For decades it has retreated into a self-inflicted isolation focusing on communism in order to avoid being overtaken by the interests of its mighty neighbour, the U.S.A. So far Cuba has succeeded, by its isolation, in sparing most of its people a comparison with other countries. Some successes like general health care cannot be denied, in which medical professionals serve the community in a more appropriate manner than their free democratic counterparts. These professionals often are prepared to commit themselves to working within a community. In other fields however, progress has largely stagnated, as private initiatives are strictly subjugated to general community issues—everything belongs to everybody so that finally the individual has very little he/she can call his/her own.

The initiative to perform is taken away from the individual and nothing is passed on to the wider community. People's capabilities differ in accordance with their characters; some might be happy with just enough food, the Cuban sun, music and a relaxed lifestyle. But there are also others aiming for more, and asking them to feed the expectations of the other side, calls for human nature to move into line with everybody else, before being exploited in return for no personal benefit. Whereas a democracy might have too much, a communist society has too little in terms of personal freedom.

No system is spared changes. Where systems in the future meet halfway, better solutions should come about for both. Dialogue failure between adverse parties is the main reason for a failure to advance everybody on both sides. The other side needs to be convinced by the 'superior side' to change its course. We are supposed to apply this in bringing up our children and in dealing with other people. Why then can't we apply it also on a political level with other nations? Coming down heavily on another side won't help the process of convincing that side to change.

As many politicians fill their position at an advanced age today, they should be more aware that we start as children and leave life again as 'children' in a more humble experienced existence than we used to live as 'adults'. Upholding principles is 'adult business', which has always been a trigger for discord. Surely business would not be a priority in a more conciliatory political environment, but the benefits of lessened confrontations would also feed back to business interests.

A democratic-like system has to respond primarily to the mandates given to it by its electorate through a dialogue, where all sides have their say. Also democracy has moved away from original principles, towards a 'demo-crazy'. We are not determining any more the course of political decisions; interest groups interpret instead the mandate given to them by an electorate in a way that steals the show. It is often only after an election that they pull in another direction that suits them better.

The public sits on the fence watching what is happening. Civil courage from the people's base comes out strongly only in openly controversial times. As long as controversies can be kept under wraps, mandates are regularly sidetracked, telling the public along the way what it likes to hear. In other words, we are moving away from democratic principles more quickly than we are prepared to admit. Which is more corrupt today—a communist or a democratic system? There is no easy answer any more because of the many interest directions needed to satisfy today's democracy.

In a race there is only one winner; all others have to wait for their chance again, including presentation of their political direction. Governing 'mega-societies' has become a complex issue, which is not covered any more by the initial principles of either democracy or communism. Both systems borrow elements from each other, leading in time to an approximate ideology, opening both sides up from their self-inflicted isolation. In such a process, democratic ruling becomes more social and communist becomes more liberal. Further down this track will the question arise—the changes of which system will surpass the other and enhance new powers? It is also natural that each system tries to outrun the other in its pursuit for superiority, which is acceptable as long as it doesn't lead to confrontation, which sends everybody back into harmful positions.

Liberalization in a democracy is pushed so far that we lose sight of the principal necessities. When will education for instance come to a point that only money will drive it in **privatization**? We are not far away from allowing a 'cycle' to go first too far, before coming down again to a more widely acceptable, responsible level. Power, transport, post, health, to mention only a few, also receive this liberalization treatment until the 'clock' has to be turned back as the changed conditions again call for correction. Most of the time those 'excursions' are marred by renewed sacrifices at the public's cost.

A look at **China's** past will not prevent the country showing the world, especially during its Olympic Games, how they have run their affairs so far. No country in the world is exempt from its share of internal problems. Nobody likes to point fingers exclusively towards a country's problems when invited; a guest has obligations. Despite a different political system, China is seeking recognition in its efforts to better the situation of its people—efforts that have moved the whole country into new directions. By acknowledging these efforts, China will only continue with pride towards further changes. Also we have to make an effort to understand where China has come from through history and what has been achieved so far.

No system is ready to be installed straight into a society without some adaptations. There are issues such as demographic composition of a society, historical facts, religions, and traditions; all ask for consideration. Every country has to raise the conditions on its own to become transformed. Such a process cannot be induced from outside through disproportionate measures of force. This would only unleash proportional resistance as demonstrated at present in Iraq and Afghanistan.

Patience, dialogue and seeking acceptance are also measures that help convince a country to move towards democratic ruling. Stages to get there cannot be ignored; they depend on the make-up of a society in terms of its culture, tradition and living standards. In some cases a wide gap appears in such a comprehension. We should not forget that we did not get to where we are today in a hurry. A new democracy in any country has to go through its own developmental steps as we have undoubtedly done. For that reason new democracies are bound to struggle to get somewhere with a new system. Hasn't the situation got to get worse before getting better? Support is the only effective measure from outside that can help to ease somebody's burden. Punitive measures rarely if ever work. Let's remember how to deal best with our 'children', because in a world community of nations we are all 'children' that should learn together and not patronise or bully each other.

China's population dictates fundamental considerations in order to make such a 'mega society' workable. Complex issues out of the past and present largely determine the process a society can adopt. It is not only China, but also the rest of the world, seeking answers to their citizen numbers. The control of population growth determines the future of all of us. It should be declared an irresponsible dogmatic view that 'God sends the 'rabbit' and its necessary food.'

A democratic China of today would probably have inflicted the feared 'Yellow Peril' on the rest of the world—simply, a catastrophe. China had to start somewhere on its own terms from its own history to gradually control the changes towards a better China. Give China time and a better understanding and the so important trust will have a better chance to slowly rise even between different political systems.

How much does leadership count in a democracy or a communist rule? A call for strong leadership often rises from a failure to appoint the people's representatives in a direct single line, where people try to get direct answers and not through the complex channels of a system. Single rule would be the most effective and least costly but only if this could be achieved by a leader so that he/she could keep a dialogue open to all people. Decisions have to be scrutinized by a majority of the public before they become effective. A convincing process has to take place in which a leadership is 'morally' bound. Until now it has proved to be an illusion, because human nature is not perfect. It could never deliver a leadership consistently or responsibly. Perhaps technology could help one day to overcome on one side an administration explosion of governments, to connect people on the other side with a better leadership and in return a leadership with the people. Could computer systems perhaps help to create the direct connections?

A leading figure in governments is represented in many ways: President, Chancellor, King, Queen or Emperor. Most representations are nowadays rather excessive, making everything else highly inefficient. We don't need full representation of governing authorities on all levels. It is time to apply progress also in people's representation. So far mainly democratic governing principles have been expanded without implementing satisfactory changes. A small team of experts could have the task to prepare a dialogue and 'sell' it to the people through media technology. In this case, a dialogue is initiated across all representations of a population requiring some sort of majority approval to feed back from the people in a referendum.

Part of such a process is implemented today in the political arena of *Switzerland*, which has been a frontrunner in the early days of democracy (but didn't sufficiently move on with time). Switzerland's improved wider version of a democracy could become, with technological back up, a more just democratic system in the future. If individual citizens could ignore their part in such a process, it would mean, there is no need for a change. Nor are people ready for it, which would also be in real terms an answer. The case has to go back to the 'drawing board' to attract the required attention. This way people would always have their say without somebody else taking over instead. People understanding a submission implement it better and therefore control the political process more efficiently.

New initiatives to improve a democratic rule should be undertaken so that everything remains at first unchanged, while the new concept runs parallel, allowing a constant monitoring process. Further down the track, when all the arguments have been put on the table, a decision for a change receives support or refusal, relative to new majority consent, without offsetting the current agreement. Never throw out what is currently accepted before its replacement is thoroughly examined—otherwise a setback will occur instead of progress.

When discussing China, it would be almost mandatory to refer also to *India*. Currently the largest democratically ruled nation should be seen as one of democracy's most significant achievements. The diversity of its people, religions, languages (estimated at approximately 1,500), art expressions, and history, is overwhelming. Still only one system rules the country—democracy overlays all the differences. Undoubtedly India's determination for independence has played a vital role in its recent history. Today we can hear on the news the explosive expressions of opinions and also at the same time the powerful existence of a superior mediation, settling conflicts by means of peaceful responses most of the time.

Mahatma Gandhi set a good sample in the past. How a nation with a good leadership could achieve the goal of independence through mainly passive resistance and not active aggression was a powerful message. India still maintains a strong caste culture, which in the past was more a spiritual 'tool', giving people in a diverse society a place where they belonged. An order to rule a mega-society like this had in the past its justification.

Religion first tried to organize people of this huge society so that they could be ruled ethnically, religiously, politically and socially. A subjugation of the individual towards more important community needs was already a 'password' in India in earlier times. Today as education has entered all areas of a society in India, caste culture is losing its significance. More people can nowadays compete for better living conditions, not only through education, but also through new opportunities in a more open society. Democracy has opened India in recent times showing that a diverse mega-society can also make use of democratic rights for the wider benefit of most people in a society.

What works in somewhere like India doesn't necessarily work somewhere else. As previously mentioned, other countries had also to go through developmental stages throughout history. This accounts for why there is more than one democratic face around today. Different cultures reflect differently on democratic views and on the requirements of understanding other nations. All forms of a democratic rule are changing constantly anyway; therefore it is no use looking at a democracy with 'blinkers' on.

Parties in today's governments grow in their mandates, inevitably leading to closer results. This in turn asks for a strong leader to make a coalition work. Here is a similar, crucial approach in different systems; parties still represent the mandate of the people, but a strong capable leader is required to bring party differences under control. At present in Germany, the Chancellor, Angela Merckel, fulfils this requirement.

In democratic developments where mandates are nearing equality due to growing voter input, the leader has an important role in balancing controversies and achieving results, even if subjected to compromises. Clean-cut solutions are desirable but not the norm anymore. Stalemate can become a political reality if neither side emerges strong enough. The choice then is either one party out of a number of others or a single person as leader to guide the nation through the political process. New avenues in a continued democratic process have to be found when avoiding political inaction in the future. The many individual voices have to become unified in less controversial circumstances. And how is that achieved?

As more people bring closer the possibilities of a more equally balanced voting result, the longer such a process takes and the more the differences in a repeated election process are reduced. Chances for clear solutions however are rare, which only encourages compromises to become the norm. A leader has to 'tackle' these increasing compromises or else nothing will be achieved and the whole fact finding process through voting repeats itself at the community's expense.

When following this route, a political process can come to the brink of bankruptcy which nobody can afford any more. A good example of such a direction has been Italy in the last decades. Its 'political circus' is sending the country into possible bankruptcy. A way out of it in the future will lead towards the 'ant society', where individuals' tasks in a 'mega-society' are reduced, thereby allowing a society to function.

As a matter of fact, a leader in a society can be more easily replaced by voting power than by parties. A leader, as long as he/ she can unify parties and deliver a mandate, will be the right person for the job. If this is not achieved, the parties cannot unify and the process goes back to the ballot box in order to form a more realistic political outcome. Issues have then to be addressed so that the voting becomes more conclusive and not divisive. An 'ant society', the result of originally adverse parties in a society, which has halfway amalgamated successfully, could become the answer. The 'ant society' serves a purpose in simplifying life of mega-communities, because 'only through limitations will a master emerge.

One last example of a democratic rule, which should be examined, is **Italy**, which has notoriously pushed into a re-election mode. Just now in 2008, one single Parliament member in the only recently introduced government has again caused instability. Meanwhile it is openly admitted that personal power struggles within government ranks is responsible for this constantly repetitious 'election circus' in Italy. Sixty-two governments in as many years—what an abuse of power! Italy shows the limitations of democracy and how it can turn into a 'demo-crazy': too much representation of the people in government levels can ambush the idea of a democracy through undercover interest groups that can easily steal the 'show'.

An advanced stage of a democratic rule with its close election results asks for more direct mandates from people and less representation. People must become more active in the political process instead of giving governments 'blank cheques' through their representation. No matter what name governing authorities claim, a call for excessive government representation usually ends the people's representation.

There is a balance in representation, which each nation has to find to fit its needs. This way, the 'ups' and 'downs' regulate democratic representation and not the other way round.

EPILOGUE

Is this an attempt to translate some of Socrates' messages into today's understanding in 2008? Whether you agree or disagree with it, you are invited to carry this dialogue further so that others could benefit from somebody else's understanding. It is however important to come out in the first place and initiate a dialogue. I have taken the first step; the 'ball' should be now with the reader in an open democratic 'game'.

Having said so much about democracy is by no means the end of a collection of thoughts. A reader should be able to add to the dialogue, which when extended raises awareness about democracy. We all sit in one and the same 'boat'. A future direction can only be achieved when a direction for a society like 'democracy' is constantly discussed. Such input from the people is what best characterizes democratic principles, whereas input from the people's representatives more readily indicates a communist rule.

As nothing is spared from changes, it is reasonable to expect that initially opposing systems like democracy and communism will eventually meet, over time, halfway in a new understanding. Will 'Demo-comm' (Democracy + Communism) be the new ruling for future society and hopefully not a democracy off the track, 'demo-crazy'?

CHAPTER THREE

ECONOMY

PROLOGUE

I s there any reason to have confidence in an economy, which is driven by capital?

'Confidence' should be left to other fields of a society and not mixed with incompetent practices of financial domains. An economy is a power instrument born out of society. Its existence has changed or imposed its power in a polarity-competition between 'capital' and 'work' throughout history.

The best 'mate' of the economy today is the share market. Daily television news gives us their interpretation of the state of the economy. People however lose trust in how money is managed today. In 2008, it is about time to sit down and have a good look at how we do things and implement new directions instead of clinging to antiquated rules that keep us in our comfort zone. The political game looks the same—namely that one thing is convincingly said and something else is conveniently done. In the end the public has to pick up the bill and those responsible get away, often with a 'golden handshake' and are replaced by someone else for another 'trial'.

What does this really tell us? Honestly—not much! This is because we receive interpretations of monetary definitions tailored to a more commonly used understanding. How much truth is in this? As long as the public is pacified, has it served its purpose? Economy is at the core of our society like the proverbial 'holy cow', accepted but with difficulties connected with it. It is more easily said that something is too hard to understand than to give the benefit of doubt through simple explanations. Simplification usually takes 'the sting' out of difficulties and opens a path to a better understanding.

I am not an economy 'guru', but I endeavour to put forward common sense thoughts with which readers might agree or disagree. I have no doubt whatsoever that economists reading this topic will probably disagree with some presentations, but maybe a second thought might lure them into a different direction from their current set understanding. A reader can be the judge; who has the more blinkered view, the economy experts or me? I give you, the reader, my common sense briefing on the economy. Also keep in mind that changes are not meant to be easy. They have to be born out of many dialogues, one of which is presented here. Even disagreement helps in a dialogue because it makes an individual's opinion firmer and should be seen as a valuable contribution in a search for necessary better changes.

START OF AN ECONOMY

Economy serves the materialistic needs of societies. During history, economy has started off very small. Once, the head of a family roamed the country to hunt deer. His success determined how he could feed his family. When this step of the early economy was satisfied, other steps followed. A neighbour who was not so lucky with his hunt heard about the other one's success. Firewood stored at his place was bundled up and carried on his back all the way to the hunter's place. The firewood was very welcome because all the meat from the deer could be processed over its fire for immediate consumption and storage. One party had a rich prey and little firewood, whereas the other party turned up filling the firewood deficit and negotiated in return for his efforts some of the processed meat. Thus both parties undertook to have the meat prepared. This exchange basis of available natural goods was the beginning of the first economies.

From there, other goods entered a changing economy. Goods that had been modified from their natural state were more valued products and thus became worth more. Also, the greater the rising demand, the more value was added to a product. Exchanging goods became more sophisticated with the growing diversity of societies. Over time demand for different exchange methods grew and therefore money found its way into the economy. This was mainly through growing customer demand in which many people couldn't supply the same goods because of their different lifestyles. Services, as well as goods exchange, entered a rapidly changing society.

Money of high value was initially represented by coins of precious metal, which helped to spread and diversify the early market in the economy. The money market received its main impetus as early as 1367 through the foundation of the *Fugger-sche Handelshaus* (Fugger-Trading-House) in Augsburg, Germany. A refusal by the trade guilds of the time to allow the Fugger family to enter a trade business became the start of the financial institutions. The Fugger dynasty answered their trade 'isolation' by developing the monetary system and lending money as an initiative to the trade businesses in order to produce goods that were in demand. A money lending profit, and goods trading out of it, quickly surpassed production margins in a 'race' to win consumers over.

From such a start developed a power, which rules the world today—money. It is neither natural goods nor skills that underlie today's economies; it the 'money carrot' the world is after. Goods have become a mere stimulating factor in a consumer chain. Out of a makeshift beginning an emerging power subdued the forces that prevented the small dynasty of the 'Fugger' taking on the trade market. As a consequence of this, the 'Fugger' prepared the money lending system offering a powerful tool to those later seeking the power behind the money.

The groundwork was prepared for those without developed skills to find a job suitable for them in the money power game. The initial skills market became the 'underdog', greatly undervalued by the non-skilled section of a society. And this happened accidentally, not as a planned process as we look at it today. The system that developed with a money-driven economy mainly served its own purpose: lending money to energise activities in society, which brings in return 'yields' which then is expected to keep up a cycle of growth. For what purpose is this type of economy developed? It is solely for the purpose of profit in terms of money to keep the cycle going. The economy we have now has developed more by chance. The system we want to see in it is not much more than an interpretation of a development. How well a system works in the economy shows the turmoil in the financial world, which happens right now in 2008. One current explanation is that these are natural cycles occurring every six years. Certainly the public receives only the 'tip of the iceberg' in terms of information. There is much more behind it than classified information will let us know. Many more people burn their fingers in today's financial world than we conveniently get to know.

It does appear that 'consumer confidence' has already taken over financial powers in a new shift of power. Such a focus dictates many measures taken in a hurry at the time, until consumer confidence cannot be sustained any more and the next shift has to come. Which one that will be is the current question. It could well be something we can control even less, like a downturn in our world of expectations. Eventually a major correction factor sends us back to the basics of the economy—effort first.

The financial power around the world today has the potential to drive up as well as down, not only the world economy but also all the public related institutions of all societies. Can the powerhouse that we allowed to be established in the financial world be controlled now? A lot of new thoughts and ensuing actions should enter the present discussions; the free economy has gone astray in its liberal position. If we were appropriately in control of the economy and its branches of manufacturing and trading and then finance, there wouldn't be a constant need for adjustments in fluctuations as the world experiences on a grand scale in 2008.

In today's economy of 'capital' versus 'work' the economy exists in cycles. Money maintaining these cycles is one of the main reasons for constantly changing its ownership, while its value is 'floating' from one hand to the next. The cycle usually starts with a newly printed banknote. Somebody who has performed work receives banknotes to enable him to acquire also consumer goods other than he is providing. Let's say, he/she has made furniture, which sells for $500—the furniture manufacturer partly hands over his banknotes to a shop to pay for groceries, pay a bill, put petrol into the car and eventually something is left for other expenditures.

Each time money changes hands, the service is paid for, it drives its value up and down. Next time this money is received by a car dealer, a dentist, a garbage collector, a public servant, a tourist, an unemployed person, a pensioner, a broker, a student, a tradesman, whoever might be the recipient in a seemingly endless consumer chain, the nature of service will also change the performance level. Electronic transfer of money only reduces the transparency of how money value changes. When the performance towards the value of money drops, inflation and eventually further down the line a recession or at its worst, a depression can start. In all these cases money has lost its value and we have the names ready to explain at least the cycle behind it. All money measures either to cut or stock up money supply follow cycles if they relate to consumer confidence. The hard lesson to be learned will always be at the end of cycles, when we have to start performing again and winding down our expectations.

By recognizing the conditions described here, we could have a better chance to look at options and improve on aspects of the economy. Our views to get us there have to be very clear and free of the many clichés. All societies live in conditions largely determined by real efforts. Direct relations between efforts and their outcomes have shifted economic positions throughout history in societies due to an increase in the participation of people. Nowadays not everybody has to come up individually to what he/she is exactly claiming. Systems have diverted from the initial effort-related issues turning instead beyond the individual, which happens when efforts change their nature through progress.

Individually we hardly ever create something from scratch anymore, particularly where we can actually see ourselves as the originator. Our tasks become minor in the face of progress and we increasingly back away from real efforts. Already 'draining blood from somebody else's efforts' in the past was managed during colonization periods. A widening competition with other economies through better access was partly facilitated through the transfer of know-how, starting to correct an effort imbalance as new economies 'fight back' with 'tools' given to them.

A new shift takes place here and fewer 'traditional partners' remain in a race for economic superiority. It does appear that an age-old rule applies here: 'If you can't beat them, join them,' 'them' being the new emerging economic 'power houses'. 'Joining' however means cooperating in a mutual interest that both sides have—that is to maintain efforts to constantly stay that 'nose-length' ahead. Otherwise the party failing in this appointment will inevitably disappear from the 'table'. A new order in an exchange economy will then take its place and a 'new war' emerges: not solely with armed conflict as in the past, but with superior efforts, which have enabled the originally 'disadvantaged' party to 'fight back' with the efforts often learned in exchange with others.

We are talking today about 'foreign investment' through 'technology transfer'. Exchange of goods is not the only commodity anymore in an economy. Since money entered the early economies other 'elements' of an economy have also joined this exchange-game. Perception of power replaced the direct connection to a product and has gained with time the upper hand: a personal input is not measured any more with goods-criteria but by a system of bargaining power that has entered instead to enable even 'small contributors' to benefit disproportionately. A money system was the first to lead an economy and as already indicated, consumerism became the next dominating economic factor of that generation.

Today in a society with stock exchanges, money is more and more driven as a new measure, putting an artificial challenge on to market indicators, which leads to a gambling situation where somebody always loses to make somebody else a winner.

Here is a license to exhaust freedom of expression to its limits in economic terms. This all happens mainly on the back of the people who depend on employment for their livelihood. Where is the social responsibility in this? Everything has its limits and so also has a stock market, until the 'bullet' comes back and 'shoots' its originator! Any form of a war, even a new 'French Revolution' could become an escape door, forcing new considerations to take over, but with wide reaching consequences for a stability-seeking society. A failure to deliver changes in time builds a barrage of unforeseen problems, which the majority of the public again has to bear just as it has in history all the time.

In a society, intellect should be the understanding to balance 'diverging polarities'. When one side has become 'stuck', power interests offset a balance by taking disproportionate advantage, which can end up in an economic crisis for all. Small problems can cause big problems with time! War has always been the first and the last resort when parties got lost in their problems. It is said: 'War is the father of all things'. It renews everything that is put out of balance under coercion. The price to pay is very high, because war always claims the best. A start without the best becomes then a lingering process asking for sacrifices to continue.

All this amounts to the wrong interpretation of what civil liberty actually is. Liberty requires a high degree of intellect to attend towards timely needs and subordinates individuals to it. Exploiting liberty to everybody's liking can lead to conflicts between competing parties of similar interests instead of becoming unifying efforts under necessary restrictions.

MULTINATIONAL ECONOMY BRANCH

The growing power of multinational enterprises is one form of liberty going astray in recent times in an economy. The 'cuckoo' is growing in its nest, throwing everybody else out. Explanations to justify takeovers are always on hand. Original efforts out of one source transferred into another place can work for an exchange, as long as other economical considerations don't move around those first initiatives to maximize profits.

The original basis of an exchange in 'know-how' and the provision of work for others become a vehicle for political purposes. Takeovers then prepare new expressions of power. They are not working all the time, as two major car manufacturers (Mercedes and BMW) of Germany have experienced recently in their takeover initiatives in England (Rover) and America (Chrysler). We are talking here not only in terms of economic losses, but also people's efforts being sacrificed for a bit of superiority, which has turned into an 'act of gambling'.

The same happens when corporations shift production facilities with the know-how to other places. Such competition can work when the economic infrastructure is organized to suit the new 'recipient' in its own development efforts preferably for a longer rather than shorter period. Suppressed demands regulate practices in an economy, which are by no means easy to uphold and control, considering the different circumstances in which societies live today.

In cases like China, a government sits at the table with its own economic initiatives where it is advisable to be cautious of any sort of exchange practices. Initially, foreign investments to build on the economy in China seemed to work as long as the foreign party is able to offer benefits to the Chinese cause. China is set to grow and the power behind it is growing too. In China, an initial foreign presence faces, with time and investments, a stronger partner as government and economy is a united powerhouse. Officially China does not operate in a 'liberal' way. Its flexibility to change when it is required constitutes a challenge however for the 'foreign players' in a 'dragon territory'.

Obviously, China knows exactly what it is doing with its vast traditional wisdom, probably better than many of the foreign investors, who could well be on a 'gambling tour'. Any benefits out of such economic power-games have still to show up today and in the future. The foreign parties help China with their presence to become more flexible, but it remains to be seen at what level which system will emerge the stronger? Anybody entering this foreign investment 'game' has to be aware that changes in China will effect all the parties involved and apart from that, will feed back into the countries of the 'game partners'. Original economic inputs will also feed back into China.

China knows quite well what it is doing. While pushing its interest regardless of other countries, the big rush to the 'profit Mecca', China, dominates. If foreign investors don't display through their presence a support capacity to the changes China wants, problems of a scale not previously anticipated could force changes through those bilateral economic contacts.

The liberal economy of the investors can then become corrupted in a new environment of China. A multinational 'superiority' role will experience its downturn in the face of a stronger partner. The need for changes in both 'camps', the foreign investors and the beneficiary, arrives through the individual country's 'back door'. Many problems, such as a balance of capital control with work ethics, receive through changes their different aspects. Enhanced changes and the new conditions attached to it could cause considerable disagreements on political levels, fuelling either a 'new revolution' or a war.

The latter would again bring down all that has been achieved and call for rebuilding sacrifices with renewed efforts—the meaning: nothing has been achieved through war; the clock has only been turned back. Whereas with time, an internal revolution would make many differences disappear in a halfway meeting process. Opponents can play their roles independently only as long as the other side is prepared to look at it. Ultimately everything has to come down to a more widely accepted level in economic terms.

Our 'mega-societies' are becoming our driving forces. The 'ant society' is including the economy in its evolution. As laid out previously, the 'ant society' is an advanced social system in which every living form finds its place through a reduced individual function and allows 'mega-societies' to survive. All initiatives of a society, when practiced long enough, lose the 'sting of controversy' with time; each time when something gets 'worn off' in such a process, it leads to results of a less controversial nature.

A balance in economic terms is then eventually achieved, but prevents progressive solutions; this applies to all society-related 'institutions'. Deadlock can only be overcome when institutions like 'democracy' and 'economy' receive new impulses through changes, which will determine a new balance either in a smooth continuation or radical change of a society, depending on societies' readiness for changes. Also an economy depends equally on continued changes within an existing framework always waiting for the 'better' solution and vision.

Today's economies are often driven by capital from sources crossing all borders of a society. Religion has taught us the 'belief' and for various reasons our understanding connects to it. A growing economy is believed to be 'good'. We also believe that more capital drives more work and already a new 'spanner' has joined the economy system—the consumer. Lately, consumerism was declared the main driving force. Population growth is brought into the 'game' where more people mean more consumption. Is it really responsible to believe this way and act upon it? Whether responsible or not, enough people strongly believe that everything around them is just fine.

One experience however shows the fallacy of this belief. When a majority of people is content with their lives, a condition is reached where foregone conclusions neglect a continuation for changes; catching-up is logically taking place in the aftermath. Self-caused deadlocks are societies' biggest traps. Undoing laziness happens most of the time through forced issues. Before this can happen, it would be wise to remain active and alert towards necessary continued changes. Those who rest for too long will rust! If we are true to ourselves, deadlocks have been reached in many ways keeping us going, but it shouldn't release us from keeping our heads out of the sand when it comes to looking further than the nose on our face.

My writing perspective is to keep one's head out of the sand. I am also concerned about the present and would like to see the lights in the different tunnels rather than say, 'Why should I worry—after me the deluge can happen.' Such a view cannot be responsible, because with our existence we are obliged to pass on a future for our descendants so that they also can reasonably survive through caring for our children.

My intention is to develop an understanding out of the past, which leads into the present and discuss at the same time with a reader, where we are right and where we have possible room for future improvements. The people's input is also the only control in an economy surrounding us. To display contentment without constructive criticism invites a cycle of forced changes, which could catch up with us at any time from within our society and from outside as well. Hoping that a reader has by now a better understanding of the need for constructive criticism, I continue with my observation—why are consumerism and capital driving 'work' in a society?

Action was first, the word followed: from the beginning of earliest human civilization 'action' was around first. The 'word' came in afterwards with time. Increasingly the 'word' has taken over and replaced the action in its leading role. The 'word' has also become an excuse for not being able to perform actions. Here is one major reason why 'action' and 'word' have drifted apart: 'words' are always lacking behind action interpretations. I refer again to the 'glasshouse' situation. The ones in the 'glasshouse' try to interpret the actions from outside as they see them. Rarely do both sides meet on common ground, in which each side has a real understanding of the other side.

The secret would be to stay alert to changes and get out of the 'glasshouse' in order to remain open to a wider team, even if problems are hurting. Problems shouldn't be addressed only from 'higher ranks' in the 'glasshouse', because this way our 'managers' find themselves 'cornered' with the creations of their own problems.

To know about something can solve often half a problem, whereas the other half of it can come together in a wider effective dialogue. Also, management has to respect the changes around, as one would undoubtedly recognize in wider cooperation, but we all know too well that we do not easily recognize our own mistakes.

What is the role of 'work'? Has 'work' really become the 'underdog'? Is misinterpretation causing imbalance? We believe that capital growth makes 'work' grow as well as giving more people a way to make a living. How long is the spiral in consumerism, capital and goods production sustainable? Not everybody could possibly take part in such a 'race' worldwide. Prosperity for everybody in the world is an illusion! We have to get away from illusions and learn to deal more with realistic facts. Neither is necessarily obvious nor easy to obtain. Renewed efforts have to bring forward more conclusive directions also in economic terms enabling us to stop and think where we are at a present and where we possibly could move. Growth in economies can serve only a limited number of societies at a time. 'Roulette' shifts fortunes around giving stability very little chance to develop over a longer period of time. People across all divides have the same understanding of stability, which should guide all our economic goals.

Zero growth or even negative growth in an economy is bluntly rejected at present by the 'establishment'. If you ever dare to think in that direction you are declared ignorant and immature. But wouldn't zero growth as a gradual opening target deliver more stability? Strong systems like the financial market of today have ambushed the efforts of 'work' establishing their power base from where they act with one-sided control of their own. 'Work' with its performance has become the 'underdog' and discrimination of 'work' has never been far behind. The power we unleashed, we cannot control any more. Systems like the financial market can superimpose their 'grassroots' by degenerating from its originator, which leads to a 'self-purpose'. Zero growth in this case would enforce the balance between the opponents: capital and work.

Yields, including the mixture of foreign capital interest, are said to determine the course of every economy. To service such demands at present managers have the quick answer ready by axing, in the first place, employment. Alternate measures would require efforts also from the 'managers' for which they claim: no time is left to waste. Everything has become today a 'race', which unfortunately doesn't allow time to consider other options. Who are the organizers of such a 'race'? It could only be us! Therefore we can only blame ourselves for not having enough vision to manage internal changes from outside.

When 'managers' turn into 'mismanagers' they often leave their field of responsibilities with a 'golden handshake' and are not much worried about what is left behind: others can have a go and sort it out. People understandably don't bank on trust any more in such cases and 'a quiet revolution' starts to build. Today more people are educated leaving no more room for a vision: 'up' there are the clever ones and 'down' there the 'stupid' ones. People however have an instinct from mother nature and they know very well to judge how to be treated; their response to tutelage can often be more intelligent than that received from 'up there'.

Controversies between a system and 'people power' can quickly lead to a disruption of social freedom in which a most likely outcome doesn't really serve anybody.

With economic growth, we always run away from stability and allow the regulating factors to drive it up and down. I don't want to be seen as a 'world reformer'. I want to show directions, which also require efforts, if not more than we conveniently are prepared to admit.

Let us go to the relation of capital and work to establish a foundation. Capital has an overwhelming position in today's societies. Not many constructive efforts have been undertaken to properly evaluate 'work'. We have rather developed a tendency towards discrimination about 'work'. For such a reason, skilled 'work' especially is directed into a short supply by economy's regulating factors so that sooner or later skilled work might drive the economy into an unwanted direction. Where an economy cannot afford its own workforce any more, demand has outstripped supply.

How many times can one experience others turning up their noses at somebody else's work? Convention keeps such an expression 'under the carpet' in order not to expose 'incompetence' from inside the 'glasshouse'. What many don't want to do is conveniently declare such conventions 'inferior'. This kind of an attitude even in an economy can't be helpful for a 'common task', which everybody is bound to follow, if one wants to succeed. We still have to learn to work together as equal partners.

An even balance in economy's activities would be a good starting point so that neither 'capital' nor 'work' would be positioned ahead of the other. This discussion is not about 'turning the clock back', but to continue the focus on gradually neglected changes towards present deadlocks. The financial turmoil at present in 2008 is enough proof for just one major deadlock. How best to go about it would be to set up a smaller trial case for an improvement in an economy on which a majority can agree—monitor it and determine eventual adjustments for the later benefit of a wider economic implementation. Never let decisions drive the whole economy unless they have satisfactorily stood up to trial situations.

More specifically, the economy has developed itself in a mostly 'free elbow room' and only afterwards a suitable 'formula' was found for it. Why can't it be possible to give existing economies new directions? Liberalism, but with attached conditions respecting other coordinated functions like work, education, research, politics, all integrate with each other. To capitalize on all these, one needs to know first, what are the values behind them in expressed money terms. These figures could tell a financial market the obligations of how to serve this market. A balance could be maintained avoiding 'shortfalls' or 'overheating'.

With this in mind, a reduction in economic growth could be gradually targeted parallel to a cost index reduction, which would then create growth on a steady wage level. Why can't we turn away from something that has developed with very little control? Inflation does not have to bring everything to a halt each time. If we understand 'liberalism' as a free pass to let everything happen in its own way, then there is no reason to be serious about control. But if we want to be serious about control, then we should make use of it. We don't want to bring an existing economy down with changes.

In a team effort, small steps can be monitored with the 'right representation' long before it is decided to take new findings on board more widely. Instead of introducing the new findings slowly and steadily, every successful business today stands on its own two legs; one is an official business version and the other one a stronger business leg, specific for each individual business, which leads in the end to success. These variations are partly responsible for the discrepancies in an 'official' and 'unofficial' business structure occurring in the economy.

Wage claims have to be related in a responsible economic environment to productivity gains, if an economy doesn't want to lose competitiveness with its own products. Other regulating factors towards wage claims, whether capital or politically driven from inside or outside a society, result always in inflation, which is a negative result for a wage claim, because initial gains quickly erode buying power instead of maintaining them.

When productivity can be raised, no projected growth is needed and people would have real gains. 'Work' would then drive the economy and no capital growth leads the way to everything. As a result of work efficiency, capital will grow proportionately. If really wanting to be 'liberal', we have also to accept capital reduction, including wage restraint, when negative work performance surfaces.

One advantage of this situation against a capital driven economy would be that inflation can be better controlled, which is directly connected to capital growth but outside the parameters of work performance. The capital growth spiral and its correlating inflation leave wages further behind than smaller 'negative' adjustments would do.

Everything that takes small steps over time into a negative territory, after having been in a positive territory, overcomes more difficult stages in an economy because everybody is moving in the same direction thus helping to better maintain stability. Things don't always go well; changes are less incisive when a move from a strong position is prepared in time in small backward steps to allow strong rebuilding for a not too distant future. Nobody in a society should feel discriminated against as long as new work efforts lead first to more capital and more income. A cycle is maintained from work to capital and then back to work.

Critics of these thoughts should be reminded that there is an urgency regarding new directions, which starts with financial organizations. For too long the 'prophets' of financial systems have cemented their positions, preventing new influences from entering. Virtually every country in the world, with the exemption of only a few, is today in a sense bankrupt; everybody has overcommitted himself financially.

At present, financial commitments exceed liquidation feasibilities; in many cases not even interest rates can be met on excess capital borrowing. Irresponsible forces are at work here aiming to get as many debtors as possible into their 'shaky boat', because they hold the view that when all are in the same boat, the boat is less likely to sink. Also with the 'debt-bug' making its rounds, there should be enough 'others' on hand to struggle against going under.

The public is meanwhile pacified with consumer encouragement while everybody puts their head in the sand and tries to avoid the realities of broad financial mismanagement. In 2008 there is more mismanagement around than management! Nobody has an effective answer to the current financial problems. Everybody wishes the problems would go away and be somebody else's problem.

This won't happen easily any more, as the present wars for oil and ideology are demonstrating in Iraq and Afghanistan. Waging war to offload problems has found responses, which makes concepts out of the past dangerous conflict materials that cannot be overcome by making others pay for our own failures. Iraq and Afghanistan, both war zones, have not been able so far to deliver the sought after results. Economic considerations have laid the groundwork to earn quick dollars in the aftermath of war. So far, the results have instead been a financial mess. Passing on the 'bug' through war seems to have stopped working these days.

Others have meanwhile become too strong to receive corporal punishment from 'culprits' as has happened in the past. More irresponsible measures are taken instead. Since when does digging it deeper fill a 'hole'? Nobody wants to face realities and tighten the belt because it is simply not popular and cannot be sold easily to the general public. Quick-fix solutions have become popular instead: worry about it later!

The cycle that brought the financial impasses is upheld further. More money is also circulated while the 'hole' gets deeper to keep the economy going for the moment. Nobody speaks out about how to stop such a destructive economic cycle or how to fix it. If we could only reduce our false expectations marginally, as indicated previously, in due time we would have a better chance to stop the negative impact of the current financial implications hovering above the entire world economy. When too much money is circulated and not backed up by work, it will first inevitably inflate prices and then have a negative impact on the labour market. Instead of creating work, the market rejects work as demand drops.

Constant expansion of interests in an economy is not realistic. Expansion not corrected with balanced measures will run out of control in time into other areas of society. Nobody really wants to know then how to get out of such a 'bottle-neck'. What the establishment preaches currently is: changes are too hard to implement and too much would be at stake. Possible changes are looked at only as a last resort, but meanwhile 'let's keep cool heads', which better serves financial interests for the moment.

The 'Damocles Sword' of a recession however remains a potent agent of anxiety, which is kept under the carpet as long as possible. If a recession cannot be stopped any more, the current economic problems that have grown out of financial over-commitments could turn the clock back to a difficult and unwanted time. What cannot be controlled can run away uncontrollably at any time.

The huge 'hydrocephalus' in administrations should have the task to work out to what degree liberalism in certain economic functions should become exposed and where restrictive measures have to be implemented in order to balance an economy towards other social needs. An economy is responsible for meeting social needs in a society. Social needs like work, education, health, transport and defense have wide reaching considerations to be addressed when coming to economize them through privatization.

The future certainly will tell where we have gone wrong in this regard. Picking up the pieces of a battered economy will then become a daunting task, conveniently referred to the future by our notoriously defective short-sightedness. The longer a task for changes is not recognized as urgent, the more difficult a correction will be. Improvements through gradual changes have to be a constant partner in a society backed with majority consent. Efforts for balanced conditions in an economy have to be bigger than just the 'let-things-slip-away' them under a false understanding of liberalism.

People with common sense and civil courage have to come out of a society where most seek security in 'hiding'. This doesn't help to prepare with renewed discussions the ground for gradual changes, which again has to be monitored for its correction requirements. But when power prevents new dialogues, problems have found a hidden 'breeding ground'. Not much better would be an outcome in which dialogues do not lead to active changes, *summa summarum*: let's prove that we have the right people to get us out of the current economic 'bottle-necks'.

If we could better use our brains, it should help to minimize the adversities in an economy and better guide us towards what to do. The action space is widely understood to be in a 'free environment'. Changes within a society bear on the relations with other societies including their economies, because nobody lives in a world economy in isolation any more. Population increases especially demand closer cooperation as previous diversity changes to density, in which freedom of expression receives a new meaning. What might be good for one should also be good for someone else in a society where a dependency has emerged through density. Neither an individual nor interest groups can exist in a denser society independently. Its smaller boundaries dictate different rules from that of an individual society.

In such a process, economies also lag behind in adjusting to new rules while the individuals are still in its free environment. The 'real world' always hovers miles ahead over the 'established world' as was previously indicated in the business world. Businesses are formally run to establish rules, but what makes a business successful, is its own in-house formula on how to run its business. On many occasions this is not recognized, especially when 'economy gurus' preach their lessons and try to rubber stamp the process. Such a 'lesson' only amounts to ignorance of different requirements on how to run different businesses. During my lifetime I have experienced managers, recruited from completely different branches, who have turned company structures upside down in their eagerness. As a consequence the business disappeared altogether not long after, along with the new manager and his ill-conceived initiatives. This is just one example of the myriad business 'failure stories' out there today.

Continuity is the key for changes! It is recommended to first learn how an existing company works. Next develop a proper understanding with its people on all levels and then in consultation with them, changes will have a chance to gradually become introduced and implemented. With the essential support of the people and without cutting them out in this process, improvements can take place. Enterprises can only remain efficient in an economy with a wider representation of its people.

All this sounds quite familiar but is still widely ignored in the 'real' business world. One problem of running a business can be an overrepresentation of staff instead of the business heads. People themselves usually know best what to do and what not to do, which usually only requires a coordination of everybody's efforts. How many times have people seen things go wrong and because of an incorrect representation by management, nobody came forward with the right answers? Those differences in projected business strategies and their real outcomes establish one discrepancy in economic terms, which cannot feed efficiently on the economy.

A key for all parties in business could be to gain access to a better understanding of each other's position. This is best achieved, not through separate parties, but with a transparent system allowing everybody to perform to a level, where he/she finds a fair position. Contributory responsibilities in an enterprise shared with all staff levels are the best warrant for any business, especially when it comes to difficult times.

On one occasion during my working life I experienced the positive outcome of open teamwork. 1968 had been a year of a recession. The company I was employed with understandably had problems, but its staff did not abandon the company. Unanimously, measures were decided to help the company get through such a difficult time. This included personal sacrifices by the staff. A bit more than one year later things turned around and everybody received an appropriate bonus for his/her personal contributions. Such an outcome would only be possible with a staff and management that work together, where each one knows the other's position. These core elements of a good economic interaction are foundations for a sound economy.

As everything starts off small, balanced work conditions feed best into an economy and not financial systems from an outside position. The 'little cells' of a system show how healthy it is! History teaches us also that all changes in societies came from its broader basis and not from exclusive levels. When 'high' levels of a society are reached, we have already arrived closer to an end.

Survival instincts are left behind in such a career, where instead exclusivity operates. This cuts off the main stream, which keeps its efforts up pushing further up an 'exclusive ladder'. The more vital mainstream pushes up the 'ladder' and rarely allows the 'top' to come down. The 'top' is more likely to disappear from the basis of a society with strong exchanges. Good management takes such knowledge into consideration and doesn't act single-mindedly from the 'ladder top' but comes down to a more common level with others, including them in a participation process. People are never stupid! Everybody knows how to contribute something to a common cause. Access into every cell of a society is an essential understanding. Only then can strained relations largely be avoided to the benefit of an economic balance in all society levels.

There are already enterprises successfully applying equal opportunities for everybody. A managing director has been here through all the performance stages of an enterprise, when he/she knows about the requirements on different levels and has each time received approval from a majority of colleagues for further promotion. This type of manager makes a better team leader than somebody who comes from a disconnected level of a work environment and its people.

As education struggles to stay in line with the requirements of the 'real' working environment, clever enterprises have united their efforts (e.g. in Stuttgart/Germany) in education institutions, where the 'real' requirements of today and tomorrow are taught. The experienced staff of such a business is contributing to the education with 'real world' current know-how. Such an exchange of knowledge from in-house and from outside works hand in hand with the constant changing requirements in technology. Work performance with the support of knowledge is a powerful economic instrument working successfully in some highly reputed enterprises.

By these industry measures the question arises, how useful is the huge outside education system, currently largely disconnected from work performance? It appears even today that there is still a discrepancy between what is taught and what is required. This discrepancy is responsible for the economic fallout of its many 'well-educated' but isolated graduates, who often cannot find useful, adequate employment. An antiquated teaching system isolated from current requirements prepares students inadequately, leaving them exposed to the real work performance environment with its many demands.

When a newly 'baked' graduate enters work-life, he/she starts in many cases as an apprentice, learning the new requirements. Many industries cannot accept such discrepancies and have therefore established their own education initiatives. This again indicates that it is important to primarily include work performance and education together but not in isolation. Another small cell feeds the economy—the inputs from many 'cells' feed into an economy, which make it work flexibly, and not through isolated measures of capital dominance.

In such a competing family environment of work and in all its supporting branches, everybody gets a fairer chance and find its proper place, capital inclusive. The close connections of today's societal functions require a transparency, in which nobody in work is distanced from others. Closer team efforts can only succeed towards new requirements with continued open-mindedness.

With history as the teacher, an impartial view on how to run an economy should have been gained today. Not everything has been good or bad as we can only learn from a distance. Everything is often first flatly condemned, before it is analysed as to whether it is 'good' or 'bad'.

A work-based economy has emerged only once in recent history so strongly that its power corrupted the 'Third Reich' of Germany like other powers have done, when humans grab for it. There can't be any justification for the 'Third Reich', but we should look from a distance today at a phenomenon of that time. The world Depression in the late twenties of last century left twenty-five million people in Germany out of work. The initial work programs of the 'Third Reich' however managed to put everybody back to work in only a few years, thus doing what financial measures could not have achieved.

Alarm bells in the financial world at the time were of course going off as Germany moved away from international capital dependence and found eventually followers. Nobody could deny that the work programs of Volkswagen and the Autobahn were measures way ahead of their time. Germany's power however corrupted the authorities with time in handling their duties irresponsibly. The brutal end of the 'Third Reich' banned everything connected to it in the aftermath.

Today from a distance, we should look at history to allow identifying with hindsight, where some good parts have been, because they shouldn't be thrown out with the lot. If we were to lean constantly towards the 'bad' of the past, we could lose the opportunities for a better future. History's cycles form our consciousness and constantly ask us to learn from mistakes without repeating or staying with them. All countries have their share of mistakes—Stalin in Russia was not undisputed and neither was Mussolini in Italy nor Franco in Spain.

It remains important that we learn from the past. What we shouldn't do is throw everything continuously into only one 'bad bin'. If we are open-minded today, we should look also at the good sides, which have eventually gone down with the 'bad', because nothing has been singularly 'bad'. If 'work' was not connected to the 'Third Reich', a closer look at it could eventually have become more popular earlier. Are we today ready to look at it in an unbiased manner without confusing matters?

What will be the role of the 'stock market', the economy's 'best mate', in a changing economy? New regulating factors have to be found to service an economy, which is in a state of a balance when it heads towards 'zero growth'. Work should create the demand for capital. When returned to work a balance has been gained, which satisfies work efforts. There would then be no need for an independent capital growth. Work-related requirements can more directly adjust to changes than capital does out of a position of self-interest. Capital should become a service industry on demand of people's work efforts. Disproportionate representation of capital, especially by foreign interest is a current problem, which is usually patched up with new regulations. Can the 'blood-giving' and 'letting' functions of a Stock Market deliver its own justification in an economy?

'Blood-letting' of a patient was a standard medical procedure in the Middle Ages, performed by medical 'professionals' in order to encourage the renewal of blood in a body. This wide practice led however to further weakening of a sick body in many cases, which turned it also into a 'power tool'. A dependence of a patient on such blood-letting procedures often fostered money transactions into the pockets of these medical 'professionals', who didn't hesitate to play the 'tongue of the balance' when it came to the power games of influential people.

How far have we come since? The medical 'professionals' are bloodletting no more but the procedure has also spread under cover into economic practices, where capital 'drains blood' from societies for its own benefits. Interest rates, currency fluctuations, and money solvency all aim to secure a one-sided dominance in societies and violate the principle of a balance especially towards 'work'. Here capital also offsets the efforts of 'work'.

Shareholders are left to shake their heads regularly in a self-declared 'volatile market'. Since pensions have also been added a few years ago to the Share Market, the individual has only 'gambling' choices in other fields like gold or property markets and eventually others as well. Where have principles been left about stability or even of a moral nature? Financial power plays its own one-sided role. There is no warranty whatsoever in a future in which economic growth serves the share market. The desire for progress is an endless spiral, which needs more materials and efforts each time to progress, which in turn cannot be sustained.

No resources are unlimited. Economic growth has to slow down if the human race and its diverse living forms want to survive in a natural environment. There will be no living standard for a mega-population on earth, unless we decelerate the destruction of the natural environment. The share market has to learn also side by side with the economy and the consumer demand to play a different role in a changing world, sharing power in a balance with work efforts.

EPILOGUE

Economy is connected very closely to a human population. 'It is more or less the same to ask a mosquito to cure malaria as to ask an economist to cure the economy.' It has become a serious question today, whether we can afford human population growth in order to satisfy economic goals? All our activities, especially the economy driven ones, bear an impact on the natural biological environment, in which we are undoubtedly playing our role. The micro-cosmos consisting mainly of bacteria also demands our respect, if we want to survive for longer. More population has to go on to be accountable for the natural environment.

In the beginning all changes are slow and difficult to register, but they accelerate unstoppably further into often unforeseeable existential consequences. We are all on one and the same planet and in the same boat. Whether it will hold us or make us all sink together, depends on how we treat our 'planet boat'. If we don't restrict ourselves in time and learn to live also with 'zero growth' in our economy, our expectations will send us more quickly than we would like into 'hell on earth'.

We might still have time to reconsider our position, but we have to be quick and determined. Cosmetic patch-ups like pumping money into a 'barrel', which has already lost its 'bottom' won't help our future. As an example, look at the wrongly directed economies that 'feed' on the wars in Iraq and Afghanistan. The consequences show up in the economies around the world. Will money be able to fix the problems it created? Are efforts available to close the gap between capital and work performance? Hasn't the economy 'boat' become very shaky here?

The main thing that remains is that the 'wild west principles' in the economy are upheld. If we don't find somebody to pay for capital failure, we might have to come up for it sooner or later all together. As long as such 'financial bugs' can be passed on to somebody else, would there be a need for real concerns? The important focus remains on restricting ourselves and joining 'nature's party', before nature is going to decide to get rid of us all together. But where there is life, there is hope. We have to anchor ourselves in the calmer waters of our economic aspirations and keep our heads out of the sand!

The 'advantage-taking game' encouraged by a liberal economy is like roulette: fortunes come and go. Is that all that can be expected in our lives? There is a fine line between 'letting it go' and 'educated measures' in an economy. Social responsibilities ask for the 'educated measures', in which the needs of societies are addressed and financial interests are not given preference. It does still appear that the longer changes in societies are put on hold with one-sided power-expressions of interests, and the more sudden and unpredictable changes will later on take over. It also would be definitely more intelligent to work in smooth transitions towards changes.

A second French Revolution today could be far too reaching in its consequences for everybody. Let us therefore keep the 'tiger of a revolution in its cage'. Have we got 'practical intellect'? Let's come forward with it and use our 'intellect' practically in an everyday decision-making for the benefit of us all and do not forget in haste that nothing was ever achieved easily.

When we embark too much on the easy sides of life, we are primed to face life's hard sides in the future. A little bit of hardship tackled at an appropriate time keeps us alert and fit so we won't succumb so easily to hardships. The views towards the economy are here largely based on 'common sense', which could be expected from everybody and gains therefore hopefully a good deal of an understanding worthy of promotion.

CHAPTER FOUR

MULTICULTURAL SOCIETY

PROLOGUE

What is a 'multicultural society'? Obviously not something to eat! Today, the concept is debated around the globe and everybody seems to understand its meaning. But is this really the case?

'As long as multiculturalism occurs somewhere else, I can live with it.'

Do most people think like this? Outside our own lives we are prepared to tolerate it, because the timely trend is, 'Who wants to be out of step with society ?'

What about when a daughter turns up with a friend who is, on a multicultural scale, further away than the family clan has so far experienced? Then you are tested as to whether your tolerance for something closer to your own home has room for acceptance. Individual 'antics' are relevant here; we look at something with the knowledge and experience we have accumulated during our own lives. Therefore, all events close to us are dealt with at an individual level as much out of ignorance as of knowledge. Who hasn't seen one side 'go over the top' when another side brings something unknown into their lives? No son or daughter-in-law could reach the expectations of an ignorant party in opposition.

Then culture often loses its inherited ground and shifts towards arguments, if not outright hostilities. However, nothing will remain completely bad. In the end, the 'wake-up call' through multiculturalism prepares everybody for a much improved future understanding. The future is coming anyway, even without the consent of any particular individual. Changes in our lives are a daily reality. We would be well advised to keep our doors open to changes and allow the so important dialogue to continue between different parties.

FROM EARLY CIVILISATION TO CULTURE

How far does multiculturalism go back in history? From as early as history was documented, changes in societies through early migration started with its initially dominant survival-needs. This led to a development, in which ultimately the 'better strategy' spread into other communities.

First, 'civilization' set a start for a 'culture' to develop. Civilization, the forerunner of a culture was dealing with the basic needs, which allowed societies to function. In the past, war was more responsible for this, regulating a transfer from civilization past the walls, which cultures have initially built during an 'identification process' of a society. Through civilization, everybody had to find the means for survival and then create his/her own cultural elements for 'identification purposes'. Civilization was always more commonly shared between societies because it served the basic needs that everybody developed with time: food, housing, basic clothing, hygiene, and practical skills.

When it came to communicating with each other, something other than civilization had to enter with the first cultural expression—language. Some societies still cope better today with civilization, others with culture. Civilization recruited the more 'practical skills', whereas culture gained a foothold in what could be called 'imaginative expressions' or theory. This split in societies is largely responsible for further divisions.

We are still recognizing 'practice' and 'theory' as two separate capabilities of individuals. There is however an untold number of individuals that achieve both aspects, the 'practice' and the 'theory'. The system of separation doesn't recognize its existence in its dimension. Divisions are like walls in societies; a build-up behind it always ended in destruction from where something new had to be rebuilt. Civilization allowed changes in societies to happen more easily. It was the culture that has built the 'walls'.

Density of societies has removed some of the controversies created through cultural isolation and introduced instead a coexistence, which is born out of the necessity to survive in larger communities. The 'ant society phenomenon' has taken over. A traditional gap between civilization and culture is closed in an advanced 'mega-society' and everybody's task is reduced to allow others to participate. Even civilization has been creative in its beginning until becoming more widely established as culture took over a more 'exclusive creativity'. On its way, culture has lost its mainly creative character, changing more into a preservation and 'copy' culture.

People are the bearers of civilization, including culture. When people meet, their civilization and culture also come face to face. How they understand each other and get along depends largely on how they come forward without expectations born out of their own civilization and culture. Such a process hasn't started only recently; it has been around for centuries. The way people meet, changes the process as well as the people. The stronger civilizations with a degree of culture have built walls between societies, which in the past were mainly dismantled by wars. These enforced changes have led to less aggression over time and they will continue to do so while people make sacrifices with their efforts. Population density and new technological transport facilities, along with the aftermath of the two world wars with its shift in populations, eased the spread of a multicultural society around the world.

Migration, a motor for multicultural societies, has played a vital role today in establishing new societies in countries such as U.S.A., Canada, Australia, South Africa, Brazil, Argentina, and Algeria. Early migration from countries of origin like England, Portugal, Spain, and France brought their economic interests along as well. Changes were imported into the new countries and they still continue to do so today with the help of migration from countries other than the colonial powers. Other languages and customs have entered the new societies, requiring the establishment of new rules allowing integration and a new society to function. Integration has become a continued process as more and more people move out of their inherited territory in search of better living conditions, supporting at the same time exchanges in goods, workforce, technology, know-how, civilization, culture, and tourism.

What started with small migration moves in history has now become an all-out exchange process, in which people are bound to learn more about other civilizations and cultures. As societies have grown, they have come closer together, reducing the chances of conflict through war. Modern warfare has become a deterrent between societies. The stakes for conflict have been raised significantly and the war options are made 'cloudy'.

A multicultural society has a good 'braking system', stopping all out war from taking place as no single part of society has the upper hand. In the past, it was those with the upper hand that enabled decisions to be made. The many opinions from a different societal background form more balanced outcomes in compromise processes. This means that solutions are less progressive, because a larger number of opinions have to be attended to.

Multicultural society prepares us for the 'ant society' and the 'mega-society', where the individual's 'elbow-space' has been significantly reduced, forcing everybody to sit at one table for unilateral decisions. At such a 'table' something would undoubtedly remain also 'under the table', which means in cultural terms, a 'cemented-culture', enabling communities earlier in history to survive.

Today's rapid technological changes brush aside individual concerns about cultural survival elements. A call to serve the multicultural society today is becoming stronger than ever before. Larger communities cannot take into account individual concerns of groups any more. Therefore, new guidelines have to regulate other forms of coexistence like the emergence of the multicultural society.

I originally came from a strong traditional society in Transylvania and experienced its disintegration during and after World War II. Until the war, an isolated life worked for centuries in favour of Transylvania, giving it the backbone through its culture to defend itself against other surrounding cultures. Changes from outside created counter-forces, putting an end to Transylvania as it used to exist. Only the future will tell whether Transylvania will find a place on the map again in a new coexistence with others. The signs are there for it, because the country is blessed with a wealth in natural resources, a richness not found elsewhere in Europe.

Years after the war, in the mid 1950's a new form of migration started in Germany too. Guest workers, firstly out of Italy, entered the labour market on time limited work visas. Their contribution to the economy soon received wide recognition so that time limits for their stay became more relaxed.

I also remember my dad saying, "No foreign workers will work in my company." Not much later the same man revised his stand, acknowledging, 'Without foreign workers the company would not be operational any more.'

Many of these foreigners were good reliable workers and therefore often remained longer in the foreign country than they had originally planned. It was only slowly though that they found acceptance by the population in the host country outside their work environment.

Generally speaking, integration into another society always proves difficult. Customs, language and even a different appearance can get in the way of an untroubled integration. Seeking refuge in their own insular communities temporarily creates a division between the mainstream communities of the country. Brazil, one of the longest established multicultural societies in recent history, is a good example of how various nations have integrated. Without creating prejudices, it is undoubtedly an experience to find out that different nations tend to integrate differently into a multicultural society like Brazil.

The relatively small number of Japanese in Brazil was holding firmly to their own culture in the 1970's, when I lived there with my family. I remember a third generation peasant family, which lived in the country and could not yet speak even one word of Portuguese, the Brazilian language. They stuck privately to themselves and produced an outstandingly 'stingy' yet resilient opposition towards foreign influence. Most other nationalities gradually lose the identities of their original country with a generation change. It is more the first generation that keeps up the customs and traditions from the 'old country'. One side effect of such behaviour is the formation of closed communities that are eventually regarded as a hindrance to integration.

Integration was however never something to happen in isolation, because it is the people who make or break it. Fortunately, time shows the way a multicultural society can 'heal wounds', which are inflicted from time to time in the adaptation process. When people start searching for records of their family tree, it can probably be said that they have become truly integrated. As soon as knowledge of the past has retreated, the present circumstances of individuals gain the upper hand, allowing a view of the past from a distance. The existence of an ethnic division in a society relates more to first generation migrants who haven't sufficiently managed to integrate into a new society. The next generation of 'new citizens' usually grows up without this problem and is more easily accepted by the host country. The bonds to their own culture weaken over time as the need to coexist gains the upper hand.

On the way towards integration into a new society, an individual is confronted with many things: a battle for recognition in language, religion, work, and family ethics. Differences can only be overcome when adaptation comes from both sides, the 'host' and the 'guest'. Some decide to return to their country of origin where they then discover that they have changed and become a 'foreigner' even in their country of origin. A second move to the 'host country' then often becomes a distinct possibility.

Integration efforts into another society help in nurturing tolerance and a better future understanding within a society. Such beginnings of the process towards a multicultural society are difficult and can only be understood by somebody who has gone through the rejections, adaptations, disappointments, recognitions and successes that lie ahead of any integration into a new society. Migration to distant countries goes through very similar patterns in terms of integration, as outlined in a 'guest worker's' situation. Migration is however earmarked with the decision of a more permanent nature.

MULTICULTURAL SOCIETY IN LIMBO

South Africa has made attempts in the past to establish a 'separatist' society, which with time failed to address the growing demands of a mixed society mainly of African and European descendants. All lost heavily when 'the pages' were turned in the 1990's. The Europeans lost their forefathers' heritage as a liberation movement took everything down a path where circumstances had to first get worse before getting better.

In the past, 'the other side' had been deprived from sharing responsibilities in South Africa's mixed society. As a result, the new government with the African majority entered a phase of learning the hard way through their mistakes—a costly process for all sides. To free themselves in such an interim situation, crime established itself so firmly that it became the number one problem. All this happened because of an impossibility to supply adequate opportunities for the masses of deprived African people.

Many resorted to taking what they thought belonged to them and were not willing to wait much longer for what their new government promised. Impossibilities to deliver have set the course back for everybody in South Africa: Africans, Europeans, Indians and its mixed population. If South Africa wants to succeed in the future, it also has to change into a multicultural society, in which all people participate to get the country's future back on track. Leaving behind new parties will not help its case. All good intentions have to unify to keep an effective check on the negative sides for the sake of the common goals in order to achieve freedom and prosperity for all that strive for it.

A remarkable move towards a correction in a multicultural society happened in early 2008 by the newly elected Australian government. Unlike Canada, who has made a move to reconcile with its indigenous Red Indian descendants by awarding them ownership of large territories, Australia had previously chosen a different path.

In Australia, territory claims by its indigenous population had been dealt with by forming Aboriginal 'reserves', mainly in the Northern Territory. These were not much better than 'lock-away' areas, failing to receive in the past the required attention. In areas other than the 'reserves', especially in city areas, the indigenous population of Australia was more 'tolerated' than actively integrated with equal opportunities into Australian society. Time has advanced long overdue changes in the Australian society for the mostly quietly enduring indigenous communities, allowing everybody, regardless of their origin, to responsibly participate in the life of a nation. Where there is a will, there is a way.

Kevin Rudd, the Prime Minister of Australia, took, in 2008, the initiative of publicly addressing reconciliation with the indigenous Australian population by acknowledging the past mistakes, thus opening the way to a better coexistence. On behalf of the whole multicultural society of Australia, Mr Rudd offered a repeated, apologetic 'sorry'. This gives a long overdue healing process a chance for the oldest culture on earth—Australia's Aboriginal culture—to reconcile with all the other cultures of modern Australian society.

Action was promised to work towards a more equal future for all Australians, in which the indigenous Australians would be equal partners. The task to address a community on equal terms will be immense because of past neglects. We have to start today and put all our differences aside in front of such an important future task. The Prime Minister also invited the opposition to come to the table and help shape the country's future together in a responsible manner for all Australians.

It is encouraging to see today that strong personalities like Kevin Rudd eventually can unite a society with better common goals. As was indicated in the chapter 'Democracy', a strong leader who can unite the people's voices with sound government initiatives is an essential part of a democracy. Throughout history, governments have brought the ups and downs to societies, which often were related to the real capabilities of a leader in any form of government.

After having outlined a few different paths of multicultural societies across the world, it is important to return to the accompanying elements of individuals in today's emerging new societies. A decision to move to another country and its society bears elements of a more decisive nature than the decision to work in another country. Especially in the beginning, more compulsions in a move to another country play their role leaving little room for a personal 'wish-list'. Whoever has integrated as a migrant makes a good 'building block' for multiculturalism to flourish in a society. Again, rejections, adaptations, disappointments, recognitions, and successes have to be addressed personally. Losing part of an inherited understanding opens however a door for 'new material' in a coexistence with other people. No such process is free of pain and as is often said: there is no gain without pain!

It is a widely known fact that all countries allowing the intake of people from other countries have to keep a close eye on the push of illegal migration. For whatever reasons, illegal migrants are more difficult to integrate into a society. Countries with a relatively small population like Canada and Australia are still classified as multicultural, despite not qualifying as a mega-society. The 'mega-society' doesn't yet refer to the number of its people, but more to the number of cultures living together in one country.

Integration of hopeful new citizens into a densely populated society can provide them with limited but immediate living conditions, whereas integration into a lesser-populated country doesn't guarantee such instant conditions as a support. Densely populated and sparsely populated societies share similar challenges when it comes to a multicultural society. A densely populated society lives more in circles, creating many of its own problems whereas the less populated society faces challenges out of a less apparent circulation. Here, citizens have to search within themselves to meet their own survival needs.

Both efforts, in a crowded and non-crowded society, amount actually to the same thing. On one side, what is a hindrance to be overcome in the densely populated society has, in the non-crowded society, freedom of more choice. It has however to be pursued with more individual efforts. In growing societies, these differences draw closer and help to form the universal multicultural society in a step towards the 'ant-society'.

I'd like to give a couple of samples out of a daily life to underpin the necessity of a more tolerant society in the world, where we all have to move closer if we want to survive a bit longer. As I have already outlined, it has never been, and will never be, an easy undertaking for anybody. Difficulties in understanding and acceptance are constant companions in the making of a multicultural society. When we don't try to live with the difficulties surrounding us, the difficulties would certainly continue into the future with little or no hope for a relief. Difficulties are there to be overcome.

Three different samples out of a life in an emerging multicultural society are aimed to highlight facts that are characteristic. The first is about a daughter/foreign friend in Germany. The daughter has been to the local movie with a friend. They take a road through the small town's centre before heading to the home of her parents. Nothing is special about this and still the news of this 'insignificant' event reaches her home address before her arrival. Who was the messenger and why? As a matter of fact, on arrival at the parent's home, the mother was already waiting at the door to their home. The friend stopped a short distance away.

"Who is the bloke with you?" asked the mother.

"He is Muzaffer. We have been to the movies."

"What is his name? Where is he from? He can't be a local. Even looking at him from a distance I can tell that."

"He is a very nice bloke if you want to know. I decide who is my friend!"

"Don't talk to me like that! All those years we have done our best to bring you up as you are today. We don't want you ending up like so many other kids that we all know too well. Our family is highly respected locally. Tell me who is that mister? You said his name before. Don't tell me; he is a foreigner. From the look of him, he must be one."

The argument continued back and forth for some time, both mother and daughter getting more and more heated. Finally the mother says, "This is too much. I can't listen to more of this rubbish. Tell me, where is this bloke from?"

"If you want to know exactly, he is from Turkey and his work is well respected in the same place where I work."

"We have never had a 'Turkey' in our family."

"It's about time that this is going to happen."

Dad yelled from inside the house, "Not even over my dead body! He is not coming into this house!"

The daughter shouts back, "Well I am not coming either, see you later."

The daughter and her friend leave but the mother is so upset that she admonishes her husband and goes after her daughter. Together they decide to attempt reconciliation. The mother returns to talk to the father while the daughter argues her case with Muzaffer. Half an hour passes before the daughter and her friend return to the house.

The house door was left open a slight gap. Mum receives the daughter first; ready to take her back into her arms. Friend Muzaffer remains outside a couple of steps behind, full of nervous expectations. Mum really took it to heart, coming out of the house, offering her hand to Muzaffer and inviting him into the house. Muzaffer needed some reassurance from the daughter to come in.

"It will be all right; my parents will be different when they get to know you. Please give them a chance. I am supporting you all the way."

"Okay. I give it a try; but only because of you."

Straight behind the house entrance the living room offered comfortable seats.

"Where is Dad, Mum? I want him to talk to both of us, but in a friendly way. If this doesn't happen, it is best to leave again. We are taking no 'shit'."

Muzaffer remained next to the seat where the daughter had placed herself, as if he wanted to escape.

The daughter smiled, "Are you all right? There is no need to get excited. Make yourself comfortable and settle in. Dad will join us in a moment. Do you hear this Dad?"

Only a few minutes later the silence broke and Dad joined the group, taking his seat without a word. After a short time he spoke, "So what's the fuss all about?'

The daughter opened the meeting. Mum helped to break the silence, 'You know, we always wanted only the best for you and that's why we have come together, so you can tell us a bit about your friend."

Dad still kept silent, only watching.

The daughter continues, "Muzaffer works as a CNC machine operator in the same local company, which employs me. He is very good at his job. His language is still a bit bumpy, but he has already proved to be a fast learner. I also want to see his country one day, the weather is so much better in Turkey than in our place."

Then Dad came out with, "How old are you Must… sorry I couldn't catch your name yet."

"My name is Muzaffer. I am twenty-five years old."

The impossible seemed to have happened. Dad was especially impressed when he heard Muzaffer answering his questions with clear sentences.

"Would you like to have a drink with us while Mum gets dinner ready?"

"Oh yes. I'd like that," responded Muzaffer. The ice was broken. The first cautious exchanges had started. In this case it proved once more that 'barking dogs seldom bite'. The initial rejection had been turned around into a multicultural understanding, in which everybody had to move away a little from his/her inherited culture to allow others to join their community and coexist.

As we know, not every beginning is easy and so too with the first multicultural contact. However, it doesn't stop after an introduction; continuous efforts have to come from more than one side to keep a 'multicultural boat afloat' in the wider society. Efforts that are instigated by peaceful means allow different cultures to live together and work for the betterment of a society, whereas efforts based on conflict work negatively in terms of coexistence in a multicultural society. The creation of a racially diverse society could be seen as the re-energizing of that society with fewer controversies. This in turn could lead to a better future

A DAY'S WORK IN AUSTRALIA

Nowhere else does the existence of a multicultural society become more evident than in a work environment, where professional people compete for their livelihood. Let me mention a visit to a high-tech tool room department of a Brisbane company in Australia.

Briefly, a 'tool room' definitely has nothing to do with hand tools like hammers or screwdrivers. Tooling has become the modern way to produce quality products with minimum labour involvement; automation is the ultimate stage in 'toolmaking'. Many parts are manufactured by 'tooling processes' such as machining, stamping, forming, moulding, casting and assembling which, along with many other processes, leads to the making of products used in our daily life e.g. cameras, televisions, cars, watches and so on.

In an industrialized world everything today is covered by 'tooling processes', which are, most of the time, very expensive to design and manufacture. It is decided at this stage how economically a product can be manufactured. Automation, process reliability and timing are crucial for a successful pricing of products. It is a fact that the majority of people never gain an insight into a 'tool room', because most companies have this facility behind closed doors, reflecting the need for secrecy about many of these processes. Modern 'tool rooms' are equipped with the latest technology meaning that today it includes state of the art computer systems from the design to the tool manufacture. People working in such a tool room environment usually have a trade background of a toolmaker. Experienced toolmakers earn good money.

The tool room in Brisbane had received instructions the day before that Japanese visitors were coming to look at our facilities. In our days, Japanese was synonymous with very fussy judges. They are used to taking everything one step further than the rest of the world has done.

Despite it being the middle of the week, the tool room reflected cleanliness and order as all is left in pristine condition late Friday before the weekend. Our tool room staff wore properly ironed marine-blue uniforms, representing, along with the spotless environment, the detailed attention the company also gives to its production efforts. A miniature Japanese flag was placed next to the Australian one at the entrance, surrounded by arrangements of tropical indoor plants. The epoxy floor reflected a mirror-finish and ceiling lights shone brightly.

The group of Japanese visitors had arrived in their organized mini-bus, a Japanese car model of course. Together with the key staff, the owner welcomed the visitors first in the company boardroom. At the reception, a sign indicated the details of both parties to 'celebrate' the occasion, as is the custom in Japan.

After a routine tour through the company, a surprised sigh of relief came from the visitors when they entered the tool room. Here the summer heat disappeared instantly in the fully temperature controlled area in front of a tropical garden which is every visitor's first stop.

"Here is our 'brain-centre'," the owner opened the tour. "Our modern machines are from Japan, Taiwan, Germany, Spain and Korea. Our staff also comes from various parts of the world: England, Germany, Switzerland, South Africa, and Vietnam. Here in Australia, far away from anywhere else in the world, we can only survive with the very best of everything."

After having personally welcomed each Japanese visitor with a Japanese-like 'bow', the tool room manager took over and answered all the raised questions.

The visitors had an interesting statement to give, 'We know in Japan that whoever makes it in Australia would have made it anywhere else in the world. Due to its difficult market position Australia has set its own remarkable benchmarks for survival.'

The tool room manager continued, 'We train our own people in collaboration with the State's education facilities. On our CAD-CAM systems, including machining centers, we successfully employ women also, who are a great asset in our workforce.

The in-house language is English, but people also converse privately in their native tongues. Over seventy different nationalities make up today's Australian society and they have all found a new home working together for a better future. Whoever gives his best every day has a well-paid job, which starts from the design to a process preparation, precision machining and a qualified assembly, all aided by the latest computer technology. Our employees are rotated through all skills over time, which gives them and the company the best indication of where the worker's individual strength lies.

We believe that to be progressive reflects well on the company's success. Our employees are our assets. Best results are achieved with a good international mix of staff in order to keep up a useful competition, which is required today in a constant changing technology. Teamwork is the key! Everybody is given the chance to move through with the other workers. Also, incentives for additional in-house as well as outside training are in place, so that nobody is left behind as long as he/she shows personal interest and respect towards others.

We are not promoting individual performers, because more heads can achieve better results than single ones. This is best achieved with different nationalities. When everybody steps back from his own understanding, this enables him/her to connect with others. This way good results can be achieved. A good team leader is important—one who can encourage employees with the right measures to focus on their efforts on a common task with various individual talents. The usual 'blindness' in the mistakes of isolated individual performers is also less likely to establish itself.

Clearly marked signs indicated that taking photos on the premises was not allowed, so the visitors had to make use of their eyes to gain a good overall picture. What we didn't want them to see was of course taken care of. Openness in the team approach is fine, but other rules dictate regarding outside competition. Certain restrictions with regard to competitive advantages remain in place in a multicultural society. As long as nations mark themselves off with borders, societies have to keep their 'sacred cow' in place. All this disappears first on a path towards the 'ant-society' while a multicultural society is an intermediate stage of that progress. A multicultural expression of a special kind can be found in Brazil during carnival in Rio de Janeiro. At least once a year carnival turns everybody into equals. The sharp divisions in the society between rich and poor disappear when everybody 'masks-up' for the most distinctive costume in the mass carnival procession. There are Indians, cowboys, devils, witches, kings, queens, fairies and flower-costumes. No costs are spared to show countless visitors from around the world their dreams. Brazil's powerful image of a few days multicultural harmony is projected to the outside world.

The poor here are in the majority, but this is not recognizable amongst the rich carnival performers. The poor in particular go to any extent to save their tiny money pool to create their own carnival costumes. They can dream for this moment of when they can escape their misery, if only for a moment, to compete with the rich for the attention of a beautiful 'Queen' or any other great figure of their fantasy. The poorer performers count often on their natural beauty that appears as 'café con leite' (coffee with milk). This appearance draws many visitors to this long established mixture of so many human races.

Brazil likes to look to the future hopefully, neither too far ahead nor completely out of sight. This could well be the explanation why the country hasn't yet reached what it proclaims on its national flag—the slogan 'ordem e progresso' (order and progress). A transformation of all participants who take part in a carnival procession with a common expression of joy, and leave everything else behind for the moment, can only be found in Brazil.

The dream for a better life—the conscious aim of all human beings, especially that of females—is winning against the odds during carnival season. Women in particular cannot reach these goals in their harsh daily lives. Who are they? Are they just one of the 'favellas' (shanty towns) millions of 'mulattos' from the city's outskirts: a secretary, a shop girl, a student or a rich daughter of an industrial tycoon? During carnival nobody can say for sure! The only important thing is that a woman appears especially beautiful and can dance excellently along with the many 'samba music schools'. All eyes are on her and this is the highest reward Brazil and its people can give her.

In line with a natural law of 'polarities', the hubbub of carnival lives side by side with widespread crime in Brazil. Where the social side of a society hasn't done its 'homework' satisfactorily, contrasts like wealth, poverty and crime live in close proximity. The authorities in Rio negotiate each year a deal with the 'crime league' so that they keep away from carnival. Depending on how this 'bribe' is accepted, crime barons might expect a better deal from their own activities and will go for it anyway.

'Life polarities' are also with people of a multicultural make-up where humans establish their existence while good and bad compete against each other. Tourists especially are well advised not to be in the wrong place at the wrong time, because the poverty behind this whole glamorous show will 'bite back'! It is advisable for visitors to stay with Brazilian connections and not rely completely on their own resources during the Rio Carnival.

Unfortunately after carnival the grim reality of daily life returns for the majority of Brazilians. Having enjoyed their own 'amisada' (fun) most seem to be content for another year with the new dreams born out of the carnival. 'What we cannot change, we don't worry about', is a strong Brazilian philosophy of life. The 'heyday of life' is for everybody, even though it is only once a year during carnival. What a superior life philosophy! Multiculturalism loses its 'shine' in Brazil straight after carnival season.

EPILOGUE

A lot still has to be done around the world to reach a fairer multicultural society. How many sacrifices are we asked to endure? Can benefits be met further along such a demand? More individuals will reduce the space for individual expressions if everybody holds firm onto his/her stand in life. Advances in a community are less likely to take place if people refuse to change and segregation can become the result with all its consequences. Then society is close to slipping into preparation for war, where everybody digs his trenches to confront each other just for the sake of his own 'identification'.

Time will have to play a vital role along with other factors to build on the 'fairer society' in the process of reconciliation, because nothing was ever achieved easily.

Controversies in communities and societies have to 'grind' away at each other long enough to lose each one's 'sting'. It is also reasonable to doubt though, whether the human race will ever get around this costly 'grinding process' to let common sense prevail.

In history, societies have always had a slump, before eventually emerging stronger over time. Such a process cannot be eliminated, but the path can be 'smoothened' in a multicultural society. Living together equalizes controversial attitudes with time, which receives its changes in a constant demand for new efforts towards coexistence. At the end, a society will be less judgmental, allowing individuals to live together less controversially.

Today many nations claim a multicultural status. To be true, we all are a long way from the goals of a truly multicultural society living in harmony. Stepping back in our traditional expectations shouldn't be regarded as a loss, as we should rather support a process in which more people live together and gain the personal freedom with others instead of keeping to ourselves. As long as we remain on track for a life together, there are chances to better overcome flare-up problems, which are usually of an ethnic nature.

Problems are not distant; they are rather with us and ask to be addressed first on an individual level. The politicians can only seize on efforts that come from the public. When talking about politicians' efforts, don't we really deal with 'great talkers' and 'paper tigers'? Every individual is asked to contribute unconditionally to the future of a better multicultural society in cooperation with others. A call for unity ranks above all.

CHAPTER FIVE

THE ENVIRONMENT

PROLOGUE

Not so long ago, when industrialization spread over the globe, the ever-present environment was introduced as an issue of importance in our lives. Today, everybody talks about the environment while very little is actually known. Only bits and pieces of information conveniently emerge for all sorts of purposes so that actions fall victim to indecisive behaviour. How long can we afford to continue like this?

Some facts gathered here aim to inform and thereby prepare a better starting point for the right actions, because the demand is for the environment to be the number one priority of modern society. Not even nuclear experiments have any justification in an environmental debate, because they are a contradiction to life. We are the ones claiming to control the nuclear experiments! Let's not forget that we are only humans with our inherited mixture of 'talents' but also with our error-driven 'disabilities'. We are not God!

What has the environment been like in the past and what is it like now? Everything we see around us is our environment. Our 'blinkers' seem to be constantly on as our range of vision can only focus on those small sections of the environment that are disabling us. But all elements of the environment interact with each other: sun, air, earth, water—these are the elements of our environment. They have interacted since pre-historic times to remain in balance, which has allowed life forms to prosper. Such a balance has evolved over millions of years slowly but steadily.

Evolution's path has always selected the 'better' way for continued survival. Nobody, including the human race, has been left behind. We have now engaged ourselves and 'turned the evolutionary tide'; our madness for power and progress has 'taken revenge' on what has turned man into the 'monster' we have become nowadays. By subordinating everything around us in terms of our environment, we turn the evolutionary clock forwards as well as backwards, which leaves us vulnerable against the elements—vulnerable, because we are changing our environmental support base through sun-reduction, earth-degradation, water wastage, and air pollution.

Our chances for continued survival within the environment are diminished in an evolutionary process. Progress under these conditions will turn against us. Looking beyond our environment to the stars looks like an escape from a responsibility we cannot uphold. Would running away from problems be an intelligent answer? Most definitely not! Let us therefore take into account what is still left in our environment and the challenges ahead. What is the time on the evolutionary clock today?

ENVIRONMENTAL AFFAIRS TODAY

Side-tracked, incompetent, powerful and seemingly significant 'experts' keep gathering in their numbers from around the world to have their say on the world climate, which is a basic part of the environment. Last time, this took place in Bali, Indonesia in 2007 and certainly more gatherings will follow in other places. Still, the rich natural environment of Bali invited many delegates to experience more or less a holiday, away from the pressures of other environments.

Don't let us become complacent because even in beautiful Bali the time clock has advanced. It is just not as visible yet as in the more highly sensitive environmental areas like Antarctica. In a tropical environment such as Bali, delegates don't feel 'work pressures' to discuss environmental changes. Such a 'meeting' would look very different in a more depleted environment like a desert or Antarctica. Messages out of these environments would be uncomfortable compared with the ones from Bali. Delegates couldn't have turned up in fashionable apparels and would have had to focus inevitably on the issues surrounding them.

I am personally troubled each time I see politicians gathering in luxury to have their 'yarn' on issues of poverty. They discuss how to 'help' societies in need or to make isolated decisions from a completely disconnected position, so that the ones requiring help cannot reach them. Isn't this an element of middle ages' feudalism still corrupting a wider population with its image? Does whatever looks great mean it has to have substance? To a certain degree yes; a work environment is however missing and so too is its workers, who deliver actions and not just words. It is still maintained, as long as people engage in discussions, that ways should and can be found to get us out of a looming environmental 'crisis'.

The Bali meeting ended with the classic solution: everybody agreed to disagree on how the planet's environment is to be treated. Binding results across a wider range of issues could not be achieved, because nobody came forward to commit himself to the required drastic measures needed in order to stop the 'looming environmental catastrophe'. The delegates enjoyed a luxurious meeting arranged by the friendly Indonesian host away from the harsh realities of environmental and climate changes before once more burying their heads in the sand. Where are the much-needed uncompromised, workable solutions? Impressions, expenses, lots of talking, more disagreements than agreements and still nobody wanted to take home the 'black sheep'.

Where does this leave our 'environmental baby' in its cot? A far cry from a caring mother! Will adversities born out of the environmental issues force us again to adjust ourselves ultimately to newly diminished conditions? Only when the 'good' has reconciled with the 'bad' can a better process of change be re-started; this painful historical dilemma haunts us repeatedly.

The question remains: is recovery possible for a 'better' environment after we have neglected and run-down our planet? The 'optimist' says anything is possible; the 'pessimist' sees it differently. One fact remains undisputed: to run something down happens much quicker than the rebuilding of it. In environmental terms, often a return is not possible as nature takes its course by putting us offside from what we have created.

If the *'augurs'* (ancient Roman clergy predicting outcomes with symbolic power) were still around responding to nature's questions, we would be better reconciled with nature. Their message would not be different from a binding acceptance, demanding huge efforts in our response to save the environment. However, all efforts other than those leading to positive action will be fruitless.

Let's leave the conference comforts for the uncomfortable reality that is the environment in 2008. It doesn't really matter where one starts. It is helpful to show how nature's elements are integrated with each other in a symbiotic relationship. As already indicated, the 'time-clock' is not far off midnight, when all results to be judged come to the table. Nature is impartial in its final judgement. Before becoming uncomfortable, a realistic account could tell us where we have left the environment and what are the chances of a correction from a negative to a more supportive, positive action.

Magazines and newspapers used for quick information are thrown into the bin again and again. Copy paper use is equally on a constant increase, delivering not only printed information but also superficial materials so that more people can take part in an 'information war'. We are not looking back to the origin of the paper; in a consumer environment everything is taken for granted and no questions are asked. But how many trees are cut daily out of nature's forests to supply paper? Our conscience has told us about 'replanting of trees', which will only change nature's slow course of maintaining a balance. Where we conveniently forget to re-plant, nature's new course will take over, making it difficult if not impossible to reverse over time what has become unbalanced.

Desert is nature's final response! Attempts to reverse the effects of deforestation are in some places made under huge financial burdens, which are higher than the initial harvest profit. In desert environments of Arabic countries, oil revenues are also used to create artificial natural environments, which are however restricted to a timely dependence on the oil revenues. CO_2 (carbon dioxide) output into the atmosphere has in the meantime become society's 'tittle tattle' response. Everybody watches everybody else and takes part in the search for willing and capable people who can do something about what effectively is a growing 'monster'. A positive response is lost in the 'heat' of the debate. Fewer trees also mean less CO_2 reduction in the atmosphere.

Regeneration of rain from the forest's storage capabilities is also interrupted, spreading further in ever-increasing circles. If the 'wounds' of a natural environment are not given a proper chance to heal, the next step after deforestation is the formation of deserts. We can't compete with nature's 'cleaning capacity' and when it comes to a certain point we have to admit that the job of restoring the environment has grown too big for us. Trading of CO_2 output is like temporarily shifting the 'bug', because a trading income would not cover the cost of processing—that is if a process to compete with the 'photosynthesis' of all plants without generating more environmental problems were even available.

Photosynthesis is when hydrogen is cut out of water through the sun's energy, assimilating CO_2 in plants instead, in order to form the organic substance 'glucose', the food for all living cells. On the other hand, the released oxygen from water during photosynthesis goes into the air, working on a balance in the atmosphere. Less rain and sun because of air pollution add to the problem of keeping a balance of

CO_2 in the atmosphere. Reduced tree numbers and plant life only add to the problem.

CO_2 in the air, when not assimilated in nature by 'photosynthesis', creates with rain an acid substance. This in turn kills plants off by disrupting biosynthesis, an inherent process in plants: the yellow/ green 'chlorophyll' in plant cells enables the process of 'photosynthesis' to take place. This single process shows how sensitive nature's environment is. Just one missing element in the balance of either sun energy or water or sufficient plant life will change nature's course in the environment on which all life forms depend.

Just who is responsible for the CO_2 output into the atmosphere? Who is doing it? Who else is on planet earth beside us? We could hardly justify putting the blame on animal and plant numbers; they are certainly not the cause for an imbalance in the environment, because they obey nature's selective laws, which regulate their numbers. We are in opposition to these laws and have to therefore bear the consequences of it.

While claiming constant superiority in our drive for progress, we subordinate everything around us for a limited time, until the environment responds surely but slowly out of a 'position of retreat', where new forces have prepared the downfall of the 'originator', our human race. "Forces unleashed, cannot be controlled any more." (Goethe)

Meanwhile, everything that can be burnt serves our search for more energy: mainly coal, fossil fuels, wood, recycling of our rubbish, and uranium. Waste burning without further impact on the environment needs to prove itself as it makes questionable an initial economic exploitation.

An historical note from the literature highlights the fact that man was at no time capable of judging properly our impact on the environment. In Northern France, today's Normandy, a citizen in the middle ages watched in a pasture the cattle's breath steaming out of the nostrils on a cold morning, raising at that time the question: if we had more cows, would they take away all the air? Today we laugh about such a comment, because we have 'progressed' and don't think any more that cattle could breathe away the air. In reality, has our consciousness about the environment gone backwards?

Physics tells us that only what has been invested can be extracted. One-sided extraction builds up debts, which when not serviced in time create the 'time bomb' we are facing today. Of course we are talking CO_2 reduction, but our growth doesn't yet allow us to tackle the pollution problems of the atmosphere credibly. Consequently, the earth, the water and all organisms become strained. Our measures still outweigh the growth factors—the explosion of human population and its activities, consumerism, the pressure on the environment caused by harmful substances such as car, ship, and aircraft emissions.

Power stations operate more efficiently but are still increasing their effects on the environment. Cars are for instance made more fuel-efficient, whereas at the same time some forty million new cars are put onto the road each year, adding to the overall increase of CO_2 output. Our growth overrides the counter measures in the environment.

We are in for a major dilemma. To reduce our impact on the environment calls for effective reduction of all our current activities. With reduction eventually in place, the activity level is reduced and with it our 'sacred employment-cow'. At present we are living in our own circle, where our activities create increasing problems that keep us in an activity spiral. To reduce one side inevitably affects the other. Will we ever learn to live with necessary restrictions? If we were serious about environmental issues, we would start restricting ourselves from this moment on.

We also claim to be 'good' at what is called 'scientific research' into environmental issues. Isn't this a bit like analyzing 'the child who fell too early into the well'? Why did it happen and how could we get it out again? The most dangerous 'well' we are facing in a growing environmental discussion is not where we would expect it, namely in the vicinity of our densely populated areas. An inevitable answer is coming up in an area where humans cannot live. The most sensitive area that controls the world climate from an isolated position keeps the extremes of weather patterns isolated.

ENTER ANTARCTICA

Changes imported into this 'resting area' of planet earth, bring changes to the whole planet. It is here where the 'time clock' ticks, shortly before midnight in 2008. Of course we are clever enough to discover previous cycles of climate changes in the ice layers of Antarctica. This doesn't however spare us the fundamental insight, because we are dealing today with accelerated conditions because of our civilization's activities. The continued growth of the human population is a result of our drive for progress in medicine and widely practiced mono-food production, which have driven us closer to an unbalanced environment. Where are we heading? Not enough people are prepared to face grim-realities; 'the head in the sand' and ' as long as this happens after me', are still the most common responses. The world has been around a while and why should we have to worry about it now?

The difference from previous climate changes, of which we have hardly conclusive records, lies in our 'unique' human population and its activities, accelerating nature's cycles to a degree we are not fully able to comprehend. Being complaisant would be irresponsible as the time clock is nearing 'midnight'. What Antarctica can tell us during a short visit by sea is that it doesn't take long today to move towards this icy wilderness.

Massive icebergs have already reached the south of New Zealand. They have become a 'tourist attraction'. Smart Kiwi entrepreneurs are turning those early warning signs into a short-lived business proposition and make people pay for their stay on an 'icy island'. It is the beginning of a coming change. The impressions are out of another world, but it should not detract from the reality, where these floating icy messengers started their voyage. Especially during summer in the southern hemisphere, ocean passages ease access to this 'hidden continent'.

A wall of ice has built around Antarctica, which is entirely covered with ice and snow, layers dating back to the early history of the earth. Many more icebergs of all sizes float nowadays in the ocean surrounding the mainland and drift slowly away from the 'mother-ice'. Only one seventh of an ice mass can be seen above water; the larger part is under water. Those factors should give a better idea of the cooling effects in the air and the ocean.

Colder seawater also has an effect on the atmospheric currents, reducing dramatically the intake of moisture for rain. The southern hemisphere faces cooler conditions with a much reduced precipitation, whereas this climate push from the south sends the atmosphere firstly further north with the ocean currents following later. As a result, the northern hemisphere temporarily turns warmer, which is what is happening at present. The 'real thing' is still to come! Let us not forget that the icy rim around Antarctica stops the inland ice cap from moving into the ocean. When the ice rim wall breaks off it clears the way for the inland ice cap to move into the ocean.

What does cause this phenomenon is not entirely clear—perhaps sun-magnet field changes. It is more likely a combination of effects, one of which could be that the ice masses on the land have grown to such a size that they escape with time into the surrounding ocean. The early breakdown of the icy rim precipitates an accelerated process through environmental changes, slowly raising the average temperature until the ice adds its coldness to the environment through the oceans. Have we already reached the second stage of a cooling effect in the southern hemisphere? Such a 'forced mixture' of the ocean and atmosphere will have, as a consequence, profound changes in climate, which changes the balance towards extremes of heat, wind, cold, wet and draught. These are already showing their presence.

THE THIRD FACE OF COINS

The inland ice cap of Antarctica is so massive that when it does move, the impact will be beyond our present imagination. Just before it takes place, it might still be appropriate to wish, 'after me the deluge'. No doubt, it will come! The moving ice masses change the earth's centre of gravity, which will mean that the earth becomes unstable. Ocean currents will most likely change dramatically and will flood the planet, drowning most life on earth.

Once this nature's 'fury' has died down, the ice can retreat with all the time it needs back to Antarctica. Then a new evolution might restart with our position on the bottom of its priority list. A disturbing fact today is that even the scientists stationed at Antarctica admit our 'time clock' is only minutes before midnight, which suggests that the acceleration of the process in Antarctica could be only twenty to twenty-five years away and all this because of our avarice. If we have not heard the alarm bells by now, we are probably not worth saving.

Having outlined a few of the environmental concerns, it is still useful to look at positive, more active responses, which could help us to move into a rosier future with the environment. Coming back to the elements of the environment, the sun is an essential component in our existence. While stopping the reduction of radiation by a polluted atmosphere, the sun can supply us with valuable energy, which could be used without the side effects of environmental damage. As the sun has supported so far life on planet earth, it is reasonable to suggest that it will continue for the time being under the condition that we don't change the environment.

The air surrounding us on earth has reached a stable composition over a huge period of time, allowing life to evolve. We have to treat the air with respect and neither pollute nor process it for purposes other than supporting life. It should be understood easily; we change this support and all life will change with it. All processes in nature start slowly, accelerating only towards the end. Changed environmental elements will therefore affect us first with reduced quality of life, including the further increase of diseases that are already on the rise.

Solar electric cars, ocean current power stations, wind generated power, and solar power can, when introduced consistently and in parallel with the elimination of current pollutant power usage, help reverse the trend. All these measures will assist in restoring balanced atmospheric conditions more suitable for living forms. Regarding air traffic, we have to find other energy sources than fossil fuels. Bio-fuels are not an answer either, because the environment is then affected from another direction. There is not enough suitable land allowing food and energy production to compete! Things will suffer in the long term—the land, the people, and the environment—in other words, every aspect of our lives.

We have to seriously reconsider our position in order to 'race' after possible solutions for an immediately improved environment and sacrifice also some of our deep-rooted habits. Otherwise we will not find sustainable replacements. It is best not to argue that fact and instead move quickly to accept restrictions on some aspects of our daily lives. We have to abandon our 'growth ideas', in which we are caught at present.

Growth should only be permitted in long-term sustainable environmental applications. All this requires strong leadership! To appoint such a leader, people have to be first educated accordingly, but with an eye on the 'time clock'. How suitable democracy is for such a non-debatable task, depends on the unconditional acceptance of a clear majority of people. Will today's democracy still cover this task? Haven't we already outsmarted ourselves from our 'sacred cow', democracy? Time alone will tell! The emergency in environmentally appropriate actions however doesn't allow any fiddling around with experiments. If we want to ultimately survive, our present options are very limited, except for the ones dictated by the environment.

The earth seems to be more forgiving than we are prepared to admit and tells us with a simple language when we have gone too far, either sending us a 'stink' or refusing to grow something for us. In between there is a wide scale of tolerance, which we constantly push to its limits. We dig out and shift whatever can be found on 'mother earth'. If our rubbish is not burnt with the assistance of the atmosphere or with a substitute of other gases, it is buried into the earth and we hope that because we cannot see it any more, it will go away.

The earth itself actually holds the key for the future. It won't bother 'mother earth' that we 'have a go' at her, whether by digging or tapping into the earth's energy. It will then shrink only marginally faster, shaking us with tremors, cracking its surface more, and further down the timeline, all the water will disappear into these cracks, cooling the earth down further and sending us into line with the other uninhabited planets. It is in our hands how fast we disappear from our good 'mother earth'. Let us respect her elements a little better and not exploit them erratically; a lot of painful lessons have to be learnt otherwise. If we don't want this, we'd better wake up now.

There are better ways to deal with 'mother earth' than are currently being practised. We can practice the recycling of materials in an environmentally friendly way, but we still have to do a lot of our 'homework'. We can reduce unnecessary waste, diversify agriculture into smaller units and allow the so important 'companion culture' to work (with the right support of bacteria and insects from an intact environment, no mono-culture over vast areas, which endangers the important 'bio diversity'). Different living forms compete here in order to maintain their survival capabilities as only one living form's survival chances are reduced, allowing non-selective competitors like diseases to bring competition in on a destructive scale.

The earth should not be a 'testing field' for what it can take, neither through underground nor any other crazy weapons testing. We should never forget that we also are, in one way or another, a product of 'mother earth' and therefore have to look at her more respectfully. Other creations than us are also around, which gives us no right to put our existence above theirs by exploiting them for our short-sighted purposes.

Latest research shows that we are living in a DNA pool in which all living forms have the same 'dual spiral building blocks' from which all living forms 'start'! We have still to go a long way to better understand what 'mother earth' holds. She is not only 'dirt' and 'stone'; she holds with the sun the energies that helped to build us and keep us alive. There is usually much more to life than we can see.

Premonitions of indigenous populations, especially within the Buddhist religion, advise caution in everything that we know and see. Knowledge remains the beginning of an understanding in which we will never reach an end. Knowledge is always preceded by observations or a premonition sparked by our brain. Without observation and premonition, knowledge could not have begun. A bit more devotion from us would also without doubt help the environment.

Water plays a significant role: no water, no life! And where do we stand with that manifestation today? Most people are not aware that apart from the oceans; fresh water is a scarce commodity on our planet. Yet we are using it as if it had an unlimited supply source. For that reason the quality of our fresh water resources is reduced and visibly dwindling. Forests store our fresh water, releasing it in a slowly controlled manner into rivers and the atmosphere helps regeneration in regular cycles, if not disrupted.

One such disruption is deforestation. Only naturally coherent forest areas manage, under their canopy, protection to regulate a steady flow of fresh water. This is where all rivers start. Rain, developing over the ocean and coming down in areas other than forests, runs quickly off the barren land, which doesn't help to bridge the time between precipitations like a slow release from a 'forest storage'.

History already tells us that all civilizations disappeared because of a disrupted fresh water supply. Babylon, Egypt, Greece, and Rome all worked to secure a fresh water supply without knowing that water has to be carefully managed so that the use doesn't exceed regeneration. We haven't come much further today and it can generally be stated that there is no uncontaminated fresh water left on earth. All sources are dwindling and pollution still exceeds efforts to restore water quality.

Water supports life, but only in natural 'clean' conditions, which are determined in its suspended substances and bacteria activity. There is a very fine line between ' just-good' water and 'bad' water'. An excess of suspended substances in water reaches living cells in a reduced form, and they in turn depend in their function on a very fine 'fusion exchange' of liquid substances. Many diseases can be traced back to poor water and air quality. Polluted air already contaminates the rain and with it the fresh water supply. If the soil is also contaminated and ultimately the rivers and the oceans, then the fresh water supply has ceased to exist.

Water out of the sky is loaded 'dielectrically positive' (one property of all things) by the sun's radiation and its speed to the earth, which has a crucial effect on living forms. Water in living forms carries mainly 'negative ions', which can only take in water from rain with 'positive ions', while 'same polarities' would repel. Rain is supposed to be our cleanest fresh water supply. When this source becomes contaminated through environmental pollution, the basis of our existence is affected.

Even recycled water, despite all the assurances, is simply 'second-hand quality' compared with nature's supply out of the sky. All other sources of water have a reduced 'biochemical' effect because of their 'negative loading'. Water only then becomes a helping hand in maintaining life at the minimum required functional level, but doesn't become a support to reach a healthy growth of the vital cell functions. The effects of poor water quality can't be measured in terms of our health and well-being!

A pharmaceutical industry can supply only one-sided partial solutions to illness symptoms. We keep fighting the causes and keep feeding an economy rather than stopping and using our brains to retrace the origins of the health problems. "Don't stop the spinning wheel!" Is our common knowledge in the dark? How much does water quality affect our health? The knowledge is there, kept well protected in books and papers and has traditionally been difficult to access by the people who could do something about it. We conveniently separate the 'old' discrepancy between 'theory' and 'practice'. Bureaucracy also helps to keep actions in 'secret places'.

Looking at our 'time clock', time is running out quickly because of our incompetence.

Without knowing it, we must be nearing the 'apocalypse' (menacing decay). The signs are here. Measures to store away seeds in an icy underground safe on Spitzbergen (Norway) is an admission that we have started to think seriously about the period after an 'apocalypse', which is not considered so far away any more. The bible has already mentioned that humans end up there if they behave in a self-destructive way; the 'bill' will then one day be laid on the table. It starts again with the 'little things' in our lives, trust—hate and greed, spreading instead their 'poison' and adding further to insecurity by dislodging a positive mainstream.

A very personal observation also gives reason for concern: more and more plant specimens in my own botanical garden, especially the ancient ones like sago palms, flower lately with a greater cost than they invest into their growth. They have very old 'programmed' genes with a lot of 'information' out of the past. Do they know that they have to produce seeds for a changed future?

There are still options to save our lifeline with water. We need again strong leadership and individual discipline to subordinate us to 'must-do solutions'. Before starting the 'big picture' of water restoration, everybody can start immediately his own contribution with small steps. By taking initiatives in real water saving, by not adding to pollution, by contributing to local, national, and international efforts to achieve long-term solutions, by replanting trees, by only farm harvesting and not out of natural environments, and by giving nature a helping hand to natural water storage to overcome water shortages, we can make a difference.

As much as water conservation has been neglected, it should create new opportunities to find the small steps towards restoring water resources. This depends very much on which side we are prepared to align ourselves, neglect or restoration. The present urgency for decisive actions in the environment doesn't give much time for hesitation or considerations. Also in the environment, progress can be achieved if we really want it. Let's prove it and not wait until we face the 'impossible', which sends us inevitably into a disaster of our own creation. Nature doesn't give us second chances!

We cannot afford any more to wait and see what might happen. If we don't translate our intellect into actions, there will be no issue left for an intellect. Action remains the highest priority even if each time couldn't be achieved what was expected; at least we'd then be on track towards a better future for the environment and us. The environment may have the patience to give us the time to still get us onto a path of real changes; only from there we can improve and it is strongly suggested that we keep on that path of recognizing, approving and acting on the required environmental measures. Where there is hope, there is also a way.

EPILOGUE

The question of the environment has been explored from a number of different viewpoints. I have not written for any single reader, rather for everybody who aims to offer a dialogue, participating impartially with common sense and not solely with the commonly circulated 'classified material'. The knowledge of given facts herewith should serve everybody's better understanding. The 'experts' might argue a 'partial knowledge' and should abandon their exclusive position and join in with an effort to bring knowledge to everybody in a simple, comprehensible way. Simplifying is more demanding than making something difficult!

If your expectations have not been met in this discussion, you might be able to better it in a wider dialogue. At least the 'ball has been released into the game.' The 'time-clock' set by the environment is shortly before 'midnight'. We all have to get our acts together and unify our efforts for a far-reaching goal without delay—to survive in the future. The 'elements' around already tell us forcibly that they won't be able to support us any longer unless we change the way we are dealing with them. When engaging ourselves in the pursuit of feeding back into the environment what we have taken out, chances are better to 'dampen' the environment's negative response in the not too distant future.

We can all benefit from a 'restored environment', but to get us there, we have to roll up our sleeves and do something about it and not waste time with arguing and talking.

We should all unanimously agree that the environment has become the biggest challenge we are facing today because of our way of life. Failure to respond decisively will leave us open to nature's courses, which we have helped to instigate and accelerate to the end of the evolution of many living forms on earth. Such a burden of a responsibility couldn't be borne!

Yet it is not too late. Let's put all our positive efforts together in continued smaller sacrifices in order to distance the otherwise inevitable 'mountain' of sacrifices. Some steps have been suggested here, but nearing a completion of a wider understanding, everybody has to be prepared to take this dialogue 'his own mile further' and not leave it to a 'discussion paper'. Putting down on paper thoughts that go out to readers, who otherwise could not be reached, is one step of my contribution to the environment. If the message hasn't been conveyed adequately, it's no use calling for action. I don't claim to have reserved the exclusive right of justness, but it is hopefully another wake-up call on behalf of our environment, which is in danger of getting stripped of its unique diversity and beauty. Let us plant another tree today for a future better environment.

CHAPTER SIX

EDUCATION

PROLOGUE

The word education derives from the Latin '*ducere*', which means 'guiding'. Guidance, especially in the field of education, is understood to succeed with the support of 'modelling actions'. The quality of this guidance is a measure of success in education. Society puts teachers into a formal position where they act on its behalf. This in turn puts teachers to the forefront within a society. Also, teachers are not born to educate and, as nobody is perfect, they can only act within the education framework if they have wider community support, where everybody is asked to come forward and pass on skills and knowledge.

Where can we see the signs of education in daily life? It starts with the little things: a clean appearance, legible writing, communicating with each other, proper behaviour, working for a living, eating and living a healthy lifestyle, keeping a balance between work, rest, enjoyment, hobbies, plans, staying positive and much more. Education, a central asset of a society, interacts with all its other domains: socially, skillfully, knowledgeably, unitedly, and defensively. It also balances the constant present oppositions to it: antisocial behaviour, incompetence, ignorance, disunity, and aggressiveness. All of this can only happen when all parties get involved in education efforts, coming to one table and mutually enhancing the talent development of individuals, not only in official public schools but also in the private domain.

With respect to individual peculiarities and desired conduct within a society, a societal improvement is more likely to become a reality for everybody. Despite constant changes, education is of paramount importance to a society's realistic changes for continued benefits. The complexity of a society reflects also on its systems of 'upbringing' and education. New emerging ideas have always competed with traditional ways of 'upbringing' and education; the 'battle' for superiority doesn't stop here either.

The overall performance of a society, not forgetting the 'upbringing' of children, is the ultimate measure of success in education matters also. A society's failure to perform sends clear messages that changes haven't materialized, which begs for increased efforts by returning to a more modest base from where correction becomes more viable. Only continuous efforts from across a majority in society can spare societies from 'upbringing' and education preconditions that indicate the 'big fall'. Independent of varying conditions, an analysis of the 'pro' and 'contra' arguments for an education revolution, spanning history into today and the future, will indicate the strengths and weaknesses. 'If we were perfect, nothing would be left for coming generations to do'.

Education has always been a high priority in all communities. Throughout history, education has developed in a close context with a community's progress out of a desire to pass on present skills and knowledge to the upcoming generation. It has gradually included more fields of a society's activities, originally more the social aspects of life, which allowed people to live together in greater harmony and decency, regarded as a prerequisite for any further education.

New experiences have introduced new community needs such as health and strength, skill and knowledge preparation, work competitiveness, teaching and research, staying creative, defending one's own important territories, but also respecting harmonious coexistence with others. Failure to reach perfection in education, which is only human, has led by gradual stages throughout history to where we are today.

AS OLD AS THE HUMAN RACE

Where did education start historically? First education efforts date back to the first communities of the human race. Life had already been reflected in the education movement by passing on skills and knowledge: from experiences of hunting, food collecting in nature, seeking in nature 'a roof over one's head', building then a protection against the seasons of the year, starting a fire for heating and cooking purposes, making tools to assist skill efforts, communicating with others and starting a goods exchange. All of these aspects of education started with 'skills' and then later added 'formal knowledge'.

The growth of communities deemed necessary new ways to pass on skills and then knowledge to others so that more people could participate in a quest for a more secure and improved life. Even from the beginning, 'exemplary action' had been the preferred method of educating others, as long as a community remained small. The larger community did not allow skills transfer only by example, 'formal education describing skills' however found its way into a broader education. As this 'formal education' required also its own set of skills (communicating, teaching, displaying and exercising through other means than 'per example') information was stored and transferred. The field of education had started to grow in direct relation to progress in communities and later in societies.

The splitting of the two tasks, skills education and knowledge education, caused the 'skills action' aspect to move towards being a 'description task' from where, ever since, skills and knowledge have tried to catch up with each other with varying degrees of success. Only our very early stages of learning skills have continued with 'example actions', long before we learned to comprehend through language communication. Play, an early form of 'skills learning', is not only a vital tool for the child, but also for us through our whole lives preparing developing skills. We need to stay on that educational path, because only from a 'playground' can we develop our own contribution to 'further education'. At the end, we have to respond individually with our own skills and knowledge to life's unpredictable situations.

Education has also been from early on an instrument to exercise power. There are other domains of education disciplines in a society. For instance, professional training, research and science, religion, and military training were all subordinated to a 'new power formation', which finally allowed 'the penny to drop'. He who runs the 'show' of education exercises a great power already through education's own justification in a society. No matter what a situation in a society might be, education has to stay, thereby giving an undisputed advantage.

For such a reason it has always been slow and difficult to bring education in line with progress. Too many secure human existences hang on to it and are reluctant about implementing changes. A 'self serving monster' developed with time, always ready to serve education, but under conditions aimed not 'to rock the boat' and govern without the usual uncertainties of 'real life'. Stability at the basis of society has become the justification. Later on it will be shown just how this justification stands up in the demands set by progress even in an economic recession or depression.

An 'upbringing' of the family, alliances with schools and 'further education' have to prepare a 'conduit' flowing into education's efforts. Education was always wasted, when 'upbringing' didn't correspond with formal education discipline. Talking about the constant facts that rule education, it can be said that discipline is one of the main pillars in all education efforts, whether in skills training or formal education. A spiritual focus on life gained access in early history in a growing education field through religion. As long as knowledge could not challenge religion, its followers carried it into our days with the support of tradition, maintaining the claim of a given order into our existence.

Changes in 'upbringing' and education were regarded in the past very conservatively. Therefore progress always surpassed education. Only recently computer technology has allowed education to better catch up with progress, but not with success all the way, because shortfalls in the basic elements of an education, like creativity supported by efforts, have changed education today to an almost unwanted degree. This is highlighted later in the section: 'Education Today in 2008'.

We cannot deny that education has introduced new levels in a society through a 'backdoor' replacement of the system of inherited aristocracy. The tradition of inherited superior characteristics lost credibility as a greater amount of knowledge surpassed such tradition. It is only human that as soon as humans handle something, it receives, through expressions of power, the human touch.

What were in the past relatively small groups claiming superiority in society, have turned into a more divisive people masses, where everybody tries to place himself according to the possibilities, which an education promotes. Is education the key for success in life? If we don't balance it with wider efforts than through formal education, our living conditions will catch up with us in another progress. It is this never-ending struggle for superiority that is guided mainly by intellect, which offsets efforts, leaving us therefore divided so that we are never completely right or wrong.

The more we do, no matter what it might be, the more we create problems, keeping the 'carousel' spinning. The 'wrong' side on that 'spin' always provides the extra work, so that an education system can find its justification in the 'carousel'. As soon as the education system with its 'appendix of upbringing' became complex and reached a superior position in societies, it could be called education's recent history.

EDUCATION TODAY

Education has become a firm institution in today's society, covering with its formal aspects virtually all areas. Prior to skills education and then the ensuing formal education, there was an equally important branch in the 'self motivated education', which was meant to follow us for a lifetime. Formal education should give us the preparation we need to get us started to operate tasks safely and efficiently with others as our competitive race demands.

Despite the level of discussion taking place, what should happen after a formal education? If formal education hasn't given the incentive to continue educating oneself, especially through existing underlying personal abilities, it has become only a personal 'attachment', which will fade and fail to activate with time one's own creativity. There is of course a balance between what we practice and what we learn. Focusing on one of these two skill levels is widely accepted, which has however become responsible for the division between practice and theory. Tradition has managed to put theory ahead of practical skills, establishing an unjust advantage for one side of society.

We should not forget even today that all advances in knowledge leading to inventions were derived from a skills basis e.g. the motor car by Daimler & Benz, the bicycle by Drais, radio by Hertz/Marconi, the telephone by A.G. Bell, the electric light bulb by A. Edison, etc. We have more problems creating practical results from pure knowledge than from a practical intelligence with its skills to establish the knowledge behind it. First was the action—everything else followed!

What does action in today's education look like? Often we are dealing with antiquated methods, in which a teacher still heads a class and teaches out of a book. 'What we have in writing can safely be taken home.' This is still the password for education; formality has become the 'mother' of many things, which asks for respect for what is taught over and over out of books, isolated from actions and traced afterwards only to theoretical knowledge and not skills.

Education has to start somewhere and therefore a steady formal process cannot be denied as it is established. Its division and isolation from skills and knowledge are however subjective enough to consider changes. Other ways of education are also around in many fields such as 'on the job training', which is usually lacking behind formal recognition. Tradition out of the past has helped to embody education firmly into a society supporting on one side continuity and steadfastness within a teaching process, but favours on the other, stagnation.

To ensure a balance in education is also a high priority. Progress in education has to be built into existing systems and not be served for throwing something out of it. Today's revolution in computers has changed the 'landscape' of education as never before. Yet we shouldn't forget about the basic principles in education that remain subject to pre-conditions like discipline. It still remains mandatory to start education with its elements of personal examples, before advancing from there. Progress without the basics is like building a house without its foundations.

Children who start education on computers run the risk of focusing too early on economic considerations of others, cutting short their own efforts, skills, and ingenuity to a large degree. Too much is presented at an advanced level which prevents the individual from retracing the origins of this knowledge. Foregone conclusions settle instead with individuals, making them the 'know-how servants' of a higher intelligence.

Surely concepts can also aim to have more people participating in work processes. Through computers reducing a task and thereby controlling more operators from one and the same level of intelligence, the number of participants is reduced. It ultimately depends on the individual, into which level his intellect allows him to become classified. More people are asking for changed approaches in education. Do we really want almost everybody highly formally educated? Who controls these people then? Specialization has developed so far that more people can participate in a complex task reducing at the same time however higher intellectual demands, which are very difficult to gain out of a progress-driven society. This in turn makes any system more vulnerable to economical changes, in which individual specialization cannot move any more with the changes.

Books can tell us only so much through the written word, whereas people have got more 'real' knowledge and when coordinated, people's knowledge from the 'real world' is as equally powerful as knowledge out of books. In a society everybody who is engaged in 'training on the job' knows about the benefits of such an education as opposed to a more formal education isolated from action. A good ' job training' has the advantage that it translates from action with a support of knowledge straight into results, which by all means is economically sound. The job training supplies already the job, builds on it and with the experience coming out of it, secures a job; whereas formal education has to go down first that road of experience, when a job will ask for it. Clever people in leading positions lean therefore very closely to the world of action, which alone can deliver the results. Any disconnection from actions in the 'real world' leads nowhere.

During the course of my life, I have personally experienced enough cases of people with a practical intelligence having no trouble in picking up book knowledge, when the opportunity was given. On the other side, we all know the stereotype of the absent-minded intellectual, who has trouble in performing a simple task like putting a nail straight into a designated spot. These people would be quick to respond, "I have a more intellectual task to perform than this nail business." Is there any substance behind such a statement? Doesn't everything require the same attention in the search for what is done right? Our education system is responsible for such a division, which still discriminates against practical intelligence by putting formal intelligence ahead of it. How capable would our teaching be in performing practical tasks?

A disturbing trend could also be called today the 'privatization' and 'capitalization' of education systems. Since when could money rule efficiency in education? Private education claims a right in a selective education for people who can pay for it, aiming at the same time to position themselves ahead of graduates from a public education system in the future. Ambitions in the private education system ignore however the obligations a society has towards all its citizens, i.e. equal opportunities. Only with equal opportunities can excellence emerge out of an education. Segregation stands for disunity in education, which fails to perform in open competition, producing our real champions. Education should be regarded as a 'right' for everybody in a society in order to gain access in relation to an individual's natural intellect.

A society has always been renewed from its broader base of citizens; the ones having reached the 'top' are already out of the race for superiority. The real 'battle' doesn't happen at the 'top'. The 'top' can only exist with a supporting base and is well advised to seek an open dialogue for its own benefit. An isolated 'top management' ends up in a 'dead end road', where everything becomes exposed to the detriment of those at the 'top'. Institutionalism for the purpose of securing privileged positions lasts only as long as resistance from a broader base brings an establishment down. Temptations in establishing authority ruling within a society are old one-sided instruments of power as old as human society. Education is not exempted from it. Real progress has always needed to 'rock the boat' in order to take it out of 'calm waters' into the 'stormy sea of changes'. Formal education has been advanced to a degree at the expense of a skills education so that sooner or later everybody will be knowledgeable as far as he/she can get and hardly anybody can do practical tasks any more.

Here is the key for rising economies: to better-educated knowledge with a broader skills base. An initial lower income from a skills basis will later on justify a better income, because the 'rest' has reluctantly abandoned skills, which are harder to reinstate than knowledge.

Abandoning skills through a wrong understanding of a living standard would become a perfect example of a modern decline of a society. Practical skills already involve a practical degree of knowledge, which is inherent to the skills or are developed from a person's skills level. Formal knowledge can only add to an existing practical skill; formal knowledge alone has never brought us far.

Equal partnership between skills training and formal education is a precondition for any education system to succeed. Differences between the two sides are detrimental to education efforts. Only together can they succeed. When recognizing the equal importance of skills and formally acquired knowledge, it supplies also a balanced distribution of intelligence and a work force, which would avoid the concentration of a formal educated intellect, detrimental to the skills. Through equal opportunities an outcome should be reached, in which skills and formal education are likewise desirable in a society as well as in remuneration and recognition. We should stop putting formal education ahead of practical skills abilities, otherwise we will run out of skilled people quicker than we would like.

Most people follow education paths with a view to better their future life prospects.

Therefore it is the responsibility of those people appointed to direct education, to provide the right 'switch positions'. In 2007, the elected Prime Minister of Australia, Kevin Rudd, courageously asked this question during his election campaign, 'What is the difference between a professional further education and a university education?' There is none and we have to recognize that both sides are contributing equal efforts in a society. Academics have no mandate from the public to lower other people's standard. How right or wrong is that? There is more truth than questions in it!

EDUCATION IN THE FUTURE

What else should education do in the future apart from what it is doing at present? First of all, it should take the 'blinkers' off and look past the 'establishment'. There are lots of things around us of which we are not always fully aware. Coming down from our own understanding to connect to others has never done any harm. Outside us is more to explore than we conveniently acknowledge and so is the case with education. Before wracking our brains for progress, it would be much easier to investigate first what others do in education. Only if compared with others can it be established where one stands with education. Nobody is perfect and can claim superiority over others. If doing so, we'd cut ourselves off from progress and instead go backwards.

Where are the other examples for a future improved education worthy of being investigated? The biggest mistake would be to classify from the start, where to look and where not. Reaching for new horizons in education, one has to be unbiased towards other approaches. We also have to look in such a process past religious, political, and social boundaries without limiting our equal and just opportunities through a comprehensive education.

In 2008, it became public knowledge that two countries, Finland and Taiwan, were selected as having the best education systems at the time. What do Finland and Taiwan have that makes them better in education terms than so many other countries? As I have family connections to Finland, I can refer to its education system from a personal point of view. It is basically an open one-institution system from the start right through. Nobody is discriminated against because of class barriers. Everybody performs to the level he/she can reach in a mainly free education system, which is regarded as a public obligation.

What in Finland is the liberty of the education system would, in Taiwan, be more the discipline, both reaching top marks for their system. The benefit from an advanced education reflects directly on the living standard. Finland is considered to have one of the highest living standards in the world. Even from Germany, I received news posted to Australia that Germany keeps regular contacts with Finland in order to find out what Finland is doing better within its education system.

Such an approach can only lead to real improvements on both sides. Many countries like Germany are locked in their education system by tradition, which has its merits in stability, but can also act as a brake system in a push for progress. One foot is usually in the past and the other one in the future, trying to make up for the discrepancy in a few branches of its education at a time, instead of performing right across the board. The system cut up into many branches prevents its universal performance. A 'perfect solution' wouldn't be desirable either, because there is no such a thing as perfection in the world. Everything is constantly changing, as is the education system required to do. The 'perfect system' would take out all the 'fun' we experience endeavouring to find new solutions. Apart from 'formal education', how are the skills treated, which should rank at the same level of importance for balanced employment reasons as was indicated before with formal education.

"How green is the grass in another field?" Back in the early 1960s I remember meeting a young man in my hometown in West Germany. He had successfully fled the oppressive communist system of the East. However, he expressed his surprise at the low standard of knowledge that school-leavers had in the West. Acknowledging the obviously better living conditions in the West, it came out that the education systems differed considerably from each other. The young man said, 'I didn't go through a university, but at primary school we learnt more than students learn here in the West at secondary school. We were all taught skills at school, learning how knowledge finds its application. Everybody in the East knows about machine tools and many trade practices straight from school so that further education, no matter in which direction, could bank on a common skills basis. Here in the West, only a plumber knows about a plumbing job and, as I found out, asking somebody what an EDM machine tool is showed that most wouldn't have a clue.

Education in the East worked much closer with the requirements of a skilled environment after school.'

Naturally the question would come up, 'Where was the East in its overall standing with the West?' In the East the political system of communism had reduced private initiative to such a degree that even the better education could not reach its potential under such an oppressive rule. Doesn't this put question marks on the claim that education rules the future of citizens? Education can remain isolated if not opened up into other directions, which serve purposes in societies other than ideological and politically motivated ones. Let's take away the 'veil of mist' covering communism and look in this direction to see what lessons could be learnt.

Not everything in another system is altogether bad. It has never been good advice to isolate ourselves from something different from what we know and distance ourselves from everything that is inherent in it. We are never totally right or totally wrong and should therefore never close doors providing access to a different system. This has not necessarily to be followed up by everybody but people charged with education should do it. They should prepare dialogues, in which suitable new solutions are developed while still serving a system to which they are obliged. There are many more cases outside our own field of activities worthy of investigation.

If putting a wider range of innovations to the test in an education system, what would a better education then look like? First of all, there should be one united education system with the commitment of the entire society. It should include pre-education, base-education, further education, and advanced education, all starting from childhood and continuing through to adulthood. Professional education should be a constant part of it, because all education ultimately has to lead to a professional activity if it is to contribute realistically to the life of a society.

All participants in such an open education receive confirmation of their present abilities and how far they can go in education. Nobody 'fails' on this open education pathway, as there is enough skills training providing at many stages opportunities to find employment through such connection to the real world. There should be no division between skills and formal education when everything is channeled into one direction out of which a future job becomes part of an education from an early stage. Even the economists could find approval in such an economically streamlined education process. Nobody could deny that education is also accountable in spending public money.

When coming to the so important 'teaching body' of all education levels, we have to make sure that it also serves the purpose of a newly defined education system. Apart from sound knowledge and the personality of a teacher, the system would be better off with teachers coming out of the real world and not from the 'school bench'. A good teacher is one who can connect education to the materials that are working in the field outside the education system.

To get there, it should be mandatory to collect experiences first through skills and then, for a number of years, knowledge in the professional world from which individuals who have the will to teach others should make their decision. The suitability of a teacher supported by pedagogy is easier from this side to be established than the other way around through isolated pre-education efforts. Additional pedagogy training could be more effectively implemented with candidates knowing the field in which they will teach.

To understand all this, we have to be prepared to get our foot out of the past and focus more on future requirements, especially in education. In the past, knowledge became cemented in a system, which as a consequence derived its justification from it. Today we should have advanced ourselves a bit more and have at least one foot out of the Middle Ages. It might as well be that all this discussion is rejected, because it asks for too many changes in the existing education system, which could however be wrong again.

Nothing has ever happened overnight, neither the present education system nor the future one. It is also well known that a desired result can be achieved, especially long term, by breaking down a task into smaller portions. People of 'high caliber' need to get involved and look at ideas instead of throwing conventionally everything overboard because of a lack of enthusiasm for changes. These people have to work out the details of how to incorporate into an existing education something long overdue—monitoring. Communicating openly and making adjustments when needed ensures that everything is then for the benefit of all.

I have started here a discussion and others are asked to participate in a wider discussion and eventually take it further. Not everything I have said here should be rejected outright. Despite not being formally recognized as an education 'expert', input from 'outside' should never be underestimated. As stated before, the 'experts' are often too close to their subject, easily losing therefore common-sense approaches by 'missing the wood for the trees'.

EPILOGUE

Isn't formal education a bit of both, 'ruminating' and eventually writing book number 13 after number 12? When it comes to education, our understanding should not be like this! Education is too important to be subjected to such narrow interpretations. If we can leave behind what history has created in education and learn from it, a better vision for a future education should develop. There is certainly in an education system the 'official side', which may not entirely agree with what is written here. But also we have to learn to accept independent views, which should be examined for their validity rather than disregarded by the establishment out of self-protectionism.

Over time everything has changed. It is up to us to deal with those changes. The more changes are disregarded and left on the 'back-burner', the more an explosive situation is favoured. Tradition always was a close ally with education, which in a sense has its benefits in a timely, limited stable situation. This 'calm' should not prevent a continued dialogue.

I have initiated here a dialogue from the early beginnings of an education, and looked at how it has diversified into the many different directions of today, suggesting also that it is time to unify all these directions with the focus on equal opportunities for all in a new education system. It is not only 'supremacy' of formal education sitting at a discussion table, but all those other forms of an education should take part in decisions in an equal partnership and contribute to a wider education system, especially to skills and self-education. Divisions in the system do not help in developing common education goals; a will to overcome those divisions for the benefits of a better education has to emerge instead.

Isn't there a system in place that is working? Why all these remarks? This certainly would be one view; probably a quite commonly adopted one. But why do I bring suggestions here, which ask for changes? People carry a lot of opinions around; many are never expressed, either verbally or in writing. Writing should be considered however one-step ahead of a verbal expression, because it reaches out to people we would otherwise not meet.

Not only people responsible for education should make decisions in their field, but also people dealing with other aspects of a society, as they know also how to contribute a good deal to a wider, open discussion. I found it personally interesting collecting my thoughts on education as an 'outsider', putting them down on paper for judgement by the widest possible reader circle. Where individual readers will disagree, it will still help to unleash their own thoughts. The absence of a constructive criticism wouldn't bring a discussion together, because criticism always was and is the essence of all discussions; to agree on everything cannot foster a worthwhile discussion.

Also no progress can happen without the element of criticism. Criticism should not hurt other people's opinions; when presented as constructive, it should have a firm place to prepare decisions, which can lead to newly balanced actions. Agreeing or disagreeing, regardless, if there is somebody else following me and writing down his or her views after this thought-provoking analysis, I would have great pleasure in a continued demonstration, in which the 'ball has entered the game and is passed on.'

CHAPTER SEVEN

HEALTH

PROLOGUE

What is commonly understood by 'health'? Regardless of divisions or borders, nationalities, races and languages, all people have one and the same understanding regarding health. According to the World Health Organization, health is an individual's complete well being in physical, mental and social terms. Health is an all embracing concern in human societies and it is therefore rated as a fundamental human right in which all human beings have equal rights accessing available services for the maintenance of health.

Where are we placed today in 2008 with this claim? Isn't health still subjected to preconditions that satisfy materialistic terms? Health maintenance is very much linked to economic and social achievements. A number of preconditions for health maintenance cannot be satisfied everywhere and all the time, because of economic and social fluctuations in most societies. The right for health care as the World Health Organization declares it, is in real terms a target to which all humans can aspire.

How the history of health care has been developed and managed throughout time into a common understanding today by individuals and societies across the world is worth examining. The aim of this discussion is to raise awareness about health issues. A great number of diverse personalities and organizations such as Florence Nightingale, Albert Schweitzer, Mother Theresa, Fred Hollow and Medicine Sans Frontiers have served and still serve humanity with health concerns, dedicating their health expertise to the maintenance of health care for so many underprivileged individuals. They are pioneers helping to ease the suffering caused by ill health.

Contrary to this is the fact that even the best human intentions cannot prevent controversy occurring in an oppositional attitude. It is here where individuals meet with the daily realities of risk factors influencing the individual's health. Health has always been a powerful issue, because it deals with the quality of human existence. Therefore it is only natural that our human power game has also firmly established itself in today's 'health industry'. Health has always been an important 'capital'. Its importance is however often realized only when health care is in short supply.

HEALTH, A TIMELESS ISSUE

To better understand where health issues stand today in 2008, it is useful to go back in history and trace the path that health care has travelled along with human societies. Already in very early history, the importance of health was recognized in a short Latin formula: *mens sana in corpore sano* (a healthy mind in a healthy body).

What does this mean? To have a healthy body housing a healthy mind is linked to a partial individual responsibility to recognize it and support a given health standard from generation to generation. There is a correlation between body and mind and vice versa. They both depend in many ways on each other, which is sufficiently established in the medical sciences of physiology, biochemistry and behaviourism. It is not the purpose to analyze here detailed medical science, but rather to foster a broader common understanding of it.

When going back in the history of human society, early records already cover the issue of health. As knowledge started to build up throughout history, health was considered an external power, having magical and demoniacal influences on a human existence. Medicine men, exorcists, magicians, and clergymen all exercised considerable power from early on in the area of health issues in communities.

Hippocrates was the first known doctor understanding that 'body fluids were wrongly mixed' in a case of ill health and not something acting magically from outside. On the Greek island of Kos in 460 B.C., Hippocrates established a medical school for doctors, teaching for the first time medical science. Even today, during medical studies, doctors take an oath on Hippocrates, in which is expressed that a doctor is solemnly serving to protect life and helping to maintain the health of all living forms.

Together with the continuous changes in our living conditions, medicine and health maintenance are also changing. This way medicine has gone through controversial phases in history, mainly because of human power perception in everything that we do. Polarities in health maintenance have naturally followed a path through history, in which one polarity is a beneficial outcome, whereas the other one stands for 'human error'. There have been times, especially during the Middle Ages, when people expressing any kind of criticism towards the establishment found themselves often denounced, persecuted and died at the guillotine or were burnt at the stake.

Leonardo da Vinci (1452-1519), the universal Italian genius of the time, secretly performed autopsies on dead bodies. At that time the powerful Catholic Church did not tolerate any knowledge obtained from inside a human body, because it was 'sacred territory' under God's authority. Only because of his influential connections was Da Vinci spared persecution.

In later times, the criticism of writer/dramatist Moliere exposed the weaknesses of health care in his comedies, e.g. *Le medecin malgre lui*

(*The Doctor in Spite of Himself*), 1666, and *Le malade imaginaire* (*The Imaginary Invalid*), 1673.

Below are quotes from a couple of extracts from Moliere's comedies:

1) Medical examination

   Professor: What do you do with a sick patient?

   Student: Bloodletting.

   Professor: And what are you doing when the patient isn't sick?

   Student: Bloodletting.

   Professor: What is your answer when the patient is rich?

   Student: More bloodletting.

   Professor: What is done when the patient is not getting better?

   Student: If he is poor, don't waste your time; but if he is rich, let repeatedly more blood.

   Professor: You have answered everything correctly, passed the exam and are now a doctor.

2) Extract from *The Imaginary Invalid*

   The doctors are only educated enough to give fancy Latin names to the things they do not comprehend. They will kill their patients with the best of intentions, but they will still be dead. All one can do is rest and let nature take its course. All of his previous doctors contradict everyone saying his doctors were idiots, while she blames his one arm for taking up all the nutrients, so he could have it amputated so as to make his other arm stronger.

"Where there is bright sunshine, there is also shade!" There are medical professionals worthy of community respect, but at the same time there are less gifted professionals around as well as is the case in all human endeavours. One secret in life has always been in finding the 'sunshine' and staying out of the 'shade' or 'winning the other side over to the sunnier side'. All our lives are filled with psychology; he who better taps into it has the chance of a better run in a life.

Moliere, the French dramatist, escaped persecution mostly because the influential people around King Louis XIV were too preoccupied with the scenes in Moliere's comedies, not recognising the ridiculous parts of it. The establishment had degenerated through its privileged lifestyle to such an extent already that they didn't notice the social criticism in Moliere's comedies. Only the King is said to have commented, 'It's only a comedy.' This fact alone helped to protect Moliere and his travelling theatre from persecution.

Still in the late nineteenth century, medical training was widely based on Latin terms, which was a relic from way back in history. Both Catholic liturgy and health care, communicating in Latin, were living in a close relationship for many centuries giving the 'magic' to the people instead of the 'irrevocable knowledge'. Also, medical professionals understood well to protect their interests against curious patients wanting to obtain knowledge. The Latin terminology had perfectly cut out any understanding from outsiders. By preventing a team approach, in which the patient is a crucial supporting player, this isolation only widened the gap between patient and physician.

Apart from criticism and evolutionary 'hiccups' in health maintenance, another aspect of the development of health services also shows extraordinary efforts and individual sacrifices to serve health progress. They have given health a lasting mark more than anything else, outweighing long term the weaknesses of a system. Here is further evidence that positive efforts and sacrifices will prevail upon negative ones during history.

The connection between health and medicine is quite obvious, as each needs the other one. For that reason, the subject of health is not just a concern for an individual's attention but also for medical professionals. From early history, attention to health was always restricted to progress in knowledge, in which at least two sides competed with each other. One side realized the power to gain control over individuals taking advantage out of others' misery trapped in ill-health, but there were at the same time also efforts in place to limit human suffering caused by ill health. Those antagonists are a fact of life and they are always with us as a universal demand by nature asking for a balance in everything. Let us focus on the forces that have supported health. As there are an untold number of great personalities who have served humanity in health, only a few past and present examples are highlighted.

Florence Nightingale (1820-1910), an English nurse, selflessly helped to limit the suffering of soldiers caught in the war conflict with Turkey, England, France and Russia on the Krim Peninsula. When she returned to England, Florence founded in her name the School of Nurses, setting her point to a future nurse training and mission out of her experience in a war zone. War has always created a situation of greater need. When common sense is lost through war, we can learn however best through our mistakes. This message became the trigger for Florence's activity from where she gained her experience and passed it on for future generations of nurses. Her emphasis on health and knowledge about it came very much out of the 'real world'.

Albert Schweitzer, a German theologian, musician, doctor and philosopher, lived from 1875 to 1965, devoting most of his life to Africa. He founded the Tropical Hospital of Lambarene in Gabon, where he selflessly helped people most in need. Schweitzer's universal intellect enabled him to reduce the human suffering in Africa on so many fronts. The power of one strong personality is outstanding in setting positive examples, which endure past the present and into a future. We constantly learn and should continue to do so especially from great personalities.

Mother Theresa was a more recent example of human determination to curb human suffering which started most of the time with a lack of health. Mother Theresa devoted her life to India, where the greatest number of people in need confronted her. Also in India selfishness was the key to any help. The 'thank you' of a person in need looks quite different from that of receiving help in an exchange as it is practiced in societies with higher living standards. We have first to be humble enough to be able to read the signs so that help can be given to people in need. Bright happy eyes can already tell so much to the one who can read such signs. Mother Theresa also experienced the greatest satisfaction with these seemingly modest signs that kept her active during her long life.

Fred Hollows of Australia couldn't have better profiled himself and his medical foundation as with his words, 'An eye is an eye, whether it is the one of the Prime Minister or that of an unknown citizen; help can only be understood on equal terms; to see the eyesight restored by a surgeon is the same relief and joy for all'. Fred was a strong advocate of the Australian pioneering spirit for human equality by serving the people in real need with his skills and knowledge that still live on.

Our world needs more of such people. I have just mentioned serving and not exchanging their skills and knowledge advantage for a personal benefit. One conclusion emerges here; that all outstanding personalities are active people, who therefore live, in most case, a long life. Activity driven by brainpower obviously supports a long life and stable health.

Marie Curie (1867-1934) from Warsaw, Poland, who worked mainly in Paris, is the modern face of science establishing 'Radiochemistry' which finds its application also in 'Radio Diagnostics', a very important 'tool' in today's health services. Exclusive devotion to her work was also the pre-condition to her success. Success has never been cheap or quick; personal sacrifices are still today common 'ingredients' of it.

Epidemic diseases were in the past serious health hazards, wiping out large numbers of citizens in communities across the world. Therefore, personalities who contributed to stem disease outbreaks, are also worthy of mentioning here. In 1796, E. Jenner succeeded in developing a vaccine to stop the spread of smallpox, a disease with devastating effects on a population. Rudolf Virchow (1821-1902) and Robert Koch (1843-1910) were pioneers in modern medicine with their research groundwork in bacteriology, pathology (establishing causes of diseases) and hygiene, setting also the conditions for future success in surgery.

Adding to the endless list of pioneers in health-services is surgeon E. Ferdinand Sauerbruch (1875-1951), who revolutionized methods of surgery by making possible for the first time access to organs within the chest, which are functioning under a vacuum.

One particular organization operates today across all the divides of societies in the field of health. *Medecins Sans Frontiers*, according to the name, has its origin in a French initiative in which qualified medical personnel provide health care to everybody they can reach. Often where politics fail, this organization of volunteers succeeds in helping people regardless of their nationality, race or social stand, even in war-torn areas.

It is not only a mountain of misery and corruption in the world around us, but also hope through shining examples of human determination to help more people to have a better life. Progress in medicine improved the health conditions in societies and as a consequence raised the life expectation of the population.

After an excursion into the past, let's have a look where the health issue stands today in societies. As stated before, health care is still provided in relation to the all-over performance of an economy and its direct dependant branch of a social security system of which health care is a subsidiary. The dependency of social services on the economy also drives progress. The environment reminds us, especially in recent years, to rethink our ways sooner rather than later. How we live and act on new approaches in health services, not only because of economical fluctuations but also wider changes in societies, will have a continued impact on any kind of social services. Recently 'smart economists' have managed to bring health care in line with industry requirements by transforming it into a so-called health 'industry'. Like other industries, the health industry was tailored to satisfy current industrial norms to be most of all financially viable and to operate within profit margins.

In this type of management where is the help left in health care? As long as the rest of the economy can provide people with extra money besides what is needed for a living, the health industry can live side by side with other industries. Even under good economical conditions, differences emerge. How many people can pay for health care? The ones paying smaller contributions or none at all comprise a second if not third class of health care recipients. It depends then entirely on the ethical standards of medical professionals to deal with the different conditions.

Money plays a vital role in today's life and can easily determine people's focus on health care, depending on how the available funding can cover health services. The connection to money is in fact an economic consideration in the health industry. Whether it can sustain demands for equal help is an open question, because money can mainly bridge differences in health care as long as it can be raised sufficiently for such a demand. If money is however in short supply and cannot satisfy the demands any more of the health industry, where will a broader health care be left then? Will it come to a point that we cannot afford its service any more within a social field? Financial tricks of credit only postpone the imminent problems.

When we can accept fluctuations in health services as they are driven in a competition with money, service, staff and equipment, then we might live as well with the unpredictable outfalls of it. Isn't health care a community responsibility to be available to everybody on equal terms? Liberalism in a health care system will develop its own limitations as it cannot satisfy equal services at all times. Fluctuations in the health industry feed directly into its services unless constant adjustments take place, which are however subjected to affordability in long terms. It is understandable that in economically good times, system trials were undertaken also in the health industry as developed in recent years. Positive economic times have never been a guarantor and therefore health care should find a better partner than that of an industry.

Throughout history we have always operated with a certain short-sightedness, only adjusting from time to time to newly emerged requirements often only as a last resort.

Liberalism became deeply rooted in America when its people seemed to have opportunities in unlimited supply. Those conditions have been wrongly transferred to other countries with different conditions creating timely advantages for the 'exporter' of liberalism until the conditions of other countries stood up and will continue to do so by putting their own mark on liberalism. What this means is that conditions of countries and their societies still focus differently on imported achievements from other countries and these societies. Not even progress can be imposed effectively on other countries, unless the other side builds up its own efforts.

The health care industry of today has to also go down a road and adjust hopefully in time into a more sustainable system for all individuals across the whole of a society and not just selectively. Meanwhile everybody has to put up with what the current health care system can provide. As long as a vision towards a realistically sustainable health care system is not lost, we have a good chance to stay in relatively good health.

What are the criteria for an individual's 'good' health? In order to establish health criteria, its need of a support and service can be best drawn from here. Fact number one: we are all born and given on our life's journey a 'package', which we are asked to 'administer'. The content of this 'package' is our physical, mental and social well being as our ancestors have passed on to us, even in its 'accidental' form. From then on we are asked to look after this 'package', including incorporating the help of others in respecting the environment so that it can feed back and support us.

We can build on our health, control inherited deficiencies or wreck our health. The value of health in a life often is recognized only when well-being falters and ill health has taken over. Sometimes such developments can be reversed, but more often we have to first learn the hard lesson when health is not self-evident any more. Maintaining health is a complex issue starting with one's own attention accompanied by education measures; an upholding of a personal discipline and simply by an entire lifestyle; these all can support health.

We never become sick for no reason at all! Mostly we have lost our way in the way we live or we simply don't know the causes of an illness. By ignoring health pre-requisites, later a wake-up call from a doctor usually tells us that we have let our health down. A health service then takes on a rehabilitation process, making us dependent on other people's skills. How much has been personally contributed to this ill health? Whether neglected, inherited or accidentally inflicted, it is not always obvious.

Doctors, nurses, surgeons and medical assistants can only do so much about a patient's awareness that can actively support those efforts to help. No doctor can heal in the widest sense without the patient's cooperation. Generally, medical professionals are confronted with so many options leading to ill health that a correct diagnosis is difficult to establish, as a patient often is ignorant about his/her condition. Medical professionals are only human beings and it wouldn't be fair to expect miracles from them. Miracles happen mostly in our fantasy, but not in the real world.

Across all professions people create their own scale of skills and knowledge, which can naturally differ considerably despite efforts in equal education standards. Once there is an end result, one knows whether or not all the efforts to stem a disease have been successful. It also can never be guaranteed that health is fully restored in a patient's well being. Looking at the facts around health and ill health, it is obvious; losing a good health status can happen much quicker than trying to restore health to its individually original status. As health is something very difficult to plainly see or measure, it is important to give it our proper attention daily in order to learn how to keep it in check.

What would a healthy lifestyle, one which can decisively support health and well being, look like? There are nearly as many suggestions around as individuals. Despite that, simplicity still allows us to reach a universally valid understanding; supporting health requires an intellectual insight into it. Lack of knowledge is the most common source of neglect in health care. The next common cause would be indifference until a wake-up call demonstrated by ill health, inevitably reminds us of our health duty.

It cannot be emphasized enough how important it is to incorporate more practical knowledge about health through education. Only practically focused teachers could attain such a goal. Even if it might appear trivial, a good place to start is with a lifestyle guideline, which everybody can understand. A focus on a balance in life's activities is almost mandatory in learning to live with our own restrictions.

As this could be difficult for many people to follow up, the fact remains that human nature has problems restricting ourselves, therefore missing so many points in health education. We first have to accept that we are a product of nature and therefore have better to learn about nature's course in order to stay natural. It starts with everyday life and how we go through it: the rise of daylight and its decline has a fundamental impact on all living forms. Life starts with a new day and ends with night taking over.

Many birds for instance can rise into the morning sky to catch an earlier glimpse of a newborn day. One species of them stands out when a day passes. Hardly any other living form expresses its mood stronger than the Long-Billed Corella. We have been able to observe this Australian parrot, as it has been with us for over twenty years to date on our property. Its noise is a lasting surprise for the one who witnesses this for the first time. What is the message behind it, day by day? An order in life! This is what nature has given to every living form in order to survive. When we put our intellect above nature's ruling, we can only expect unnatural responses in return to our way of life. One of these messages can be widely seen in health symptoms, which we put away with civilization sicknesses.

Getting up with daylight and resting with nightfall should be nature's rule also for us.

When proving to ourselves how easily we can bend this rule and live more the way we like to do, by indulging ourselves, things get out of balance. We extend the day into the night only for our convenience and by doing so we violate two basic rules: firstly, we miss out on a balance in our life between activities and rest; secondly, we upset our natural organs' routines as a consequence. Why for instance have we two kidneys? One for a day's function and the other to relieve it during night. Liver, stomach, heart, brain, they all need these balanced operational relaxation phases that a good night's sleep gives.

An imbalance here can easily lead to an increased organ function, which when not curbed, usually leads to 'neurosis', an often hidden pre-condition for sicknesses to establish themselves in many ways. The emphasis in our lives should be on regular patterns in which everybody can individually build on his/her physical and mental capacity. In doing so, a body-resistance towards irregular influences can be strengthened to a certain degree. Sports for instance, when practiced regularly in moderation to an individual's capability can build strength, assisting body functions positively under the condition that regular relaxation is part of it.

Every individual is equipped by nature differently and has therefore to find out what is effective or less so for his/her body. Connecting one's own intellect to these requirements plays an important role in achieving an individually tailored balance for wellbeing. So many details play a role in a healthy wellbeing that not everything is necessarily good for us unless an intellect can determine the good and less good for an individual. e.g.: working, sleeping, eating, exercising, enjoying, all of them have many versions of good and less good. It would take a whole book of its own to write a detailed account of the options of good and bad working, sleeping, eating etc habits, which are individually set on top of it. Health is connected to everything we do; being such a complex issue that it cannot be measured, it stays with us as a hidden agenda, coming to our attention often only when it is bad enough to be recognized.

Health requires a lot of attention in order to support and work for us. Also, the complexity of our modern daily life as a life in privation claims our attention to such a degree that health issues are often primarily neglected. Without going too deeply into details, one example shows the complexity of a health issue. Let me analyze the issue of sleeping. When can it be said that we had a healthy sleep? There are more options not to get there! A good sleep is like maintaining a 'battery'. Not enough maintenance makes the 'battery' lose its power, meaning that there is a relationship between working and recovery hours. Sleep is never the same; one person needs more of it than someone else, depending on a range of facts. Fitness is a measurement of how quickly a person can restore energy to its normal level when tired or exhausted. This already determines the amount of sleep a person requires; obviously the fit one requires less sleep. Fitness is however driven also by brainpower, which relates to the fact that a body and brain work closely together; no healthy body without a healthy brain and vice versa.

There are additional facts surrounding a good healthy sleep. Firstly, individual issues such as contentment or worries, tired disposition, health condition, food intake and its timing, personal hygiene, sleeping position, resting with or without dreams, hour of getting to sleep (every hour of sleep before midnight counts double!), age (youngsters can sleep like a 'flour bag' while age reduces the hours for a required sleep, because of a 'nerve system loading' during life).

Secondly, there are other contributing issues such as bed condition, correct mattress (no springs!), proper bedclothes (cotton), not too little nor too much sleep, proper pillow (not too soft and the right height to support the head with the neck), fresh and clean air circulation at a median temperature with moderate humidity (10-25°C), surrounding conditions in materials (wood, brick, stone, wallpaper, type of paint, old, new), bed temperature, noise levels, single or double bed for desired comfort, and weather conditions (changing, dry, wet, stormy, moon position).

To get all this right for a good night's sleep could become possibly a task preventing us from ever finding sleep. Education from an early age and one's own intellect should provide the common sense leading to a healthy rest. Especially with advanced age one has to find his/her own rule for a rest when sleep is not so easily come by as during adolescence. Despite being only one of many facets, a healthy sleep is a very important one and not to be underestimated, because a good sleep is the best 'partner' in life, a 'mother of life' and not the 'devil of death'.

Also progress can have an adverse effect on a society's health as it has recently come to light in parts of Europe, America and Australia, representing mainly the 'Western World'. After World War II, I can remember my stepfather saying, 'During the war people were neither as fat nor as sick as they are today.' As a matter of fact, today in 2008 the social health care has become an 'industry' of its own. An industry wanting to survive needs to be kept going, has become a requisition turning as a consequence into an institution on which growing numbers of people have started to rely. Often achievements others have worked hard to provide in the past are taken for granted in developments further down the track. People relying in such cases on service provision lose the focus on their own health responsibility.

Of course ill health is always around as well as good health, in which accidental or inherited conditions play their role. A great number of people however can become sick out of negligence, overly laid back attitudes or deliberate risk taking. Some of these might not be able to be controlled and a person will seek therefore the help of compensation from a higher authority for their part in a personal failure. Because nobody gets sick without a good reason, it is us not knowing about such reasons that can lead to trouble.

Authority ruling has always replaced individual responsibilities. Where such developments move today in societies, one only has to look closer into a doctor's practice. Every patient seeking the attention of a doctor asks for a treatment, coinciding with the medical professional appointment in which a patient expects to be rated the highest and most important priority. A doctor on the other hand can't possibly deal exclusively with highest priorities and important patients all day long and not lose his/her own account of variable patients' conditions.

The number of patients seeking medical attention can turn a health care into a 'conveyor industry', clocking patient attendance with time in order to manage their numbers. Many cases on that 'conveyor belt' could however be considered 'mild', likely reducing the attention for more serious cases. Even with the best intentions, such a mixture of patients makes it difficult to establish proper diagnoses (aspect of a disease) in a society where everybody claims the highest importance with very different health circumstances.

Let's not forget that medical professionals are also human beings subjected to human errors through personal dispositions. The moment we ask for help, we entrust ourselves to others thereby often losing control over our own health in this approach. Only few individuals might control health symptoms with their own insight and behaviour, reversing them to a degree, which requires a high level of commitment in the overall understanding of health issues.

I am also suggesting that too little by far is done for a wider community in terms of education in health and medicine. If everybody knew more about health, we wouldn't need such a big industry to serve it and could save valuable community resources better invested into a wider, more effective health practice and education. Medical knowledge has always been kept exclusive; allowing only limited numbers of specially selected people to gain access to it. Latin practiced in religion and medicine in the past created a suspicion of a close 'kinship' in both fields. Today intellect should have brought us further and opened also a better, wider medical understanding for the benefit of everybody's health.

EPILOGUE

Into which direction should the future health care system move? Natural fluctuations in economies cannot prevent a 'health industry' following in footsteps of the past and jeopardizing health standards in a society.

One direction could be to abolish an 'industry ruling' in health care, because economic considerations divert from the universal appointment to help every human being in need of medical attention regardless of age, race, social standing or nationality.

Such a reinstatement of an original concept from which we have moved away with time, asks however for changes also in medical ranks and in their way of thinking. To practice responsibility by supplying equal health care must start from authority levels. These must reach individual citizens in a socially balanced way and they in return can also effectively be reminded of their personal responsibility towards their own health so that the system can reach out to them when in real need. It is only what we are prepared to contribute to a system that can be expected in return.

Responsibilities like health in a society should be shared with all parties so that no one is left aside in sharing responsibility. In health matters, not capital but a broad readiness to contribute and help our most important common cause should rule. The still 'exclusive position' of today's health industry has to change into a forgone conclusive position within a society. Such a standard wouldn't belittle a professional medical reputation but rather open new avenues pointing towards a wider societal education and practicing co-responsibility as more time could be allocated for health care further away from 'mild' medical cases.

Also, not every patient's assumption of his/her health status is medically necessarily correct, mainly in the first place because of a lack of health education, making the task of medical professionals even more difficult. Teamwork has also the upper hand over a single performance in health care. Distributing responsibilities through a wider medical education would better balance the task of health care and help ease an unnecessary workload especially of medical professionals. The task should also be to simplify; this can only be achieved in a sharing of responsibilities.

The aim here was to bring some common sense issues into the health debate, adding also basic knowledge so that a wider circle of readers may benefit from a better understanding. In closing, here is something to think about.

A doctor tells a colleague, "I lost one of my patients."

"From what did he die?"

"Oh no, he didn't die. He became healthy!"

CHAPTER EIGHT

JUSTICE

PROLOGUE

What is 'justice' in the eyes of 'ordinary' citizens? Is it something hard to reach like a 'hot iron in the fire' carefully placed out of reach for safety's sake, but which eventually could 'burn someone's fingers'? Is it better therefore to keep away from it? Isn't justice, along with medicine and religion, in a similar 'boat', having exercised power in societies mainly through their exclusive position? Even today tradition gives them a helping hand. Because of its exclusivity, justice has always served those best familiar with it and who could use it for their own good.

Education has also failed here so far in reaching the wider community with an understanding of justice. Exclusiveness in justice has been, and still is, claiming an intellectual position, which discriminates in real terms to a degree against other intellectual groups in a society. If every group in a society claimed exclusivity from an isolated position, all of us would live in our own separate 'glasshouse', making for a society in which it is impossible to function properly.

Of course, nothing has ever been totally 'bad' or totally 'good' and so it is with justice. One definition could be that justice is an order under which a society should live by regulating its internal and external affairs in order to avoid conflict in the widest sense. Individuals are subordinated by legislation to this ruling based on tradition and majority consent. Even in this definition, 'justice' doesn't say much, because only 'educated' field experts have accumulated so much in justice 'provisions' that the interpretationscan hardly be understood by non-experts.

Bryce Courtenay best illustrates the dichotomy of knowledge and ignorance in the world of justice.

> *Simplicity is the key to almost everything. If something can be simply stated and simply understood, it will generally translate into a workable concept. Law has chosen to neglect this fundamental truth and as a result has allowed itself to become reactionary, complicated and, for the most part, unjust.*

Extract from *Tandia*

Because of exclusivity, the wider community has difficulty participating in necessary dialogues for progress. Things are never cemented into a fixed mould even with the law, which is the basis of justice. Laws upholding justice are often in isolation from reality if they do not stay open to the changes happening in societies. However, the need for a steady position of justice in a society is an impediment in itself, preventing adaptation to necessary changes. Therefore, justice is always trailing behind, trying to catch up with reality. It seems that the focus is more on not changing as societies also ask for steadiness. This works in a beneficial way as well as acting as a braking system on *ad hoc* change.

The 'white horse' of the Public Service also keeps justice in its place, which can be a perfect hiding place as long as changes do not loosen the grip on power of the justice system. Such persistence in a self-declared isolation makes understanding difficult for 'outsiders'. So it's no wonder that a large percentage of the population develops indifference towards the justice system, not out of ignorance, but out of an impossibility to fully comprehend the motives leading to justice. Unjust behaviour leading to crime could be one consequence of this.

How do 'ordinary' citizens receive justice through legislation? Logic usually doesn't deliver a comprehensive answer even in this case, because there is more behind legislation than any understanding could show. It is not so easy. Here is an attempt to shed some 'daylight' onto 'justice'—on its 'third coin face'. It is not a much-discussed topic, claiming an exclusive position because of a missing dialogue, which should be nurtured through a wider education.

FROM THE PAST TO THE PRESENT

Where and when did ' justice' emerge? Has it always been with us or developed with time? Did 'injustice' create 'justice'? In early history, individual family leaders from the growing communities were always the first to mark their will upon a community, imposing on others what to do and not do. A rule came into place, which only then changed when defeated by a rising opposition. Such competing forces asked in later societies for accords accepted more by a majority in order to stem rising conflicts between the interests of too many leaders.

Written rules started to control the activities of society. Those rules remained subjected for some time to changes through continued power competitions between rival parties from within the society and also increasingly from outside beyond the society's borders. Competition initially brought more conflict, which societies regulated by introducing laws internally, keeping safely and independently away from the 'battlefields' of a daily struggle. The increasing complexity of societies through progress demanded regulations in the political arena in which justice and law are positioned outside, avoiding any conflict of interest.

Not so long ago Latin also served as a communication vehicle within the judicial system, bringing legal terms in line with religious and health terminology. This was a relict of the past. Latin kept an understanding of justice away from everybody except the legal professionals. There is no absolute 'right'; whoever interprets an existing law best has 'right' on his side. Therefore justice representation by lawyers has always been the winner in justice claims, because who else could possibly find a way through the legal 'labyrinth'?

The power battle for legal rights has shifted with time to a competence level establishing dependencies; even Kings had to toe the line. Different levels of justice systems competed for a just verdict. Whoever has the 'longer breath' for perseverance in such fact finding between 'just' and 'unjust' is likely to find justice on his side and become the 'winner'. Also, justice is not meant to be gained 'cheaply' and financial 'hurdles' put in place by the justice system must be overcome. Everything is supposed to have its own 'price tag' especially when it comes to 'quality delivery'.

And who would argue the 'quality' in a justice system? Money generally speaks for quality. Is this why justice cannot be cheap? Justice systems have moved with their operation into exclusive territory where it is mostly accessed today only through substantial financial commitments. Therefore gaining justice often means losing somewhere else. The real winners become the legal practitioners who can pass the bill on to somebody else.

Also, justice systems in today's societies have reached an exclusive position in which citizens are best advised to ask this question first before using the justice process. 'Can I afford to be right?' For such a reason, the right for justice has developed into relative power expressions allowing attainment of these 'high ranks' of the justice system. Removing the veil of myths will however reveal that human beings only envisage true justice.

To cover the eventualities of 'human error', different authority levels have been established. The independence of each justice level is crucial for scrutiny of the judicial system. Our conscience has allowed justice systems to 'step down' to 'ordinary citizens' in order to argue legally their cases, an admission to the tenet of equal rights for all. Justice has been subject to law divisions not only through today's diverse societal needs for legal representation but also through recognition within its own history. It started with the 'law of nature' relating to our survival behaviour. The next influence on justice occurred in the rise of religious power, classified as 'Divine law' and based on ethics. In a society's evolution of justice it was first recognisable that what was needed for a just individual social life in an unforgiving nature were rules. Only then came the perception of better expectations.

Human rights declarations began as early as 1215 in the Magna Carta (first documented moves in England to secure rights not only for royalty but also for the other groups of society; a first admission of guilt towards unequal justice), reoccurring in 1776, in America during the Declaration of Independence from England with its thirteen states of that time, and in 1789, in France during the French Revolution (at the time a decisive rise of the people against the establishment in French society). In recent history the United Nations Assembly upgraded the Declaration of Human Rights in 1948, receiving signatures and commitment from a majority of countries around the world.

History has also taught that the power to determine the 'right' or 'wrong' in societies has developed into an institution without links to other societies' institutions in order to curb power interests connecting to each other. According to the 'textbook', this is successful. In reality, justice works by upholding its reputation of an independent balancing power as symbolized by the scales balanced by the 'Goddess Justitia'. 'Lady Justice', a Roman Goddess, holds in her right hand a double-edged sword positioned downward in which 'the power of reason and justice is wielded either for or against any party'. With her left hand she holds up a balanced scale. Being blindfolded (before 15th century her eyes were uncovered) indicates that justice is meted out objectively without fear or favour regardless of the identity, power or weakness of those seeking justice—blind justice and blind equality.

Developments in societies and the accompanying experiences are initiators of change and show how justice is recognized. In societies the main problems release a conscience towards mutual responsibilities continuing especially in recent times with the newly emerging knowledge that we overestimate our existence in a coexistence with other living forms. So far our cases have always enjoyed first priorities therefore neglecting the rights to live on equal terms with all other living forms of Mother Nature. If we don't change this position and include the exclusive understanding of justice, also documented in the Human Rights Declaration, we isolate ourselves even more from nature's course, which doesn't know about independent moves.

When 'injustice' seeks justice, the general perception is that it takes 'ages' to find a just verdict. The legal side argues here that justice needs its time to get through all possible impediments surrounding legal cases. Only humans come face-to-face attempting to fight injustice with justice during which the better arguments with perseverance can win the upper hand. To stay within the rules, both sides in a justice finding process are usually legally represented, making a legal case a battle of legal arguments, which gives both sides, accused and prosecutor, the 'legal weapon' in front of a judge resulting in an enduring battle.

Politically motivated cases take particular time as more than two interests are battling a case. A direct line from an established unjust case to justice cannot find a majority support because of evidentiary shortcomings. All this makes the legal system time consuming. Each level of jurisdiction is difficult to comprehend and last but not least, expensive. In justice fact-finding exercises, the legal systems have become more and more a 'glasshouse' situation in which a 'legal crop' is not only cultivated independently but also in isolation from the outside world. Prices out of this 'glasshouse' have lost ground claiming what a quality service could ask for.

When will the time come that we cannot afford our own justice system any more? Aren't we already close to it? The original task to simply identify 'bad' from 'good' has degenerated into a complex service industry in which all 'powerbrokers' of society quarrel for a simplified justice. Courts are appointed to determine justice. They underline their important appearances and formalities based on tradition, which brings them in line with ceremonies staged elsewhere in churches. Is there still an invitation to look at 'trust' and 'belief' as it was demonstrated in the Middle Ages?

Critics of these views should realize that people outside a legal system have very little understanding of it and as a result they are in a distant position from each other. Just because people do not understand something completely doesn't mean that they are less intelligent. There are often reasons why somebody is not sufficiently informed, because a one-sided exclusive position in a society prevents a wider dialogue.

As the system grows, 'purpose' and 'target' move further apart. Therefore it is no wonder 'missing a target' becomes the rule rather than the exception, especially in first 'hearings' of a legal case. How is it that in a verdict such discrepancies are from time to time published, for instance reporting a case of 'abuse', which receives eventually ten years imprisonment, whereas a murder case gets only three years deprivation of liberty in some cases? Isn't murder one of the greatest injustices inflicted on humans? For instance, extreme circumstances shouldn't allow psychology to reduce justice and a competence of exercising responsibilities by throwing arguments into a legal case. Can the power of arguments distort justice? When too many powers act on justice, a simple outcome is less likely to occur. Is there a better remedy to achieving justice in a simpler way than is currently still practiced?

As no 'time clock' can be turned back, it is appropriate to continue on the existing path with a renewed focus on simplification. The 'pro' and 'contra' in a search for justice have to be placed properly to allow clear definitions of justice and injustice to gain priority over other considerations like psychological ones. Too many different opinions allow weaker arguments to often gain the upper hand by undermining the stronger ones.

In the early history of human society, strength determined largely the right for justice, which has become without doubt incompatible with today's scenario. However, sympathy towards weaker expressions cannot always allow stronger arguments to retreat from justice because of a majority ruling. If justice is meant to be independent, it should stay between polarities and not take sides. Justice of the right is a matter of a definition in simple terms and as it is well known, simplicity is only achieved after all difficult solutions have become exhausted. All difficulties are first created in a 'training field' before simplicity can be reached.

How do 'ordinary' citizens live today with justice? Perceptions of justice do not vary only between individuals of a society but also between different societies. The degree of personal freedom determines largely the complexity of a judicial system. Justice can individually have a broad tolerance while everybody has to live with conditions not necessarily ' just' in every detail. Many things are not working in daily life the way we would like, but we still move within a tolerance of justice as long as others don't feel discriminated against or harmed.

Discrimination or harm towards other individuals is recognized by law as unjust as soon as an agreement in legislation has been contravened. Processes herein have turned very complex in history. Failure mainly in judicial administrations sparked the changes, which in an adjustment process hasn't come yet to an undisputed perfection, making a general understanding difficult in many ways especially for people not normally dealing with legal terms of justice and injustice. Processes of perception in justice have become extended in order to cover more and more possibilities of an injustice, which are not identified as such due to the lack of simplicity in judicial definitions. Consequently everything takes a long time whether dealing with a minor or a capital injustice.

As time is also money, the administration of justice has decided to lean towards both, time and money. This raises the question: has money become a key in justice, thus not giving access to all citizens, because money has always divided societies. Efforts to spread a more even justice go onto the account of societies, which makes justice still expensive if not out of reach in the future. To avoid such an impasse requires new efforts in which intellects other than legal professionals should take part in a broader dialogue so that eventually the 'blinkered' view receives a wider vision out of the legal 'glasshouse'. It is mandatory in today's world of 'dense conditions' to bring to a common table all possible contributions for the wider benefit of society and not exclude other inputs.

Education could play a vital role here so that more people gain access to a common understanding of justice and could therefore also participate in a wider discussion on justice. Exclusive positions, which have no place in societies of the Second Millennium, prevent this from happening. Also, legal professions have to make progress and get one foot out of the 'historical tradition' and closer to the realities in which we are all bound to compete for more sustainable living conditions. We neither want criminals to roam freely in societies to the detriment of others nor have half the population 'accommodated' in jails.

A majority society living in relative justice will, especially in the future, require more common efforts from all societies' branches and coordination of positive inputs from varying social backgrounds. This would demand however a special leadership, which is able to head such a task and bring together the better results. These 'managers' wouldn't necessarily come from a legal background. Experiences from other fields brought into the legal field couldn't do much harm. On the contrary, recently approved system inputs from other fields will only help to eradicate from the existing ranks a certain blindness to the truth. A legal system living in self-declared isolation from mainstream society for the purpose of independent legal immunity cannot serve society effectively.

The independence of a legal system has to be scrutinized more in consultation with the societal groups it is legally representing. There is no such thing as being 'right' and ' just' out of an exclusive isolation towards other citizens who represent the majority. Also, justice is not spared the changes that societies are going through unwittingly as well as wittingly. The clinging to antiquated rules only postpones until the future much needed adjustments, while it doesn't help a broader, better understanding born into society.

Sometimes it does appear that even in justice we have run out of 'our Latin', especially when looking at crisis management during war. Where is justice left then? Has schizophrenia (a withdrawal from reality) taken us over? All justice established in peacetime receives its contradiction during war. Are different justice standards accounting for different circumstances? How close do justice and religion become when a priest blesses men and materials moving into war? Human behaviour is still driven in survival situations by basic aggressions for dominance, suppressing our 'sacred cow'—intellect. In other words, conditions surrounding us are the generators of our endeavours.

When conditions change, our possibilities change with it and justice is no exception. Laws representing justice and injustice always seem to lack behind societal realities. Is the legal side, the society watchdog, taking its position safely in the back of a field from where it gains a better perspective? To prevent injustice from occurring out of a forward position would be a very different 'kettle of fish'. This would mean direct involvement with the realities and being asked to 'nip' justice 'in the bud'. Maybe better cooperation with other branches of society could foster better injustice prevention? A circle of argument returns here to a wider education, which could help prevent injustice more effectively through a better understanding. The question arises of course: how much time should be spent on a school bench for a wider education? Knowledge not put to the test is again useless!

In Japan, justice approaches injustice to the degree that perpetrators are counselled systematically from the moment they are caught. This is a measure comparable with the 'dog' being caught and remanded with correction instructions on the spot. Remorse is known to be addressed mainly in direct connection with a wrongdoing. Anything that happens later, becomes more subject to legal terminology as it is cemented in legislation distancing however 'action' and 'reaction' from each other. Offenders put straight behind bars eventually miss out on a path to correction, in many cases receiving instead adverse materials from inmates, which can rather support a re-offence at a later date.

Japan partly shows a way to deal with justice education out in the field of injustice and not on a school bench in an isolated matter. Injustice correction through educational measures is also more intelligent than punishment, which can affect a reverse attitude from guilt into revenge behaviour. Every human being has a conscience and when caught *in flagrante* (Italian for 'on the spot') with justice, everybody knows that he/she is wrong, even if only partly. This is the time for educational correction before 'camouflage' and 'escape' set in with time into a fact finding process.

A medium measurement in a justice resurrection would be the preferred option where an offender is first effectively remanded by education and then by work therapy. Locking away the offender in 'comfort' can foster unwanted social behaviour, as it is a known fact that a number of people turn to an offence in order to gain relative comfort by getting imprisoned. Winter, for instance, can trigger such behaviour in people lacking a regular life and accommodation. They gain, through minor offences, the care of the justice system, receiving a roof over their heads and a proper bed with regular food.

These 'little cases' are a possible beginning into a re-offending pattern, which can easily worsen, because everything that starts off small can become bigger later.

Appropriate work therapy would be the best option to correct antisocial attitudes expressed in an unjust behaviour. Work has always been the best medicine for a just social attitude. Depriving an offender of work therapy could be seen as a wrong measure in correction efforts. Work is not meant to be a punishment but a control mechanism of laziness, a distraction of mind that can all disconnect the offender from rehabilitation.

As an ordinary citizen I ask myself what, in 2008, justifies one unjust correction into justice, performed at the expense of a community? What surpasses education efforts for one citizen? The question mark would not be with the principles of justice to secure in society safe living conditions, but the correction that is rather done in an expensive and ineffective way. One legal system grants bail to an offender under certain circumstances until justice is done, whereas another (Roman Right) system denies bail. The one granting bail gives both sides, accused and prosecutor, time to prepare a case during which the legal system is freed from pressure of an urgent jurisdiction.

The bail money paid in such cases could easily be regarded as a time-buying exercise, which requires however sound judgement and control measures in order not to degenerate into a justice-avoidance scheme, whereby the accused outsmarts the legal system. Does today's environment still allow applying for bail conditions? Is the person who is not able to come up with bail money disadvantaged or advantaged in front of justice when the case is not deferred simply because money has not been paid? How much can money play a role? No bail requirements can eliminate that question.

Is our 'high human self-esteem' expressed in 'Human Rights' weakening justice awareness in 'confusion' with injustice? All sorts of arguments can turn injustice into justice and vice-versa when clear common sense cannot prevail and finally the 'weaker one' consumes the 'stronger one' at the expense of everybody else. Fear lingering between unjust correction and insecurity in justice maintenance often keeps a legal system off balance, allowing fear to take over insecurity and vice versa depending on society's movement towards 'soft' approaches. We seem to err first on the side of extremes, before eventually finding a middle way in all we do.

Justice perception is no exemption and it can be suggested that we are still a long way away from a balance between justice and injustice. Balance could become a great achievement in the future, because 'perfect justice' in 'polarity-driven existences' of our lives is only an illusion of a wishful human way of thinking. Nothing however has been wasted. Whether ' just' or 'unjust', it has rather become a 'building block' to where we are today and will continue to do so even under controversial circumstances. Courageous actions to continue on an existing path and allow changes to take place over time have always saved us from fear and insecurity, bringing us out of isolation and closer to a future balance.

After having read this topic of justice, you will most likely unleash your own thoughts ranging from facts, questions, controversies, confirmations, and disapprovals.

'Ruminating' over and over a topic aimed only at confirmation wouldn't make any sense, because it misses the point of fostering a continued wider dialogue, which I intended to start from an ordinary citizen's perspective and reach out also to a majority not legally bound in justice.

We should promote wider dialogues as everybody has an opinion. Only then can progress be achieved in a comparison with other views by taking off our own 'blinkers'. If justice has been given here only partial approval, this should indicate that it is only a beginning of a dialogue asking to be carried further, which in the end was the objective. 'What rests will rust.' Here is a move away from a resting mind towards contemplation of a complex topic. Let's not forget that this topic of 'justice' has a 'third face to its coin', too.

EPILOGUE

Conventional justice, when it is not in the hearts and minds of men, has only the power to corrupt...

How often men seem to initiate the greatest injustices and repression in the name of preventing chaos. The prevention of chaos was what brought the German people under Hitler and led to millions of Jews being crushed...

Violence and guns; they are invoked as often in the name of law as they are in opposition to it. The trigger is a poor debater but the bleeding-heart liberal, filled with dogma and cant, is equally ineffective.

Extracts from *Tandia* by Bryce Courtenay

Imagine you are asked to put on paper what you know and understand about a topic like 'justice'. I don't think the view that this is a matter for 'others' can facilitate a valuable dialogue. A prerequisite would of course be that the answer doesn't come from somebody in the legal profession who knows to argue with his own terminology. Everybody else in a society except the legal representation will 'scratch his/her head' when confronted with legal terms.

It can't be argued that people not entirely familiar with legal terminology could also intellectually reach this field. It should rather be said that every profession other than the legal one has a problem to reasonably come to terms with how to understand it. Who is wrong here, the outside world, the inhabitants of the legal 'glasshouse' or nobody?

'Justice' has traditionally been an exclusive field in which an intellect has established itself without much dialogue with the outside world, all under the promotion of independence. Is that independence defensible not only in the judicial system but also in the environment where justice is practised? Justice today as part of a modern society has started to open its doors allowing itself a better insight into life outside the 'glasshouse'.

Somebody who wants to reject here the views of ' justice' should not only consider what is said but also why it is said like this. Only then can a door be opened to a wider dialogue. This is not an excuse but rather is meant to be a start in which people other than legal professionals can benefit from a wider understanding. Nobody has an exclusive mandate any more. In a modern society everybody should compete more on equal terms. Wider education would also be the key to a better understanding and an attitude of more preventive unjust behaviour in 'justice'. Whoever has a better understanding is more likely to act justly.

CHAPTER NINE

TERROR: A DISEASE

PROLOGUE

Where is the cure for the disease, terror? The answer can be found in views expressed here. I am not referring in this script to any literature, but rather appealing to everybody who has an opinion, to participate as a reader in this dialogue process. We have also to understand the mechanism that leads to this disease and how to prevent it.

Supporting facts are introduced throughout: symptoms, diagnosis, remedy. We learn that terror is deeply rooted in societies, beginning at an individual level, right through to the family of international communities. It can remain hidden for some time, as diseases do, before emerging into the open as a common threat. A result points to the strength of dialogue—a must to hold the balance and maintain responsible economic outcomes by peaceful means. People making decisions in our societies perhaps might consider comparing this information with theirs. A dialogue is the preferred solution to settle conflicts.

INTRODUCTION

We are confronted daily with news of terror from around the world. We cannot say any longer, "I am lucky. I was spared," because terror reaches all of us eventually.

Why is that so? To find the answer we have to go back, to where the foundation of such an expression was laid. We should acknowledge the fact that we are all responsible for expressions of terror to a certain degree. Only then can we understand the mechanisms that lead to terror.

The word terror, which means 'fright', has its origin in Latin, and in as much as comparison can be drawn with disease; it is frightening in intensity yet steadfastly invisible. Along a similar track, the detection of disease is oftentimes preceded by the realization that it is in fact, already well established. Thus, to fight a disease at this point, it is wise to use a good measure of precaution. We kill the body and not the disease when we don't understand it or its origins, following the premise—a disease 'can mutate or spread'.

With a measure of understanding, the causes of an expression of terror can be traced, and then we have a firm basis on which to either work our way out of such a 'bottleneck', or establish a new direction, hopefully one that may lead out of any prevailing impasse. There is the opportunity for even hostile parties working in a joint effort to bring this to fruition, although critics will almost certainly dub this attitude of coexistence with others 'a theory with risks involved'. An alternative that is also not without risk is to attack relentlessly that which we cannot resolve.

One after-effect is emerging more clearly by the day: the expenditure of confrontation is disproportionate to an eventual negotiated outcome. The way we tend to live in today's world—with constant claims for superiority through power—prepares the ground for terror. Expressions of power always have a tendency to ignore the needs of others.

In the past and still today, we nourish ignorance towards change. This persistence 'hardens' others and the more this situation is maintained, the more of an imbalance is fostered, which is yet another pre-condition for terror. In the following thoughts, I endeavour to expose the beginnings that lead to the disease of terror, and what I hope to be a simplified system of identifying it.

ANALYSIS: SYMPTOMS

Symptoms of terror are widespread; we find them close to us, even with us. Let me start with forms of terror that are not necessarily found daily in print but are most definitely with us and can determine our behaviour.

a.) **Consumer** terror is a new form of terror. To satisfy economic goals in our industrial societies of today, we are spending money on goods that also serve purposes other than our own. Individuals can lose control in such a process by over-committing themselves. As a result of this, frustration and blame can often set in: blame that is more often than not directed towards everything except the individual.

There is an expression: some things start off small and can lead to something bigger at any time, which is why the processes of terror's inherent nature have therefore to be identified and closely watched, before those processes can take over. This applies to all 'symptoms' put forward here.

As I have indicated, 'symptoms', by their very nature, at times have a tendency to remain in hiding, undiscovered, and are able to progress from this position. Early detection is the key, before a 'symptom' transforms into a 'disease'—the disease of terror. There are many symptoms around, capable of supporting pre-conditions of a disease. Even sub-conscious factors might prime people for the reception of conditions, where they are caught in their own ignorance. The result is an 'imbalance' that we can identify as such in the section 'Diagnosis'.

We have here an 'imbalance in materials', originating from consumer self-assertion, that is for the most part in opposition to poverty. One example is when we are shopping at a supermarket and we are confronted by an overwhelming number of products. The products again are represented by large numbers of brand names. Which one should we choose? To help us out of this confusion, unlimited advertisements prepare us for this choice; the last information we received waits subconsciously within us, until we are prompted to make a conscious decision about which toothpaste, washing powder, or toilet paper to purchase today? We focus on packaging, prices, colours, quantities and all kinds of information, which diverts from the real thrust—the pressure to consume. In the event of a cash shortage, a credit card assists the process. A form of terror goes one small step further. In today's consumer environment, everything is controlled by money, whether we like it or not. Is it that a state of having little or nothing, brings us closer to sympathizing with terror?

b.) *Psycho* **terror** can be classified as a less evident form of a symptom. It is quite widespread within friendships, families and whole societies. The symptom of 'psycho-terror' is very often not recognized, yet it utilizes emotions, as well as elements, that are crucial to our existence. Whole societies have been misled by 'psycho-terror' in the past. Probably the best-known example of this is the propaganda machine of Hitler's 'Third Reich'. It is not my intention to go deeper into definitions. Rather, I wish to foster a wider understanding. People in our society that are given the mandate to make decisions in particular should compare this information with their own. This should enable them to gain a more balanced judgment prior to making decisions.

c.) *Knowledge* **terror** is a form of terror that could be disputed. We seem to readily accept that more knowledge should be better for us. Is this really the case though? Isn't knowledge also making life… uneasy? Knowledge obtained outside life's actions has the capacity to mislead to directions that are not in accordance with us; formal education can fit this description. This can sometimes be experienced with people who are knowledgeable, but their personality appears to be in open conflict to said knowledge.

Knowledge can destabilize individuals and they will support a basis for others to join in. Here again is a starting point for a behaviour pattern towards 'terror' through knowledge. To avoid such conflict through knowledge, the focus perhaps would benefit from redirection through teaching towards a 'balance of knowledge' along those avenues that closely match life's realities.

During my school days, an outstanding student named Martin Klar appeared to be a dangerous leader of the 'Baader-Meinhof' group. The whole school, especially teachers, were taken by surprise; nobody was able to explain such a radical change in an outstanding student from a decent family background. The events from 1965 to 1970 demonstrated just how destabilizing this individual became, especially at German universities. During 1966, I lost a whole year of study at Heidelberg University in Germany because armed conflict at the doorstep of the University forced its closure.

Unbalanced knowledge nourished an intellect that then engaged a number of followers into a circle of terror, changing the society not through constant dialogue, but through mechanisms of terror. The leader of this group, Klar, even engaged special police taskforces to help gain his freedom with their helicopter when he was cornered. This is a good example of how unbalanced knowledge can feed dangerously on a high intellect, resulting in terror.

d.) *Industrial* **terror** is the result of a battle of interests: where one industry often emerges stronger than prevailing political systems that should control and drive our societies. The philosophy behind it is, 'Life is a battle. Who battles better will survive.' The party left behind in such an elimination process usually disappears 'silently'. Oftentimes it grows to a recognizable force; a new opposition that raises the status of 'terror' higher eventually leading to a 'social conflict'.

Car manufacturers around the world enjoyed a powerful stance for a long time. With their product highly in demand by consumers, they position themselves between possible 'consumer-terror' and 'industrial-terror', whilst the number of employees in these industries constitutes a powerful mandate towards political expressions.

Experience shows that with smaller winning margins, manufacturers escape through other activities such as cutting the workforce, developing, buying and selling the original 'task' in order to manufacture and sell a product, and providing people with employment chances. With time, new activities superimposed on the original task, become dominant.

Therefore, financial considerations end up coming first in priority of employment responsibilities. Here is the avenue towards friction, when more than one activity cannot be satisfied. Friction is a starting point for possible future 'terror-action', if not dealt with by much effort involving constant dialogue.

e.) *Political* **terror** emerges from misuse of power. In this arena, we are commonly talking about 'people power' and understand with it the political control mechanism from people's basis. A mandate of power, departing too obviously from its original understanding, corrects itself first in a form of protest, which can often lead, unheard, to a strong action of opposition and becomes a trigger for terror once again. Most 'terror news' relates to one of these 'symptoms' as outlined above.

The recent military coup in Thailand in 2006 is a symptom of political-terror, providing much food for discussion, perhaps with a view to increasing awareness of what is actually happening. An outcome leaning towards terrorist action is a strong possibility in the event of a military coup. The outcome in Thailand appears to be related to the strong cultural institution of its king, and culture can be a stabilizing factor within a society, provided that the majority of the society identifies with it.

Even our prophets for democracy stop to argue when they become aware of the fact that a long cultural institution can regulate conflict from time to time. A trustworthy individual decision can successfully cut short a conflict situation, but only if the focus is set firmly on trust. A broad base of democratically supported decisions better deals with uncertainty.

ANALYSIS: DIAGNOSIS

The diagnosis of terror is always related to 'imbalances', which can be of a very different nature. Recently a gentleman within the United Nations' World Health Organization made the comment that:

> *We shouldn't have to help so many nations in this world. If we could find a way that non-industrialized nations get a fair price for their goods, they could exchange with industrialized nations. Fair is not what we consider fair, it is something which has to be worked out to the satisfaction of both parties. This way they would be in a much better position to deal with their own affairs.*

If these comments did not come from the U.N. Secretary General, their importance should not be related to a person's status. Our feedback to nations instead, is what is more or less left or put together after an exchange process; this becomes then a patch-up process, still allowing an imbalance to continue. Therein is the key to our past and present; one that we have to learn to move away from.

To reach a fair level of exchange, we must demonstrate a will for change. To do so, we have to think with an open mind and listen to what others have to say. This would be a good way for us to learn. The imbalances listed here all have a common denominator—missing dialogue isolates one party from the other, with the result that one side retreats into an obscure position, which then becomes a starting point for terror.

a.) ***Imbalance in materials*** is best presented in example. Crude oil is pumped out in many places all over the world. All we commonly know about it is related to the impact on our lives—the price at our petrol stations. Less commonly known though, is how much the owners of this oil receive in other countries from mighty multinational companies. There is also a pre-condition in place; somebody has to forward the money to find the oil. In most cases, the owners of oil have neither this sort of money nor the know-how available to undertake this task. The imbalance begins already, complete with dependency.

Nobody can deny that progress is also happening in most of the countries classified as Third World. Today, intelligent, educated people run the affairs of their countries. They are fully aware of their requirements, including the fact that oil from their countries doesn't only drive industries, but whole governments (with their excessive administrations) on derived tax revenues. Inspection of the price of petrol at a filling station does not tell us the price composition. We call ourselves intelligent by applying regulating factors like 'supply and demand', as long as this serves the industrialized nations well to do so.

China as a new power emerges with a new concept. They avoid the conflict through imbalance by putting themselves in an owner position and buying negotiated deals as a whole. This is a new approach, about which the multinationals are already becoming nervous. China is breaking into our economy monopoly. Such new moves open the door to negotiating better conditions, which the 'other side' must learn to use.

Imbalances are created. Poverty is one expression of an existing imbalance in materials; people with little or no material possessions may not fully develop the sense of an ownership, which in itself gives a measure of this so-important identity in return. This sequence may lead to poverty—people have nothing to relate to and, as a consequence, also nothing to lose. Poverty in its many forms is undoubtedly widespread. People trapped in poverty often will accept, with very little consideration, anything that gives them something of substance. Very often it does not matter how little or of what nature this might be. This is a starting point to channel poverty into terror by sidetracking with relatively little effort.

Imbalance in materials goes back in history. Back then, colonial powers established mainly self-serving rules, the aftermath of which still haunts the world today, both in economic and political terms. Groups of interest have shifted imperceptibly today; new impulses enter and lead into new directions. The rate of such occurrences is on the increase, and rapidly so. Will we ever enjoy a future without having to patch up the past?

b.) ***Imbalance in intellect*** originates from historical differences in culture. Throughout history, cultures have developed more in isolation. Technology has moved our world closer together. In today's world, a lack of understanding for that difference becomes evident. Some cultures retreat to secure their identity; others can either open themselves to new horizons for their benefit or lose their concept in the melting pots that are today's societies.

There is also a shift away from tradition, one of the main pillars of a culture, as a result of an economic vision. This shift in cultures creates a new intellect, which represents an imbalance and as previously discussed, when dialogue fails this is often another starting point for dissolution into terrorist action.

c.) ***Imbalance in religion*** is related to imbalance in intellect. Religion itself could be considered as part of a broader culture, which, when extrapolated, means that similar mechanisms of cultural history also apply for religion. Imbalance in religion needs its own attention. After an historical overview, it could be stated that religion is still today a trigger for terror through war.

Most religions claim exclusive 'justness', which is, from the outset, torn apart into so many camps and sub-camps, that no justice is established in real terms. Therefore, religion can only be referred to in terms of individual satisfaction of traditional knowledge. Camps, by their very nature, prevent free dialogue. Again, the inability or the lack of readiness for dialogue creates the imbalance, at its core, the main causal condition for terror through religions.

Indeed, most wars were started from that premise—people were sacrificed to uphold principles of ideologies. Nobody has ever put a price on losses through conflict by terror. Its means hardly justifies an outcome. The custodians of ideologies have never failed in their quest to engage others for their purposes.

d.) *Imbalance in power* reaches out to encompass all human activities; more activity links to more imbalances in power. Here are two different categories of imbalance in power:

1) *The Family Unit*: Families have experienced through history, generation changes. Parents are doing their best to prepare the younger generation for life and there are naturally different ways to do so. One way uses authority; another is more liberal and involves 'letting things go', and then there are all the variations in between. But there is also a way to constantly adjust to new requirements by setting an example and giving advice, and allowing a necessary dialogue to grow out of it.

    The strict way of authority does not take into account the present needs of the younger generation. If authority is strictly upheld, it will lead towards an imbalance in power between parents and the younger generation. Similarly, no authority applied at all, causes the same result. A golden rule for this dilemma in the change of generation lies in the capability to show a way through with partly applied authority, but leaving enough space for dialogue. The dialogue helps an emerging young generation to form its own, very necessary decisions.

    An imbalance of any form is a starting point for activity with aggressions. We know also that cause and effect can be very much apart through time. Something unleashed today might surface much later. The outcome of an imbalance is unpredictable. Next, we look at outlining situations that could conceivably be decisive for a society, if not for the world.

2) ***International Conflicts*** Recent events in the area that we call the *Middle East*, demonstrate very clearly where an imbalance in power leads. Over a number of years, the State of Lebanon has allowed an organization to operate from within their territory. Hezbollah has developed to a power that simply cannot be ignored by any party. During a recent conflict with Israel in 2006/2007, it became apparent that Hezbollah has been underestimated in its capacity to exercise power. Because of that, the state of Lebanon has reached a level where Hezbollah has offset Lebanon as a whole.

A number of factors have contributed to instability, from both inside and outside the country. The lack of reconciliation with tradition and new elements of power, have not been given enough importance through constant dialogue. There are some camps that barricade themselves over years to a degree, the end result being that dialogue is increasingly difficult to undertake and quite likely out of immediate reach. Developed imbalances ask to restore a balance. The stronger a side can play its role against another, the more the other side is able and tends to escape into an unknown underground to secure their position. The two sides have then lost touch with one another; the imbalance in power begins to establish itself into an unknown degree. Both sides are in real terms, 'in the dark'. When efforts of dialogue do not set foot in such a process, the ensuing imbalance translates with time into an act of confrontation.

How is this imbalance in power related to the events in *Iraq?* Saddam Hussein upheld power, despite representing only a minority. Additionally, he used his mandate of power disproportionately, which called for balance. Dialogue was not given enough of a chance to establish itself and as a consequence, the power behind the international interest in oil stepped in with war machinery in a heavy-handed fashion. The 'quick' solution ended up in prolonged terror—an imbalance in power.

Failure in balancing power has the nature to spread into other camps, where an imbalance in power regroups. This is happening in *Iran* today. We cannot exclude that forces meant to combat an imbalance in power in Iraq may regroup for a new battle, if new efforts in a dialogue are not given a chance on a wider field; no matter how slim a chance might appear, even at an advanced impasse. I repeat again, an effort towards dialogue must be given priority over any other form of power expression. It is cheaper and stops an escalation of imbalance in power. Even if this can be achieved only for moments, it aids in reducing the spread of injustice.

In *Afghanistan and Pakistan*, indeed we could include *India*, the power expressions between these countries operate at a very fragile level; further power battles will only destabilize the situation in this area. Whether we can call upon dialogue efforts at an advanced phase of conflict, depends largely on whether or not we find a way to temper by dialogue efforts the hardened position adopted by the party seeking refuge. For the sake of peace in our world, we must work towards dialogue. Failure to do so will not lead to intelligent or effective solutions to problems around us.

What of the military action in former *Yugoslavia*, over ten years ago? This was a correction of injustice through imbalance in power. The partial success of the military action was only possible because the imbalance in power in former Yugoslavia requested balance. The risk of failure through military action is always present; where an imbalance in power before a war turns to afterwards is anybody's guess.

The outcome in the former Yugoslavia has also to be seen in relation to the disappearance from the political platform of Tito, the author of this imbalance in power. The partner for a dialogue disappeared with his death. His successors did not reach to his heritage, a vacuum of power prevented Tito's regime from a continuation. His monopoly in power deprived people of Yugoslavia the right to exercise control in their own right. In such confusion, ethnic cleansing between ethnic groups gained a foothold.

There was no effective defense inside Yugoslavia when the war entered from outside. Military force stopped ethnic cleansing, but not the disintegration of the country in the aftermath. Nor was the search for justice brought to fruition. Two considerations arise: during this conflict, dialogue was never given any deep consideration, in addition to the war not meeting an effective resistance from the majority of the people of former Yugoslavia.

The art of dialogue has to draw from a wide field of possibilities to get it off the ground, politically, ethnically, ethically and socially. This might include economic measurements, which also means that exercising such pressure should never derail the goal of a dialogue. As long as dialogue takes central position, limited actions like economic measures can support a process within as dialogue.

A military coup took place in ***Thailand*** in 2006. The limitation of that coup under the maintenance of a broad dialogue, also can deliver a solution. A democratic view should not be considered in a narrow definition; different cultures, different circumstances require different views, as long as an outcome stays within a wider democratic understanding. The authority of the king in Thailand is a special cultural element of Thai society, which has to be respected as an important part of dialogue, as long as it functions towards the original destination.

The recent coup in Thailand could be regarded as a forced dialogue in traditional cultural elements; if this were the reason for a coup then it would be fair to say that its justification depends on an outcome that remains in line with democratic principles. This coup by the military has previously been reviewed in political-terror—a coup tends to draw from political-terror and an imbalance in power.

The recent conflict in **East Timor** is a remnant of colonial disregard for the needs of a country. It is no wonder that Timor as a whole was given no chance through history to learn and adapt their own affairs to modern changes. Even after military action silenced internal confusion, the country still today experiences difficulty in running its own affairs.

The military action has reinforced the status quo of two separate states, a situation that should not be in the first place. Instead of strengthening Timor as one country and supporting its people towards one identity, two external powers—Indonesia and Australia—have contributed to its division with the risk of renewed conflict.

Calm, on the surface, has returned. The fundamental problems of unity, sovereignty, how to get an economy off the ground and to govern in its own initiative, how to close a gap in a development, still remain current. All these problems have failed to be properly addressed through an open and impartial dialogue. Imbalance in power has been reinstated by a shortcut via military action. A new responsibility lies today on the shoulders of the two external powers, to find ways to activate unity and sovereignty in Timor. We are back to the point where dialogue should have been initiated.

The recent developments in **North Korea** were dealt with initially in the wrong way. North Korea expressed fear of a nuclear strike from America. Where was the effort for a dialogue, regardless of a pretext or not? Why did North Korea express this fear or feel threatened and abandoned in the face of its own problems? Everybody rushed to condemn North Korea, instead of seeking a dialogue, the only way to reach an understanding of existing positions. Condemning the other side and avoiding any contact, looks like the game of generation-change, when the bigger, stronger, older, whichever, creates its own problem by disregarding, underestimating and mistrusting the other party's position.

Failing to seek dialogue hardens the other side and raises the imbalance of power. It will predictably do what is in its power to reinstate the understanding of balance in power not through a dialogue, but through actions of possible terror. This is a typical situation where misunderstood parties could stand up for the wrong reasons. A wrong representation flavoured with distrust forces the parties further apart. A negative view produces only negative responses; neither party then is achieving a desired outcome. A successful dialogue incorporates much effort in openness, impartiality, and patience, trust building, time- and space-giving; all this based on practical psychology.

e.) **Social imbalance** is the result of a link between material imbalance and imbalance in power. The degree of imbalances in material and power translates into social imbalance. To balance it, a starting point has to be set with the power of active dialogue.

Emerging terror is the result of failure or absence of a dialogue. We do not have to look far to encounter social imbalance in our own backyard. Our social understanding in particular creates its social imbalance through our own understanding: we assume everybody is socially covered in a functioning society of today. Many do not care for others, because they take for granted their position and expect others to be 'in the same boat' as them.

How wrong such a view can be; we will only experience when we abandon our position of taking things for granted, and look around us more conscientiously. There is a vast amount of help required to get people out of a social imbalance; a social conscientiousness is needed to become pro-active in help.

Exercising power with a background of possessions is easily perceived to be a success; this shouldn't however disconnect us from people in need. A continued broad acceptance in societies works for social balance; acceptance in isolation works for social imbalance. After linking all these cases of imbalances to a dialogue, I'd like to give a recommendation here in a remedy that is required to succeed in such a dialogue.

MEASURES: REMEDIES

One pre-condition has to be set for the start of dialogue: each party has to respect the other as it is.

Dialogue begins with the purpose to meet and talk.

Everybody must be prepared to listen to what another party has to say.

Develop a position where everyone can still remain in a meeting or can come back to new meetings.

Do not take a position where others cannot follow you.

Remain on a common ground with everybody else.

Superiority emerges at the end of dialogue; other participants give this.

Allow a controversy to take part even in dialogue.

Nobody's sovereignty should be jeopardized.

Always leave a door open to dialogue.

Never close doors during dialogue.

Elements of pressure within dialogue should be handled with care; they also have to serve a purpose within a bigger picture that must run into a solution.

Give time a chance to work for dialogue.

Break down a plan into steps to ease dialogue.

Avoid hardened positions; they can lead to the end of dialogue.

In dialogue nobody can win without accepting losses.

A trust has to be built into dialogue.

Do not hesitate to be the first one to display trust of another side.

Check a position of trust during the process of dialogue.

Recall trust when this is required.

One disappointment cannot be the end of everything; consistency through dialogue is the only way to dismantle the 'wrong side' of a party.

An end of dialogue should not indicate the end of efforts towards dialogue.

When we cannot stand up and produce efforts any longer, dialogue is vanishing; the result may be action through terror. Thus, the effort must be made to continue.

We claim to be intelligent; therefore we are bound to stand up in efforts to continue dialogue. These recommendations are nothing else but common sense.

Everybody, who is serious and applies a measure of common sense, must succeed with the help of time. I'm not suggesting here in detail how to document and follow up minutes of a dialogue; this again is common sense based on experience.

9/11 WORLD TRADE CENTRE

Will the 9/11 World Trade Centre disaster follow the pattern previously outlined?

Analysis: Symptoms

Industrial terror combined with political terror was established in one organization: Al Qaeda.

Its residence: Afghanistan and Pakistan

Its leader: Osama Bin Laden

Reason for terror: 'Changing the world'

Statement: This is neither the first attempt of an 'ideology' to 'change the world', nor will it be the last.

Response: All nations should be regarded as equal partners. Differences have to be solved through dialogue, not with acts of terror, or war. Controversial views beg to be heard. If they don't receive appropriate attention in due time, they will affect, with an increased response through terror, an outside resistance to their understanding.

Analysis: Diagnosis

Imbalances in intellect and religion: for identification refer to section II and III of 'Imbalances'.

Measure: Remedies

We rarely extinguish fire with fire. Dialogue needs to connect to the symptoms; this is where a correction has to commence. We have to learn to deal with uneasy partners through dialogue. There is a saying: 'Good medicine must taste bad,' which means that we have also to endure the bad taste, to cure the disease called 'terror'.

EPILOGUE

Opponents of dialogue will argue their case; they might receive one concession out of confrontation. Nothing lasts forever; a weapon long enough in use, will lose its sharpness. A decline of power in such a process invariably leads to dialogue at its end, albeit through questionable detours. It can still be maintained that the effort towards dialogue has the effect of putting action on hold. What should be seen as a saving in men, women, sometimes even in children, and materials is cause enough. Dialogue is always 'cheaper' than confrontation!

We owe such a saving-approach really to people that are caught in action, upheld by a party that is always sitting on the sidelines when it comes to making decisions that suit them and their principles. This could be called the imbalance in power. We are not dealing with frontiers out of the past any more; others are neither less intelligent nor less powerful. The only way to reach the other side effectively is through efforts in dialogue, not through attempts at punishment.

CHAPTER TEN

RELIGION

PROLOGUE

Religion spans the world in which human societies live. Is religion therefore humane, tending to refine and civilize these societies? Furthermore, religions and sects almost equal in number the cultures expressed in different languages. Thus, religion and language are close partners by which the power of a language expresses religion (as do other cultural elements such as education, art, and music).

In the past, religion ruled almost all fields of daily life, losing however its dominance as the power of the human mind turned towards technical progress, becoming a new reality for a growing number of people. A focus away from religious tradition started to develop in societies, competing with their progress. Does this mean society is a better place because of this change in focus? Isn't there a case here like everything else? Throwing something out is always the easier way; replacing something asks for new efforts. This is not easily achieved across a whole society of varying individual characters.

Religion can have a stabilizing effect on an individual's life, saving the search for a replacement for religion. The restrictive nature of a religious belief can be seen as a saviour in life's storms that nobody is spared. According to varying capabilities, physical as well as mental, individuals respond differently to changes in their environment. By focusing only on the pursuit of knowledge, we realize that the more we strive for it, the more we recognize how little we comprehend of an infinite knowledge. As we can never reach complete knowledge, it is quite intelligent to retreat into something away from the 'knowledge highway' which gives this so important freedom to our otherwise never ending search for answers to our existence.

An insight into religion throughout history is however marked with much controversy.

Realistically this shouldn't be a surprise as humans have safeguarded religion from their 'fellow creatures' and will always continue to do so. The 'pros' and 'cons' of religion are presented here together in a dialogue, albeit a limited dialogue in a seemingly endless topic. This dialogue leaves open the individual's right to choose between belief and knowledge, as neither of these fields can exercise sole representation. Our existence has become too complex to allow the turning back of the clock to simplistic single issues. Today, all issues somehow link to each other in our lives, which we have to recognise properly in order not to lose our heritage neither of the past nor present. The same would apply for religion when it is a heritage.

OUT OF THE PAST

The word religion derives its meaning from 'religio', which goes back to two Latin derivations. Firstly, Cicero, a Roman politician, orator and philosopher (106-43 B.C.) related religion to the Latin word 'religere' meaning 'carefully observing' which was expanded to mean 'to observe carefully in prayers, chants, images and temples, everything that worshipped Gods'. The other word-root goes back to 'religare', a definition by Augustine, a church teacher (354-430 A.D.) meaning to 'reconnect', given that a 'disengaged soul reconnects to the one and only God in reconciliation'.

These were the first endeavours in Christian religious concepts, which have since gone a long way across 'bumpy roads', reaching the universal understanding of today. Regardless of the nature of the religious belief, every individual is granted the right of this belief. This at least is formally recognized.

Religion is a very personal reference of human belief, a continuation of knowledge in which every individual can experience how far it can go with knowledge and when belief or faith takes over. Just how much personal elements play a role in religion can simply be experienced when a different religion enters the 'milieu' of a family. Religion has then come as close to us as it can. When such a situation takes place, 'tolerance' adapts from a discussion point to the different dimensions of reality.

What was before 'religious tolerance' is likely to become a sticking point and a challenge from outside for a family. It shows how religious beliefs can suddenly impact on a family. From a distance, other religions can achieve acceptance in a discussion more easily than from the close-up view of personal experience. A younger generation is quite understandably more curious and open to other religious expressions. Choice has become in recent times so great because technological advances in the fields of transport and communication have brought people from all over the world closer together.

The eight main world religions of today—Christianity, Islam, Buddhism, Confucianism, Hinduism, Shintoism, Taoism, and Judaism—all have so many sub-groups or sects, that unity in religious beliefs has become a distant fact. Christians alone live under the influence of numerous religious sub-groups—Roman Catholic, Anglican, Protestant, and Orthodox. India too, as the most diverse society with its estimated 1,500 single languages, has besides its main religion of Hinduism other religions such as Buddhism, Christianity, Sikhs, Shinas, and an even greater number of 'castes' (*jati*), estimated at three thousand, which is generally speaking another classification within the Indian mega-society.

Philosophy can actually claim a uniting power within the many diverse religious expressions. It is the only expression to bridge the human diversity in culture, language and religion by focusing on similar basic understanding in our existence of hope, balanced actions, knowledge, and compassion. They all lead to a continuation of life under renewed efforts. In our 'roundabout lives', we all have to return to those philosophical conclusions, even after war or natural destruction. Only philosophy can deliver answers across all the religious divides and it is not difficult to associate with it. One has only to ask more questions instead of pretending to know, which gives the individual more possibilities on how to gain real knowledge better tailored to an individual existence.

The individual philosophy is not necessarily a known 'house brand' as religion has already laid claim to ownership. The interpretation of an individual's existence from an authority source like religion has always been a more convenient understanding. A 'lonely battler' is more exposed to controversies in his life than if he has 'club membership' of a particular religion, in which collective answers can minimize the considerable life-burdens of otherwise potentially 'lost' individuals.

Returning to the scenario of a family, when offspring get 'hooked on' a culturally different religion is when the challenge turns real, not only for parents but also for the extended family. We are used to living within our own bounds and when something from outside demands that we open ourselves to new perspectives or keep our position secure by stopping other influences entering our lives, we can be threatened. Here is one key for past and present controversies, which easily lead to conflicts through different religious views.

It should be a common understanding that religions have been controversial throughout history. Everything we do regarding religion can be controversial. We never achieve only the 'good' or the 'bad', because those polarities demand coexistence. And as humans express religions, they are also subjected to controversies. No matter how good intentions are, religion expresses a power claim through humans, too.

Our existence is mainly expressed through power. To relinquish belief to a higher authority saves it naturally from dialogue scrutiny, because nobody would otherwise respond. Less knowledge has worked in the past in favour of a belief system, which religions developed by closing an early gap in understanding. Growing knowledge questioned first with time the religious power-claim and then minimized it. Are all religions humane and have therefore a firm place in all societies to the degree we as individuals remain humane?

What were the origins of all religions? During early 'primitive' human history we lived closer to nature and drew knowledge from a level of our understanding. Nature's displays of daylight, sun, night, moon, stars, rain, storm, and thunder preoccupied human inquisitiveness from early on. Even questions spanning birth to death have changed our priorities mainly through hardship and sickness; those questions are as old as history itself. Evolution determined our existence by developing side-by-side beliefs and knowledge out of nature into one life-polarity, which are bound to stay in a balance from where we cannot ultimately escape. Too much belief or knowledge offsets this balance, driving us into the territory of human errors. Are errors the 'tongue of balance' in our existence, whether in our actions, beliefs or search for knowledge?

Our comprehension started in nature and was formed with 'mystical images', constituting an early competition between fear and knowledge. Expressions of power emerged already that early in small communities claimed a next expression-level with 'prophets' having a knowledge-power over others, classified as a belief substituting knowledge. As the next step in such a development, 'religious tradition' helped to pass the nature of these expressions to the next generation. 'Prophets' had found their limits in consequent discoveries and intellectual inquisitiveness. Those changes in the human perception gave rise to a religious tradition aiming to safeguard individuals from the uncertainties of constant changes through progress. Such wishful human certainties became however a power-tool in the hands of religions, which have controlled people's lives over centuries. If war were not unleashed on societies in the name of religion, religions could have contributed better conditions than those in the past.

For such reasons, Christianity is probably the most controversial religion of all. Controversy started already in the cradle with the crucifixion of Jesus continuing unabated in varying forms throughout its whole history. The decline of the Roman Imperium favoured a power change to the Roman Catholic Church with its later 'head office' in the Vatican, still operating from Rome today. A claim of centralized unconditional ruling from Rome caused in 1054 the split of the Orthodox Church in Constantinople, which has survived independently mainly in Greece, Russia, Serbia, Romania, Bulgaria, in parts of Poland and the Czech Republic. The two religious partners haven't found their way back to common ground yet despite the late Pope John Paul II bringing the two religious parties back to the discussion table.

The most outstanding controversies of Christianity culminated mostly in wars throughout history. Crusades were not motivated only religiously but also politically and economically, starting already in the eleventh century lasting into the thirteenth century with early confrontations with Islam in North Africa and Asia Minor, all under the banner of 'fighting the infidels'. It shouldn't be a surprise that Islam has included in its ' jihad' a duty to fight for Islam.

Who was really the first to move against another religion is more likely a matter of interpretation. Christians had their fair share of conflicts. A new stern leadership started under Ignatius Loyola (1491-1556), the founder of the Order of Jesuits, another Christian branch, which brought human suffering upon non-followers by exporting uncompromisingly Jesuit-doctrines especially into South America. This had the serious consequence of decimating indigenous populations. Loyola created the key phrase, 'The means justify the actions.' In other words, the means that were chosen to attain a 'higher religious purpose' had also the approval of the highest religious ranks regardless of the fallout, as long as they propagated Jesuit doctrines. Tolerance wasn't exactly a 'key concept' in those 'power wars'. The stronger claimed one-sided rights through Jesuit doctrine putting at the time another division into Christian unity, in which more than one wanted to be the better, increasingly at the expense of a better Christianity.

Conflicts continued in France against the Huguenots (French Protestants) during the sixteenth century and then the Thirty Years War (1618-1648), in which the whole of Europe took up arms, staging power claims in the conflict between religion and governments. Not only in their own ranks, conflict served religious power-expressions when options seemed to run short, but it was also exported during colonization into other parts of the world. The extermination of Indians in North and South America was a joint venture of politics, economy and religion.

Will we ever learn from our mistakes? It doesn't look that way, considering that religion has still recently been involved in wars. Northern Ireland has only recently 'retired' from a war between its Catholic and Protestant populations as the extent of over thirty years of conflict has finally weakened resistance and it was not so much the political circus that brought it to a halt.

In the former Yugoslavia, religious opposition helped politics to trigger ethnic cleansing of the population groups in its territory, which miraculously had lived until recently side-by-side in relative freedom. It appeared that discord didn't like a freedom regime, seeing it as a challenge, especially when responsible leaders lose common sense by engaging in weak arguments for easier power gains. The uprising in Yugoslavia came down with a non-united population thereby allowing foreign interference to succeed for the time being.

Earlier the 'Third Reich' of Hitler staged a war of ethnic-religious cleansing that led to the Second World War. Probably the most devastating incident occurred in Germany in November 1938. 'Crystal Night' saw Jewish shops destroyed, Jewish synagogues demolished and burnt and Jewish worshippers persecuted and even killed. How many more conflicts have taken place, and still do, linked to religious involvement but not mentioned in history books?

This general historical overview shows how controversial religious beliefs had unfolded into conflict almost throughout the entire history. War has been initiated by religious, political and economic motives. As explored in previous topics, war is a 'renewal motor', always taking away the best of a population, which raises the question: where have mutual responsibility and intellect been left in our history of religious conflict? Surely already in the past responsible people have understood to engage others into their conflicting cases by passing the 'bug' on, so that people always had to suffer from such consequences.

Religiously motivated conflicts still flair up occasionally in places like Indonesia, Thailand, India, Afghanistan, Pakistan, Middle East, Sudan, Yemen and even in parts of Russia and China. Instead of a build-up into a major conflict, a constantly increasing number of smaller conflicts have smoldered across the globe since World War II, raising constantly the stakes of a bigger conflict. Fear supported by a more even distribution of 'effective killing-material' has so far prevented the breakout of a wider conflict. Omission however is no acquittance! Religion has never prevented either conflict from within or between societies being generated and it is doubtful this could be stopped soon.

Today's role of religion in societies has so far changed that it is losing its traditional influence, trying therefore to go out more to the people, contrary to the past, when religious authorities made people seek out their services. Martin Luther (1483-1546), the German reformer, can be regarded as a front-runner in correcting religious conscience, which had lost ground with newly emerging realities. The monk, Luther, studied the three ancient languages: Hebrew, old Greek and Latin, in which the Bible was written—incomprehensibly for the faithful. He then translated the Bible into the people's language starting a revolution of the written word to go out to the people. Education, knowledge and freedom of expression followed, which today are often taken for granted.

Already in the Middle Ages a growing population developed the right to have more of a say in their lives. Increased knowledge gradually gave independence from traditional ruling to more people. Luther was the one who brought out the 'sorry-state' of religious affairs of the time, correcting many overdue changes to the feudal rules of the Catholic Church with ethnic common sense. He decided to split from the Vatican rule in Rome introducing Protestantism. The timing of Luther's wake-up calls and his links to the principalities of the State of Prussia allowed him to succeed, whereas his predecessors, J. Hus and G. Savonarola, died at the stake only a little earlier in their drive for changes.

Changes in that time brought along also the Renaissance (rebirth), preparing a ground swell for the changed world that we take for granted today. Have we lost the drive for changes, because poverty is not the main driving force any more? Isn't just sitting back and doing nothing, the start of going backwards until we are told to wake up to the new emerging challenges? Our time now looks more like a testing field for achievements out of the past. At present, people lack a vision for a better practical future. Everything will run out of 'puff' sooner or later as no engine can remain on full throttle all the time. It only remains to hope that the bad times can energize our efforts to renew ourselves and not leave us out of options for change.

Humanity in Christianity reflects especially upon the Vatican, the leadership of the Roman Catholic Church. All human qualities have been expressed here throughout history until today—not only in charity or in directions for individual lives, but also in symbolic power as well as real power, which reaches almost all society domains by surpassing many country borders. The human grasp for power culminates in the leader figure of the Pope and has all the make-up of a person cult. Expressions of faith from a religious leader are practiced under the 'veil' of piety, canonizing of future Saints in order to establish exemplars closer to the people so that they can relate better to religion, which eventually helps to find individual identities. This yields to temptation of power over a great number of people who follow in a belief-dependence, easily corrupting into personal interests.

The life records of past church leaders could be regarded as one of such a derailment, bringing out the discussion of abuse. Forgiveness, which most religions offer to their faithful, at least in words is however the human answer to lead us away from mistakes. Leaders cling also to this formula and why should humans not be able to forgive humans? As long as religious leaders lead a way through human failure into credible new belief, their role will find justification amongst followers, because it has become evident that others also fail in life expectations but can maintain a claim for a leadership by responding positively to failure. Human example always responds best to humans and the role of religion can be seen here. Failure to comply with a simple rule of forgiveness has always led to human conflict. Before forgiveness can be granted, it is conditional that mistakes are recognized especially in one's own domain and a desire for rectification is born.

When such reconciliation doesn't take place, the door to more conflicts is likely to open as has always happened in the past and still does today. Likewise, religions of human societies are bound to changes. Tradition however is a brake-system towards changes, maintaining mainly achievements of the past. The key to sustainable changes lies in a balance of a transition from the past to the present and into the future. Religious tradition seems to have difficulty in moving with changing societies, because it doesn't recognise its role in changes.

Throwing religion out of an individual life leads to Atheism, a possible imbalance between knowledge and belief, in which neither side can satisfy any individual's aspirations. A difficulty of religious tradition is to be found in an interpretation-continuity of its 'substance' without losing its 'core meanings'. During such a process, human actions have moved ahead of human comprehension, explaining therefore why humans have always been behind in their religious interpretations. A conclusion is that we create our beliefs and it remains with us to uphold its truth.

As progress is cherished through knowledge, we distance ourselves from our beliefs. It all depends where knowledge starts and ends, while it is taken over by a wider belief, expressed also in religions. Knowledge constantly expands with no limits, leaving mankind without answers, whereas religious beliefs can spare, through a limited focus on life, one's own search for answers in an ocean of existences. As stated before, a polarity in knowledge and belief invites every individual to find a balance best achieved through efforts in both fields. Knowledge can be increased while a belief is personally adjusted and extended in a search for a balance and not one-sided abandonment.

Christianity has also found its doctrine in the Ten Commandments. The Bible is a guideline for its followers throughout life, a demand that has been, and still is, too high by asking the individual for the 'impossible'. No human has ever lived fulfilling the demands raised by Christianity, which puts the serious follower into an unhelpful position, affecting a personality either negatively through resignation or turning completely away from any belief. Does Christianity demand too much from the faithful? Are the guidelines of the Ten Commandments so highly positioned that an incentive always remains to get there? Isn't this a race without an end and out of reach? Christianity possibly asks humans for too much while promises for compensation in 'another life' can't last long. As soon as knowledge cannot assist in satisfying a belief any more, an individual can also become disconnected from his/her belief, because what is out of reach, loses its significance with time. Is this the key to the controversy in which Christianity is locked?

What are the outstanding features of the main religions in comparison to each other?

Are they all controversial? Christianity, a branch of the oldest religion, **Judaism**, dating back over 2000 years to its origin with the 'Julian Calendar'. The Roman Emperor, Gaius Julius Caesar; introduced the 'Julian Calendar', whereas the 'Orthodox Christians' introduced the

'Gregorian Calendar' by Pope Gregor XIII, end of the 16th Century. The 'Gregorian Calendar' has a delayed difference of eleven days.

The Christian God sent his son Jesus Christ to liberate followers from their anxieties of the 'unknown' and to redeem them from sin, a result of the anxieties. The Ten Commandments in the Bible are a doctrine of high demands. Christian religion has taken position between life-controversies offering an alternative and therefore being unavoidably subjected also to controversies with only human partners.

Islam is the second largest and the youngest of the world religions, established in 610-632 A.D. by the Prophet Mohammed. 'Islam' means devotion to God's will, in which human freedom of expression is also taken into consideration. Its disengagement from the mother-religion Judaism happened also through conflicting ideologies regarding a view towards 'profiteering' in life. Islam wanted to restrain its followers from a 'life of profiteering' contrary to Judaism. The hostile environment of the Arabic deserts asked at that time for a more conciliatory approach to coexist with others. Also, Islam acknowledged only one God and his prophet Mohammed, leaving out the Son of God in their hierarchy. Islam doesn't practice ordination of a priest, or sacraments or councils. The Koran (holy book of Islam) is a Muslim's life-guide in which every one of its followers are called to spread Islam (originally with 'fire and sword') amongst the 'infidels' which has led in the past to Islam's expansion.

Today Islam has two main groups, the Sunnites (ninety percent of Muslims living mainly in North Africa and Asia Minor) and the Shiites (mainly found in Iran and Iraq). Islam sets the rules for the whole of society, not only with prayers but also with the teachings of the past and present by claiming the exclusive right of public-order still today (in contrast to other world religions in which 'State' and 'Religion' operate by law independently). Islam doesn't recognize divisions of nationality nor of race. Formation of any party has to be in affiliation to Islam. It also contradicts a profit taking within its communities.

Five basic obligations constitute Islam-belief (Schakada):

five times daily prayers (salat contribution to charity (sakat)

fasting during Ramadan (the ninth month of the Islamic Moon Year which indicates that Islam refers in its calendar to the moon and not to the sun like many other cultures)

pilgrimage to Mecca at least once in a lifetime (Haddsch)

restraint from alcohol, pork, lottery and gambling as well as endorsement of circumcision, veils for women, polygamy (a regulation out of the past in which mainly the wealthy spread his influence to 'support' a wider population)

Controversies in religious ideologies have always constituted a main trigger for conflict. The unconditional fellowship that religions demand from the faithful, prevent a dialogue with others. One example is the terrible consequences that a 'blindfolded' faithful carries out with a suicide bombing, all with the conviction of serving a higher religious purpose. There is nothing in this world unfortunately to stop such destructive mind-power. The situation changes constantly however as our survival cannot be met any more with ideologies so that we move closer to a 'dialogue table' and face unitedly the realities in order to secure a future for all.

Islam is a strict religious order, based on some practical rules that have emerged only in more recent history. It appears today to be difficult for a religion like Islam to satisfy both religious beliefs and the demands of a modern society, in which case new conflicts are likely to be inevitable. Buddhism originated with Buddha, the Awakened/ Enlightened (original Sanskrit name, Siddhartha Gautama), who was born in the Himalayas, Nepal (560-480 B.C.). His mother passed away shortly after giving birth and he was raised by his mother's sister, married at the age of sixteen, and had one son. By all standards, this was a normal human existence.

There are fundamental ideas of Buddhism: 'To spin the wheel of teaching'; all living forms are part of an eternal creation and death, which are the incessant regeneration; what we wish and do not achieve in life is our 'suffering'; 'Nirvana' delivers the redemption bridging the gap between wants and achievements by transforming ourselves into a better future beyond our present situation.

Three simply understood maxims of Buddhism are:
Do not kill. (Ahisma)
Do not steal. (Asteja)

Work is considered an impediment to a proper life. (Today's conclusion would be an appropriate balance with work.) Monks (Bhikku) and Nuns (Bhikkuni) are the direct Buddhist followers, first having passed through a period of ascetics (restrictive lifestyle) before they become eligible for initiation. The shaved head is a symbol for purity of the whole body, to be ready as a monk. The monk-creed is repeated three times in a rehearsal between a monk-congregation and a monk-aspirant; such monotonous rehearsal serves as meditation, the first step into a trance, which enters the field of a 'higher knowledge'.

Buddhism is formed into three main groups of faithful. Firstly, the Hinajana Buddhists (Southern Buddhists), have spread into Ceylon, Burma, Thailand and Cambodia. Secondly, the Mahajana Buddhists (Northern Buddhists) live in Tibet, Mongolia, China, Korea and Japan. Thirdly, the Lamas live in Tibet also as well as Mongolia. The head is the Dalai Lama, incarnating the 'ocean of knowledge', who starts his ' journey' as a young boy within the Lama community, carefully selected and brought up by monks to become their spiritual leader. Lamas have a special place in Buddhism.

Buddhism is a religion all about making people aware of life's duties towards sustainable efforts and building with a restrictive religious belief on an available knowledge, which can give worshipping are traced back to the 'exaltation' of all living individuals a life-direction through simple answers to the many questions concerning existence. Buddhism is also said to be a philosophy, constantly searching for answers to our questions. In this sense it is the opposite to other religions supplying not only answers but remaining open to individual questions, which is an opening of an intellect into a dialogue and not the dogmatic rule-enforcement practiced by other religions. Buddhism is a 'quiet achiever' backed up by insight, support, and tolerance in its philosophy. Followers can freely make their own decisions.

Hinduism, contrary to other religions, is not a religious establishment. It has developed out of a multitude of sects but not by means of conversion. A Hindu belongs in tradition by birth to a caste. Any difference from that is the exemption, solely accepted in a mutual agreement.

The predecessor of Hinduism was **Brahmanism**. In an ideological conflict, Brahma was pushed aside by the two other Hindu-God incarnations, 'Schiwa' and 'Vishnu', who established the many castes in Hindu society continuing into modern history.

Its teaching is not entirely based on dogmas; only a few underlying principles start from a rebirth of all living forms in a transformation from species to species. Deeds, 'good' as well as 'evil', determine a transformation eventually into a 'God', 'human', 'animal' or 'devil'.

Strict compliance with exclusively vegetable diets and cattle forms (*Ahimsa*), possible stages in a migration through rebirths. Those stages are however transitory on the way to 'redemption' recognized in 'ascetics' of 'Yoga', 'God's love' (*Bhakti*) or in 'magic practices' (*Schaktism*), which help shorten the path to 'redemption' (*Samsara*) by turning away from the world as a 'Sadhu' in a step by step 'reincarnation', a fortunate alliance with 'Dschwara', the highest regarded 'Lord' by all castes.

Hinduism regards society in four groups: 'Brahmans' are the priests, 'Kschatrijas' the soldiers, 'Waischjas' the peasants and 'Schudras' the servants. Up to three thousand castes diverge from those four groups keeping Hindus strictly in their birth caste. The 'Trio', Brahma, Shiwa and Vishnu, stood out in the many incarnations of Hindu Gods, of whom Schiwa represents the 'destroyer' of the world, whereas Wischnu is the 'indulgent saviour' of the faithful. 'Krishna' gained wide reputation in the Hindu world for coming out as the 'God of Happiness'. There are besides many other little Gods like the Monkey-God, 'Hanuman'.

Hindu cult is based on worshipping expressions of their Gods in pictures, prayers and offerings in the presence of priests (Brahmans), who perform sacraments (Samskaras) on occasions of births, marriages and deaths. Hindus practice cremating their dead on a stake, during which, in the past, the other marriage partner was to follow in order to reach redemption (*Samsara*) together and not be separated through the death of the partner.

Hinduism mainly calls home the diverse populated sub-continent of India and has developed also as a consequence out of this diversity a great variety of religious beliefs. The modern society of today constitutes a colossal provocation towards a deeply rooted Hindu belief. It comes as no surprise that even the best intentions have frequently sparked violent clashes, and still do when encountering other religions as a result of a society adapting to rapid changes. Disengaging from a belief, which until recently was surrounded only by a world 'way back in history' would amount to changing 'boats' for many of its followers.

As the 'New World' is largely an unknown fact in a religious belief, the faithful can find themselves easily disconnected from the past as well as from the present. Such an 'interim-situation' constitutes a fragile social environment, which needs once more stabilization and balance in preferably more than one way, whether through religion, our progressive thinking or a compromise of both. Only the future will tell about a succession of mounting controversies and where they are leading into a new millennium.

Judaism, a Jewish religion is the oldest and the basis for Christianity and Islam. The scattering of its followers originated from Abraham and his son Isaac, who was the later child of Abraham's wife Sara. However, earlier, the slave Hagar had given Abraham, with the consent of Sara, a son Ishmael. When Isaac was born, Hagar and Ishmael were expelled and told to found their own nation, which led thousands of years later to Islam. Judaism and Islam have therefore the same forefather, Abraham; these two nations also later brought the split into the two religions.

Abraham's son Isaac had a son Jacob, whose twelve sons became the ancestors of the Jewish people. An original unity of religion and race in a 'diaspora' (dispersion around the world) strengthened initially the Jewish community. Long before Christ, Jews moved into the disputed Israel/Palestine area of today in 930 B.C. For many reasons, migration settled the Jewish minority population in Egypt and Mesopotamia (today's Iraq), continuing around the Mediterranean into Europe, Russia, America and Argentina. Its community strength was challenged with other communities and nations many times in conflicts throughout history right up to the present time.

Such an eventful history of the Jewish people and their religion reflects on their complex, rich culture. In a constant battle for affirmation and recognition as a minority population in so many parts of the world, one expression especially has marked this struggle from early on: 'An eye for an eye, and a tooth for a tooth', meaning, 'We only respond in the same way as we are treated.' This strategy has helped Judaism to survive to this day, undiminished in strength and becoming an exceptional achievement with a unity of religion. A brief synopsis will ensure a good, logical understanding of Judaism.

As the predecessor of Christianity and Islam, the Jewish religion worships only one God. Fundamental decrees in Judaism are circumcision and sanctification of the Sabbath (no work on Saturdays). Contrary to most other religions, all three religions have not created images or symbols of their only God. Moses in the Old Testament, estimated in 1200 B.C, has documented the underlying principals in Hebrew. A number of Prophets followed, completing the Old Testament (Isaiah, Jeremiah, Ezekiel, Daniel and others). The Old Testament also contains the Ten Commandments, previously mentioned in the context of Christianity. The New Testament dates back to Christianity.

Judaism is the oldest 'monotheism' (religion with only one God), which has been an 'apple of discord' in generations of three religious families, where always the succeeding generation tried to be the better until the conflict out of it usually brought all the parties down to the level of a better mutual understanding. As Judaism embodies both people and religion, the apple of discord has not been directed only at religion but also at its people. Developments in recent history have initiated the freeing of this coherence and opened a path to more tolerance with other people as well as religions instead of mixing up religion with people and vice versa.

EPILOGUE

"There is more to see than meets the eye." Two professionals, a brain surgeon and an astronaut, had a discussion on religion. The atheistic astronaut said, "I've been many times out in space and never seen either God or angels.' The Christian surgeon responded, "On my part, I have performed many brain surgeries and have never seen even one thought."

This undertaking about religions aims to highlight in general the essentials of a specific religion and also to search for simpler ways in an overall understanding of the world's religions. If asked, what do I know on the subject, religion, no matter which one is selected, I can only answer on my behalf that I would have had very little comprehensive knowledge if I had not collected the facts first and then added my own thoughts to reach a guideline of the complex religious issues.

A complete understanding of a religion is usually very vague because of its historic/traditional complexity even with its own prophets who either follow unconditionally or have lost the simple expressions. Doesn't religion stop us in our life-drives making us think about what we are doing and giving us the break to catch up with what otherwise could be lost in our rush? A 'foreboding' is not only the first step to a belief in religion, but also to knowledge; how could we have knowledge without that 'initial spark' of direction?

However, all religions have lost a renewal of their original task in the face of changes in societies. Today many people cannot understand religion any more, not because of a lack of will but often simply because of a failure of the world religions to move with the societal changes. Neither religion nor the faithful should be then regarded as being wrong; it is more a wake-up call for both sides to reach a renewed common understanding. After a long time in isolation, religions are urged to catch up with a dialogue of an updated understanding. I am not suggesting that religion has become something of the past, but it should rather become a new call out of the real world in which people live, so that the two sides can reach each other better. Also, religions have to move out of their 'glasshouses' and experience the changes outside in order to understand the new requirements of people.

In a religion, tradition can only have a stabilizing effect in societies if moving with the times; otherwise religion becomes isolated and loses touch with the changed realities. A summing up of religious justification in any society at any time would rest with humans, because they are the originators of religions. To refer to a 'higher authority' than a human one, only leads to less understanding as our ignorance is rarely in a balance with our knowledge. Religions have also been part of human controversies between good and evil. Humans need religion to balance their drive for knowledge; no balanced knowledge without religion, because the latter could be regarded not only as a 'brake-system' in our endeavours but it gives also the time for reviews, which is again the best start for renewed actions.

Only by focusing from time to time away from something, can we regain our positive creativity instead of 'putting the blinkers on in a single lane.' And religion is a man-made focus in life. Why don't we take advantage of what has been created so far and carry it further without abandoning it as a personal loss. Unfortunately, it is also humane that a loss is not realized in the making, but it often rather happens that religion can become a loss for the one who needs it. As a consequence of this, a person is socially better-positioned balancing knowledge and religious belief, which makes life for everybody around us more acceptable and easier. These reflections on religion speak to its benefit of doubt as to its assurance in order to help widen a dialogue on religion.

CHAPTER ELEVEN

MILITARY MIGHT

PROLOGUE

How is reliance on military might initiated? When logical thinking stops, do we automatically take up arms? Furthermore, we know that what comes up has also to come down—the cycle that military might calls its domain. But the downward turn is always easier and quicker than the upward turn. Translating this into human terms means that destroying something is always quicker than building something. Do we 'do' destruction better than construction? During destruction, it is not only what is visible that disappears, but also all the efforts behind it, including the human input—a high cost indeed.

Across whole societies, war has always forced the renewal of efforts as a result of military might bringing down almost everything through armed conflict. All human capacity seems to galvanize on the side of destruction through power determination, strength, discipline, pride, hate, camouflage, deception and sometimes there is even room left for intellect to call its shot. On the other side stand the losses, the nearest partners of our gains. These are never too far away to join the conflicting parties of military might; losses usually show up as a consequence of a lack of common understanding, respect, support, and a willingness for continuity.

To pick a quarrel leading to open conflict always requires more than one party. When all forces of a military might have finally evaporated in destruction, we can only look with sad faces at the mess left behind. In the aftermath, the winner also receives a bill, which can also bring him down if appropriate new efforts have not been put in place. The winner usually likes to celebrate, conveniently forgetting about renewed efforts required on his part. The carousel therefore keeps turning; the winners of today will become, sooner or later, the losers of tomorrow.

Does this all happen for the sake of nature's balance in which nothing is allowed to remain constant? Is our 'sacred cow' of intellect causing us to constantly change from superior to inferior positions and eventually restarting this cycle with the help of military might? Where has our intellect been left throughout history until today?

Are we intelligent enough to act on our insights? This should prevent the 'mechanisms' of the ups and downs in societies and take centre stage by military might instead. For such reasons, the armed forces still have their firm place in societies that come up for intellectual failure.

DEFINITION

What is military might? By definition, it is the readiness of a society to defend its sovereignty against challenges from within and outside, not only with human power but also materials, which societal progress has allowed society to obtain. Military might however is a fundamental institution of society as well. Could we live without it? It is unlikely because the defensive nature of it is deeply rooted in all living forms as a means of survival.

Already children quarrel and all animals develop natural defense abilities in the early stages of their lives mainly through play scenarios. This is the most efficient learning method. Those early deposits of life skills are put to the test in a natural survival request during life; through battles ranging from an individual's daily performance up to an organized military might of the whole of society.

All life is said to be a battle against the odds. Apparently, whoever battles better in all those fields of life when growing up is better prepared in his/her role to function alone and equally in an interaction with others. To stay alive and pass life on are regarded as survivor traits. Defense can only be effective when serving those survival principles. And to maintain effectiveness, ineffectiveness has also to play its part, otherwise effectiveness could not be recognized as such. Moreover, making use of life skills separates us from other living forms' mainstream in a way that humans do not adhere to nature's limits in upholding survival principles.

Animals defend for only one purpose—to survive, whereas humans defend everything they find in nature for the purpose of having a superior existence. 'Superior' to what has not yet been discovered, creating therefore drawbacks in human lives. Military might is one of those superior achievements that keep its originators on the survival edge as long as self-created obstacles don't change survival conditions.

It is also formally recognized that in a democracy the military follows decisions made in Parliament by the people's majority representation. Often however, internal conflict can lead to parliamentary instability in which a grab for power by the military often becomes a reality. In such a case, the vicinity to each other of parliamentary power and military might becomes evident.

The more a Parliament proves unable to translate verbal mandates into progressive actions, the more likely it becomes that arms of the military step in, filling an action vacuum. This can be seen not only in politically unstable countries, but also in all countries as the temptation of a power grab. No society is immune from such a change.

Only strong parliamentary presentation keeps the two sides in the place where they belong. However, whether a Parliament or the military calls to arms, it accounts to the same: arms usually forcibly implement what cannot be managed either by action or brains. The material of military might turns into our tools in the event that said actions and brains ask for a 'higher power'.

In today's world of 2008, arms have surpassed consumer production putting us in a position to destroy planet earth many times over, all in the name of discouraging others from making use of it. Is this impressive or deplorable? To answer this question, there is yet to be a conclusion as we are constantly torn between impression making and the occasionally pinch feeling of our efforts. Has this situation always been with us?

Looking back in history as far as documentation allows us, military might has ruled societies, unleashing the endless numbers of conflicts through wars. The expressions of power within societies almost predictably ended up in conflict, in which the armed forces represented the first priority on an action scale. When everything else fails, the armed forces of the military are still called today to establish priorities in an increasing battle of materials. Here emerges a difference to the past in which people played a more important role than war 'materials' claim today.

In the early days of human societies, war played its role understandably on a smaller scale because of much smaller societies. However, all our achievements have been successfully inverted with priority into arms developments maintaining the edge on others, the strong arm of any military might. Earlier, when technology could not yet serve armed forces to today's extent, human qualities determined more the use of arms through skills and bravery. Thus there became a competition between people where arms played initially a supporting role and men obeyed their instructions. Arms like the spear, axe or baton were meant to keep an opponent at large, fighting better from a safe distance, which was the first advantage of arms against a close physical encounter.

Whatever the reasons were, fighting for superiority is as old as the human race, whether for material gains, power or malicious motives. Interestingly, the more sophisticated weapons became, the more conflict was fought from a distance, keeping the human force further away from actual conflict scenes. Could the ultimate position become to live in bunkers and shelter from each other while we have fingers on buttons commanding our military might? One downside of such 'progress' could be that as our own prisoners, the outside world excludes us then from living a natural life.

POSITIVES AND NEGATIVES OF MILITARY MIGHT

What was motivated earlier by survival needs through a better-armed human force, is increasingly turning with ideological motivation into more sophisticated armed conflicts. Purpose and the end results have then lost practical ground in the same way as intellect has found new sources of conflict justifications. Expressions of power by politicians have established the rules under which conflicts should be dealt. This means that a majority society follows a set discipline in order to protect the interests produced by political representation from a safe distance and not with the finger on the pulse of the real world. To 'taste' the real world and produce results through military might is a task left always for those not in a commanding position.

Succeeding in engaging others in politically motivated military actions, psychology gives a helping hand to limit individual doubts by supplying not just combat materials but also the so important belief for the undertaken matter: through disciplinary measures, personal pride, purposely mental preparation supported by physical training and information feeding into the brainwashing process. Military personnel can therefore become convinced in their isolated societal role on paroles like: "Defenseless amounts to dishonourable," or, "Do you want bombs instead of bread?" (Third Reich parole in Germany). Left alone, civil power can become sidetracked into military might if people from outside the military organization hook on to these paroles.

What politicians cannot deliver is often passed on to the military to resolve. Here is a likely situation arising in which the weakness of a Parliament in its verbal capacity is overtaken by actions of military might forcing a power transition. The military might has then turned against its own authority unleashing internal conflict. Therefore, parliamentary order and military might have both to be in a strong position when the military might takes chances not to derail the foundation of democracy in its operations. Success here would mean that opposition from outside is defeated and no more than that.

Why do conflicts start in the first place and why are they dealt with by military might? Ideology, economy, territorial claims, human greed, and natural disasters can all offset an internal focus of one or more societies often leading to an attitude of blaming somebody else for shortcomings in one's own ranks, willed or forcibly. What is supposed to be a civilized dialogue can easily turn into a war of words as history has sufficiently demonstrated.

The next step towards conflict happens usually either out of presumption or desperation, which only divert from the real issues. Instead of a 'house fire' under control, the blaze is widened under the assumption that fire can extinguish fire. But even in these circumstances, no party has ever been spared from at least 'burning their own fingers' in heated decisions, passed on for execution by military might. Certainly, any aftermath of a conflict always gives the time to rethink what was abandoned first in a hurry. Moreover, rebuilding what has visibly been destroyed by military might will set back any process of continued progress for an untold number of years.

Some people want to see here a new increased challenge, conveniently forgetting about the losses that cannot be put back in place—losses like buildings and the human cost. Where is the responsibility left in conflicts carried out by military might? Everything is done to avoid direct accountability when it comes to responsibility. The daunting task of battling conflict with military might usually receives the support from all possible sources within a society. The individual 'warrior' receives encouragement, pride, assurances and even the blessing of the church, which is forgetting that he/she could lose their life during military action while its 'backers' acclaim the task of upholding responsibilities, usually from the relative safety of distance.

For those to whom this might sound like a theory, reality quickly changes when a conflict situation comes close enough. Losing people in conflicts as a consequence of military might can hardly be justified. The survivors have always found the arguments for justifications, as the victims of conflict could not so far be heard. This is a human tragedy that we haven't learned to overcome yet. Our intellect can still run strange directions making us at the end to wake up to everything we undertake. What we claim to control, including military might, we rather lose in the process.

Should we have military power at all, or can we afford not to have it? The past shows us that we have built an over-reliance on military might and the consequences out of it have so far determined history's course. Societies which have gone too far up on a progressive scale in relation to their neighbours, called for an equalizer, bringing down again what went up. In the end, everybody heads down, foe and friend, upholding the notorious cycle of reenergizing efforts to win back what was lost.

THE HAGUE, GENEVA CONVENTION

A new initiative might have started with the establishment of The Hague International Court of Justice for war actions in 1907. The Geneva Convention also introduced formal legislation in 1949 for the protection of war-torn populations from military might after the overwhelming Second World War experience. Dawn in the human conscience had started then and was no surprise, because this could have happened only after everybody had suffered enough. On one side it was the worst experience, unleashing the effective wake-up call, and on the other side it is better to happen later than never.

The Hague International Court formally observes 'fair military might', which is to a certain degree controversial in itself, because since when could a martial conflict be judged 'fair' or 'unfair'? Nevertheless court cases against war crimes of political leaders have taken and still take place in The Hague helping to relieve international conscience towards its war actions. As such a process takes place only in hindsight, a prevention of war crimes through a convention is still far out of reach. As noted previously, action has always been the forerunner of intellectually driven consensus; it has unfortunately to get worse in conflict situations before getting any better. Shall we ever learn sufficiently from our mistakes to not repeat them? Would this reduce the challenges or shift them into peaceful territory?

One answer could be in the better use of our brains and not of our physical aggressions, which obviously are less under our control. The problem of focussing away from military might is already hampered through all society's military efforts without exemption. Where should efforts go, if diverted from a power build-up in military might? It is a known fact that often more goes disproportionately into weapon manufacture than into peaceful consumer demand. Would a shift from an existing manufacture priority system be able to compensate eventually for the part of arms manufacture? Maybe, maybe not.

One reason might be that too much effort towards consumerism and infrastructure for a rise in living standards could exhaust, with time, progress as societal aggressions retreat. As in everything else, balance must also be the answer here: have a 'necessary' military might in place, but make sure you never use it, which means, all the other efforts in a society have to be significantly bigger than a focus on military might. The best insurance has always been the one that is properly maintained but not used. This way, the need for defense is less likely to occur.

What about, if conflicting opinions—the most common source for conflict—are dealt with in an unconventional way? For instance, if politicians were asked to also act on what they decide, the world would certainly be a different place. And this could be extended to all other fields of decision-making, because when the ones who make decisions cannot deliver, responsibility would also clearly stay with them. Let's spin the idea a bit further and put politicians into a boxing-ring and have their quarrels sorted out in direct personal measurements of strength. Their decisions would start to look very different from then on. Whoever wants a change should step into that ring and personally fight for it.

Unfortunately this can only be an idea, because it remains doubtful whether individuals could deliver the answers that the majority population needs to progress. Only such a thought of a more direct responsibility in decision-making could help a more cautious approach also in the political arena. The direct connection to responsibilities is a missing fact to a degree in almost all societal institutions as power expressions divert from the issues. It does appear we have to live a while longer with things as they develop before gaining something better with time. The boxing ring can neither deliver what a majority population is asking for nor do the right thing for everybody.

MILITARY OLYMPIC GAMES

Wider expression of opinions and consultation on civil matters, simply a wider democratic control, can support peace. In the ancient Greek history during the Olympic Games, 'Ekechira' (the peace time) ruled, stopping all hostilities. Men competed then in athletics, transforming the battlefield of military might into peaceful sporting events, honours of which were higher ranking than victory out of conflict. Today, the world does not only lack ideas on how to achieve peace instead of conflict but also the necessary discipline required. The original peace mission of the Olympic Games has today lost its title and nothing could substitute for it so far. As a matter of interest, women didn't take part at all in the ancient four-yearly events in Olympia; they were not even allowed as spectators.

Expressions of strength were, from early on, men's business, fuelling the rise of conflict in societies driving for power and recognition.

Women on the other hand could hardly put enough 'brake power' on men's might. Only progress in recent history could open the way for women to participate more widely in society matters which has benefited more people as women's decisions relate more to nature than their male counterparts' ones.

However, pushing for equal status with men, women shouldn't abandon their inherited strength at the expense of adopting men's might. If women had the principal say in directions around the world, the world certainly would be very different today. In what sense, is hard to project, because it hasn't happened so far, therefore remaining only an assumption. Those likely different conditions would also have cost a price. Which one would be the better, is a matter of opinion as men in particular are captivated by power and force when pursuing their goals, whereas women are better in bearing the consequences that life constantly inflicts on us. Balance is again here the key word leaving the options open as to which side in the future will tend to swing to centre-stage. Are we to continue with man-made conflict or allow for some time to pursue peace at least?

History teaches us however that peace cannot last as long as there are people trying to reap benefits from conflict. A given diversity of people doesn't allow single-minded focus on directions thus keeping up a constant exchange amongst mankind in order to serve nature's balance principles. Nothing is here to last, everything is subjected to changes within a universal higher understanding. Battles must be the little steps towards a broader understanding preparing first the ground before moving away onto an eventually uncertain ground, which keeps life's wheel spinning.

Standstill would be life's worst enemy, because it doesn't give options of where to go. Thus military might is the opposition to peace, helping at the same time to maintain nature's cycles of the ups and downs, fortunately and unfortunately. Human longing for a better life is also said to have no limits and because of that it comes as no surprise that we try to reach for the stars, not only for one reason but rather for a number of different reasons which serve our insatiable thirst for knowledge and power.

Following this doctrine, why can't we transfer military might into space, further away from us so that Mother Earth is turned again more into the underdog of its intractable human tenants. Where would we like to go then from there? Space certainly is unlimited, but wouldn't we get lost in the attempts to conquer more and more incessantly? What could become the balance to the Universe in our restless pursuit of might—our own disappearance? Luckily, we haven't yet arrived there. Let's keep our feet grounded on Mother Earth and follow the advice, tackling first our nearest problems.

A phenomenon has lately overtaken the world so that instead of past large conflicts, a number of smaller conflicts make up today for it still serving unabated the weapon distributors of the main military might. Weapons manufacture has turned today into a major economical activity of a few 'culprits', spreading troublemaking material into other yards in order to stir up conflict somewhere else and reap the benefits from it. This might be a smart way of doing business, but time will tell if the 'apple of discord' returns to the 'farmer', who drives the wedge of discontent between others. A result is likely to become an explosion of hostilities feeding into a major conflict from outside into one's own yard as might develop at the present in Afghanistan and Iraq. Terror could be seen today in this context largely as a result of a failed balance in bilateral respect.

History can also tell us that it was never beneficial for either party in a long haul to play at superiority, especially with military might. It can develop into a cuckoo's egg in one's own nest, overpowering its own foster parents if political pressure is applied on others. It is like a hot steel rod that doesn't want to lose heat and so must stay near the smithy's forge so it does not break.

Controversy is an inherited part of military might, too. It can for instance serve positively in discipline, physical training, education of special knowledge and skills providing jobs, supporting health and a strong combat-readiness as long as it is kept in house. Letting the 'cat' out however, can lead into different conditions: what has been built under peaceful conditions is forced under changed conditions of aggression to turn against others with or without defence, in which the individual is driven just by chance into survival practices. The initial benefit can quickly turn into disadvantage not only for the individual but also for the entire military power as risk calculations never add up to the initial projection.

The risks of a military might lie in polarities, where it can mutate. One example is the production of arms, the backbone of the military today. Arms are manufactured and provide initially qualified work to large numbers of people that in return can build on a personal living standard. Even maintaining arms arsenals of the military can extend employment benefits as long as they are not used to reduce an opposition by force instead of supporting dialogue. In the case of forcible use of arms, the military can turn into a might, which creates its own opposition. Benefits of employment and living conditions can change with the blink of an eye into sacrifices and losses. The good side has then turned into a bad one just because the benefits disregarded caution.

In the end, individuals have to pick up the bill of miscalculation and even victory has its price. This shows up mainly in changed individual conditions.

As already stated, the best military might is the one that is well maintained but not used to bring others down, because the strength used against others can at any time turn against one's own interests especially those of a political nature as an outcome can never be guaranteed. Even victory will haunt the better aggressor in the aftermath. To keep military might realistically fit for combat, why can't the world community compete as well in Military Olympic Games for a better future? I am aware that such an idea is likely to be regarded as impractical, but doesn't everything start off not only small but also unreal in a sense, asking for consideration?

Joint military exercises are a step in the right direction when conditions other than conflict allow competitions. Looking over each other's shoulders during such friendly encounters only prevents the one-sided military might emerging disproportionately isolated from others. There is a lot to ponder relating to our claim for superiority through military might. As long as we don't stop thinking about it, better chances will develop in a constant testing of new military approaches also at a joint table with others. Isolation in a misplaced understanding, plus having 'blinkers' on, becomes the biggest enemy of military might.

EPILOGUE

We never achieve only the best; the opposition to it, the worst, its most reliable partner, makes us wonder why we have to live with controversial circumstances delivered through military might. The answer lies within nature's mechanisms (invariably not changing conditions) in which also we are bound by accepting all we aim for, the existence of 'idle-running'. If everything could be perfectly arranged, the missing task of fixing problems would leave too many people out of work. Thus the polarity of the military might remain simply as a longing for peace creating more than one job only. Once our activities favoured military might, it is only a matter of time until they swing to the side of peace building.

Necessity doesn't mean inevitability in regard to military might. We are the creators of our own luck and our own misery, let's not forget it and make sure not to stay for too long in one field, whether in the misery- or the luck-field, while one option exists only in our dreams. Let me quote another writer, Emilie Carles, who has joined in an effort to show her 'third face of coins' in her book *A Wild Herb Soup*, expressing 'the real thing'. As much as the situation of a deserter in this excerpt is questionable, it does show to what extent individuals are driven into desperation by military might disregarding on a large scale the real human rights.

> *How many died? A million, they say it's true; it's terrible, but millions upon millions came home. On the other hand, if you desert, if you go underground, you find you are done and that's bad enough, and then, if you get picked up, it's a firing squad for sure. You are refusing the system when you desert, you are saying no to the whole set-up. You are saying no to the rich guys who decided on the war, you are saying no to the arms dealers, you are saying no to the colonels who play servants to the rich, and you are saying no to the priests who give them their blessing. War is state-sponsored savagery and its first victim is the man who goes off to serve, the worker and the peasant, the people like your brother who go off to fight because they do not understand.*

We act on what we understand, don't we? When looking at the twelve topics explored in this book, three main issues emerge each time: polarities, balance, and power. They touch irrefutably each subject and lead to the same conclusions, which means, all subjects are connected to each other by those principles. The topics can only be representative in front of many more topics that can be found in our lives. Above all stands the incomprehensive nature of Mother Earth and around it the Universe, driven by polarities, balance and power of which humans are only one product. Polarities generate life, balance protects life and power moves lives. Military might is to be seen as a power depending for its strength on maintenance of balances and polarities to other power expressions.

CHAPTER TWELVE

LOVE—JEALOUSY— HATE—WAR

PROLOGUE

All's fair in love and war.
There is no love without jealousy.
Love and jealousy can make hate.
War is a result of them all.

What do wit and wisdom say? Mostly they 'say' to reduce experience and knowledge to one simple truth! And what is the truth in these four concepts? They 'live' close to each other in a constant exchange throughout our daily lives. However, they still remain things that nobody has physically got hold of so far with their appearances and effects known mainly to others. They seem much less recognized however by us personally. Do we have a sixth sense noticing developments with and around us, which only words such as love, jealousy, hatred, can identify? War in particular is recognizable beyond words.

Controversy is probably the nearest 'trademark' connecting those four subjects with us. Where there is controversy, the so often mentioned polarities of life are unleashing considerable power into many directions—good and not so good—which depend on individual incidental actions. So can we reach the core essences of 'love-jealousy-hatred- war' through common knowledge, disclosing how they came to exist and live with us and largely determine our lives?

CLOSE-UP VIEWS

All we know is that 'love-jealousy-hatred-war' are powerful words. Where is this power coming from? Is there another word like 'love' commonly used as often and does it mean the same every time somebody spells it out or expresses it? How much jealousy or hatred goes with it and why? The common denominators seem to invite the individual to find his/her own understanding. Therefore 'love' and its 'neighbours', 'jealousy' and 'hatred', are constantly searched in order to find a safe anchor in people's minds. Who hasn't said many times, 'I love you. I trust you. I hate you.'

Newspapers, television, books, and advertisements—they all relentlessly use the individual's imagination of love (usually with an appendix called 'sex') in representing stereotypical images, which are detracting from the normal comprehension. Those images of other seemingly perfect human bodies move 'love' towards ' jealousy' as many will ask themselves (usually in secret), "Do I look like that?" or, "Does my wife/husband look like that ?"

The mass media fabricates near-perfect images by creating subconscious pictures, which can lead further to self-hatred. This can start to develop an unnoticed feeling of inferiority for the individual only growing more intense the more it becomes exposed to these so-called 'perfect images'. Obviously inciting individual discontent through the futility of pursuing the 'better picture', but undermining on the other hand personal satisfaction, might achieve a marketing goal but it achieves little else that is positive.

The positive strength of human love is seen as a general respect towards an individual as well as towards others, something that can easily become sidetracked into the negative territory of dissatisfaction, serving purposes other than those pursued by the individual. Dissolute people's own ideas can therefore often better serve other initiatives. Along the way, a shift from 'love' to ' jealousy' and moreover even to 'hatred' can happen. Finally, there is the risk of the individual being led into an oppositional attitude towards self-belief.

Our strength is always in close proximity to an 'abyss', which is able to change unexpectedly into a weakness, highlighting again the existence of life's polarities. We never reach either the purely good or the purely evil; it is either a mixture of both or first the one then the other to follow. Only strength of mind can keep us on a more valued life-track with powerful expressions of love.

Where else is love mentioned? Friends of both genders usually like to exchange words and support in a friendly love relationship, which can be regarded as a testing ground for a lasting commitment towards a broader understanding and support. All commitments ask for a constant reaffirmation from all sides and so it is with love. The common saying 'they fell in love' means that two people exchange expressions of commitments in their very personal understanding. Isn't this something we'd like to refer to as a 'romance', an understanding most of the time different from an ordinary daily life and expressing a wish to help each other? Once a 'romance' however faces the more prosaic side of daily life, requests for help are then asked to prevail more in continued commitments towards a broader understanding of love by listening to each other in order to learn from each other. When listening stops, usually previous experiences can block a further understanding.

Tradition has its own reason, referring to the fact that only restriction produces one master. Crucial crossroads in life ask for restrictions in order to meet new personal goals through a better focus on one's own discipline. Also 'love', in its widest sense, is nothing less than asking the 'master' to carry it further. A human society based on such personal commitments allows family cells, with the support directed towards responsibilities, to emerge. Love is important in an individual's search for such support that depends on its existence.

Since human society evolved, everything has started small including individual love commitments. However, the differences understood by all individuals cause families to live their lives individually as well as in a unit, which led to many of the problems of societies. In life also commitments are tested and everybody responds to them according to his/her own ability. Everything here is rather subjected to changes within the course of nature's evolution of which we are a part.

Other branches of society can however support through common focus the individual 'boat' to anchor more steadily, rather than losing direction in 'unknown waters'. Friends, the extended family, education, religion, and even political institutions can assist in an environment in which the small individual cell of a 'love commitment' should prosper also for the benefit of a community. The individual can experience love from those community branches in an appeal of mutual help to shore-up the basic existence of a society. It is not through one-sided assistance that advanced social systems have difficulties helping today but a genuine need rather than the improper claim of individuals.

Social responsibilities could be seen as a societal 'love package' put in place to move individuals out of difficulties and away from a 'help-needed' situation. This of course can only happen when the individual actively takes part in translating help into his/her own actions. The different expectations born out of all sides that receive and contribute to a process with 'love' are clearly identified in mutual help in the first place. It can again change its nature into 'jealousy', 'hatred' and even 'war' when original commitments do not receive strong enough support.

It is a basic rule that we should only expect in life what we are prepared to accomplish ourselves in the first place. Any form of 'love' receives its lifeline from the same rule. In the past whole societies have changed individual commitments into societal mainstreams, leading unavoidably to downfalls that are often recognized as 'moral decay', when even 'hatred' has lost its role and love's sense of support is gone for the majority of people.

What about those 'houses of ill fame', which are said to be the oldest institution of society? Isn't 'love' marketed here in exchange for something else, changing it only for self-serving purposes? Love has been single-mindedly traded for pleasure but not for its supportive role. The 'positives' and 'negatives' surrounding 'love' are at the same time so diverse and close to each other that it gives cause for exploration. Then the reader can also compare it with his/her views and eventually carry the dialogue further.

Nothing lasts forever and when people have reached the bottom of their expectations in one way or another, a desire for support and love always returns first to individuals out of the 'ashes', spreading then to the wider community. Such is the cycle that human societies have to live with—everything must change. Only the individual can escape the full extent of those changes by staying strong to his/her convictions of which 'love' is the most essential. It alone is capable of saving the loss of everything in a general 'apocalypse', as long as personal ground is not lost.

Strong commitments of 'love' can build bridges, especially during difficult times when 'want' is overtaken by 'must' and choices for the individual shrink to margins hardly recognizable any more. A 'flood of events' can surge more or less regularly in societies, born predominantly out of ignorance and following the path down in the same way everything else does. Having been cut off and ending up lonely with the ups and downs of life, the desire would then be to reconnect to something to receive our attention. Only making sense again by reminding us that only 'love' in its genuine order and focus on others, can bring us out of isolation, away from ourselves. Love gives in return what we have given somebody else. Acting on our own without love, amounts to 'war' with others.

It remains only a matter of time to see the seeds of our greed prosper. Nature produces in abundance that which bears fruit. A tree for instance produces many more flowers than it does fruit later on. This visible natural reproduction and survival process takes place with all living forms including us. What the flowers are on trees is with mammals a sperm selection. Preparation holds the key to 'fruit-bearing'—what comes quickly, goes quickly.

Humans are also bound to nature's course and, if wanting to succeed on that path, we had better follow it closely. Many human relations do not prosper, because appropriate attention wasn't given to the preparation stage and most of all, during the course of a relationship not enough effort went into maintaining mutual support. We cannot claim ownership of another person like negotiating deals for a car or other consumer goods and we won't find in the other person the mirror image of ourselves. Neither can the other person be expected to make up for our own shortfalls. It is unrealistic to try to change the other person to serve an individual's self-interest. An individual remains as such during life through nature's incidental selection process.

All that love can achieve is to win the other side over with continued renewed commitment. It is truly said: "To become a father is easy, but to *be* a father is difficult." Nothing in life was ever meant to be easy and if connecting first is the easy part, we have also to get ready for the difficult part sooner rather than later.

A fresh example of this complexity was reported recently on the news, showing how close very personal wishes of love, trust, and hope became interlaced for a woman who made contact with a man through the Internet. She trusted this man and thought he would become her life-partner. Helping others was one of her basic qualities and she didn't hesitate to offer it to her new friend via the Internet. Basically, there is nothing regarded as 'wrong' in the modern world, where so many changes have occurred, including the way people meet.

A considerable amount of money changed hands to help her 'friend' in his business. When the day arrived that the lady was to meet her new friend at the airport at their first meeting, she was the only one there and there was no trace of the man she had already started to 'love' deeply in her mind and heart. Such a wake-up call became an instant 'cold shower' for her as her love, trust and hope were ambushed by a smart cold-blooded con man. In the future, this woman will probably not easily commit to love, trust or hope any more. She had to learn to deal with her personal side of expectations the hard way and become most of all more cautious. Hopefully this terrible abuse of trust will never be repeated in her life.

People cannot necessarily be judged by what they look like, or what they express or wish for, as there is always more behind people's appearances than one could possibly see. Only appropriate time and cautious distance can reveal more about the true intentions of another person. Advice is always handy but could never cover everything, because what becomes one person's downfall could be another person's good luck.

As long as we stay active in life, we keep moving by leaving behind disappointments and learn hopefully to face the better opportunities, as we never know the 'neighbourhood of our longings'. Trying in the first place to avoid any disappointment would lead to inaction, which is incompatible with life's demands of civil courage, and moving on as long as life allows us to do so.

To keep private matters and business matters separate is always difficult, because what we want or have to do can quickly come on a collision course; a clean division is a good recommendation. By no means should 'love' or any other virtue change camps from privacy to business. Privacy means for us developing privately and not making a deal out of both with business interests. Again, there are people who tackle such a deal and even possibly reap benefits out of it but it remains to be seen for how long. Caution has always been the mother of wit!

When looking for something, we search most of the time for the bigger and more obvious aspects and therefore easily miss a focus on the greater number of smaller life issues. Love has also a number of issues that offer at least two sides of the 'coin'. One seeks help, whereas the other one shows greed. This double-image or polarity causes us to take different directions in our lives. Rules 'attached' to it are to regulate coexistence with others.

Past accords that have developed mainly through tradition maintain such rules, translating them to individuals as well as possible by relating to changes over time. This failure to catch up with the present, drives the individual into self-defense of his/her life-issues, which in turn becomes the start of divergence from the mainstream. This receives inputs from more than one source, contributing therefore to eventual confusion. But as is well known, rules are here also to be challenged. If everything went according to rules, life would become rather boring. On the other side are the 'romantic' longings with love as their main 'deputy'—without doubt essential in our existence.

Ultimately, our whole existence is owed to love. How love creates us is better known than its travelling stages. Everything becomes possible here, with or without time, regardless of rules, boundaries and attached strings, love reaches then its strongest human expression asking regardless of circumstances only for one continued commitment in support. Continuation of life has so far proved to be the strongest prevailing human capacity despite all the efforts that lead to the extinction of life. Everything else that happens in our lives disappears except life itself—no love, no life.

How much of this love has been subjugated today to marketing purposes? Our longings to give and receive love are successfully used in advertisements to lure people into consumerism. All 'hands' of human strength are here called for a purpose other than personal benefit. This 'charm-of-novelty' is constantly taken further, subduing love with images either irritating or stupefying. Nature doesn't wait long to give answers in return by disconnecting ourselves from love as given to us for other fellow creatures in unconditional help. We have then become indifferent to our greatest gift, love. Maybe for that reason we experience increasing difficulties in society's foundation, the family—not only in the family home but also in the individual's incompetence in raising a family.

If mutual longing for help is not taken further, love will not share a home with us.

When trying to safeguard exclusively our own benefits, we are on a path to becoming strangers in our own backyard and for what purpose? If we cannot share our benefits any more, they become useless when the end of life's journey catches up with us. Nobody asks for our benefits but rather how our love has responded to the coexistence of others. Fortunately life gives us time to learn about love, because nobody can ever claim to be perfect and therefore it is never too late to take one's place on 'life's school bench'. A fact of life is also that most of the time we wake up only from deeply rooted habits once we have lost them— even love, jealousy or hatred.

When talking about habits, the various understanding of love as it is viewed within different cultures needs also to be mentioned. In the past, survival has dictated restrictions such as monogamy (only one wife) because of the simple fact that a family-cell could better survive and prosper partly in the seclusion out of which tradition developed. Even today's tradition reflects these origins. A characteristic found in the Arab-Muslim world would be the customs that encourage the better positioned ones in a society to spread their influence by marrying more than one wife (polygamy). This custom of having more than one wife at the same time is restricted so far only to a few societies. The presence of male dominance and influence cannot be denied here.

Before judging however, let us not forget about the harsh desert conditions of many Arab countries, which are in itself a human survival challenge. The fewer the options are by nature, the more the individual develops dependence that has widely been the generator for living conditions. 'Minimizing the burden' is at least the official version with no surprise that human nature fiddles with everything to make something more palatable for the individual's likings.

Other areas in the world, in parts of Laos and the Eskimo Arctic, family customs can still be found concerning the care of young offspring, even when the daughter could not get married. Here history goes back not only to religious foundations but also more likely into harsh isolated conditions of people in which a family-expansion became a priority in order to avoid in-breeding. Conditions have in a sense mainly driven 'love' in societies asking in hindsight to stay with help-commitments on track.

Only the Catholic Church has found a simple recommendation for its faithful: "When God sends the rabbit, He also sends the grass." This is however a highly controversial guideline that lacks personal and societal responsibilities, helping to keep individuals subdued to the maintenance of power by the Church. As can be recognized today, a lot was going on in the past and still is, not always openly noticeable.

When love fails for any number of reasons in its original appointment, it can change into jealousy, hatred and finally into a war-of-words that can escalate into a war-of-action. A 'repair bill' is then almost certain not to be met any more if it were to remain on that downwards track. Where there is a will, there is also a way out of a stalemate situation and leading towards love again. People reflect on love in endless ways, nearly in as many ways as there are individuals, because love is the most personal expression of our existence.

Songs in particular can connect to people's understanding, as music is the only language commonly understood, regardless of language barriers. Using music assists languages in a powerful way as long as it knows how to connect to people's expectations, which are also changing with time. There was one song for instance from back in the 1960s: "Love is a curious game moving from one to another..." It leaves an interpretation open to everyone and how he/ she likes to understand it. Music connects people and so do the words associated with it.

There is hardly any creative human work that doesn't somehow borrow from love in order to connect to people. Probably 'love' is our most universal expression inherent in controversies. However when too many references claim love outright, it loses its strength in the wake. Those people have then lost their connection to love despite constantly using the appropriate 'words'. Using something doesn't necessarily mean, it is understood. Because every deeper understanding requires individual reflection not substituted through teaching, and when for reflection no time can personally be drawn, even obvious knowledge can retreat into ignorance.

In today's growing societies, can such developments become common when media-power relentlessly showers people with slogans designed to attract one-sided attention? Let us make sure not to lose our own judgement in such a process, which can cut us off from our own valuable experiences ranging from positive to less positive ones. Here is the key to how to experience life's ups and downs equally with love. No positives or ups in life can be recognized without the negatives or downs.

EPILOGUE

After showing a number of 'faces of love' and its 'neighbours', the question could arise: why bother putting it down on paper when everybody already knows the 'basics'? But does everybody really know anything besides the facts surrounding the love-jealousy-hatred- war that their mutual relationships create the confusions in the first place? And can they keep moving from there into unpredictable territories of people's daily lives?

Reality around us makes people rethink their positions, usually people that always 'know' but still find themselves trapped in the labyrinth of love-jealousy-hatred-war seeking desperately the 'thread of

Adriane'. (In Greek mythology a thread became the key in a desperately lost situation for Adriane.) To know means to listen to what else knowledge has to offer. As this love-topic belongs also to personal privacy, lots of hidden agendas stay with individuals without stepping out of obscurity into clarity. To argue hereon is usually the start of misunderstandings, becoming in the end the trigger for jealousy, hatred and war, not necessarily on a big scale but more often small just as every 'fire' starts.

Whole books filled with arguments are passed between 'actors' who arise really from ignorance. They have been written from constantly changing sides and doing nothing more than confusing the real issues; many films can also join in this exhibition of failed dialogue. We'd like to see others engaged in arguments and draw satisfaction in the short-sightedness of being immune from others' mistakes only as long as we won't get caught ourselves unexpectedly in the same arguments.

This is all conveniently called 'emotions', the opposite of an insight to which this 'opus' likes to refer. The choice remains ours—whether to build on the positive sides of help through love or go down the road to jealousy and hatred to end up in a self-initiated and staged war. Every personal insight takes its time to materialize in life until it readily assists the individual in circumstances of conflict. The more prepared we are, the better we battle life's ups and downs. Especially private issues like love, require therefore an open public discussion in its widest sense, which is ranked 'civil courage', sheltering individuals from isolation through self-inflicted ignorance, what this collection of thoughts is aiming for.

CONCLUSION

No matter how one looks at this undertaking, it remains a wake-up call to rethink our position in life, which we currently either take for granted by not reenergizing it with new efforts, or conveniently throw it out with a total lack of understanding.

What we need is a dialogue between achievements and future prospects under the umbrella of an equal partnership. It is not enough to economize in the present for political short gains; it should rather become a competition in thoughts requiring renewed courage to prepare the societies that want to emerge more humane. To do so, we have to abandon our routine and spin the wheel of progress in the quest for a wider participation for increased mutual benefits also outside our 'glasshouses'. Achieving balance remains the goal, neither staying idle, nor breaking with the past. Instead of fighting for a balance, we have better options to achieve it: unconditional dialogue is needed to monitor our actions in order to prepare for a sustainable progress.

SOURCES

Dialogues with people from all levels of society were the main source of thoughts collected over my entire lifetime. Comparisons between information, own experiences, logical conclusions in a continued learning-process, the "philosophical game" of never ending questions, balancing the ups and downs and much more have helped creating this written exercise which readers are asked to take further in a said continuous learning-process.

www.ingramcontent.com/pod-product-compliance
Lightning Source LLC
Chambersburg PA
CBHW031120020426
42333CB00012B/160